D0948795

How do Soviet politicians rise to power? How are national and regional regimes formed? How are conflicting political interests brought together as policies are developed in the Soviet Union? These questions have long absorbed historians and political scientists, yet none have systematically examined the crucial role played by patron–client relations. In *Patronage and politics in the USSR* Professor John Willerton offers major new insights into the patronage networks that have dominated elite mobility, regime formation and governance in the Soviet Union during the past twenty-five years.

Using the biographical and career details of over two thousand national leaders and regional officials in Azerbaidzhan and Lithuania, John Willerton traces the patron–client relations underlying recruitment, mobility and policymaking. He explores the strategies of power consolidation and coalition building used by Soviet chief executives since 1964 as well as the institutional links and policy outcomes that have resulted from network politics. The author also assesses the manner and extent to which leaders in politically stable and less stable settings, spanning different national cultural contexts, have relied upon patronage networks to consolidate power and to govern. Finally, Professor Willerton explores how, in a period of dramatic change, patron–client networks may now be giving way to institutionalized interest groups and political parties.

PATRONAGE AND POLITICS IN THE USSR

Soviet and East European Studies

Series list continues on page 302.

PATRONAGE AND POLITICS IN THE USSR

JOHN P. WILLERTON

Assistant Professor of Political Science
University of Arizona

The right of the
University of Cambridge
to print and sell
all manner of books
was granted by
Henry VIII in 1534.
The University has printed
and published continuously
since 1584.

CAMBRIDGE UNIVERSITY PRESS

Cambridge
New York   Port Chester
Melbourne   Sydney

Published by the Press Syndicate of the University of Cambridge
The Pitt Building, Trumpington Street, Cambridge CB2 1RP
40 West 20th Street, New York, NY 10011-4211, USA
10 Stamford Road, Oakleigh, Victoria 3166, Australia

© Cambridge University Press 1992

First published 1992

Printed in Great Britain at
the University Press, Cambridge

A catalogue record for this book is available at the British Library

Library of Congress cataloguing in publication data

Willerton, John P.
Patronage and politics in the USSR/John P. Willerton.
    p.   cm. – (Soviet and East European studies: 82)
Includes bibliographical references and index.
ISBN 0 521 39288 8 (hardback)
1. Patronage, Political – Soviet Union – Case studies.
2. Executives – Soviet Union – Case studies. 3. Soviet Union –
Politics and government – 1917 – Case studies. 4. Lithuania –
Politics and government – 1945 – Case studies. 5. Azerbaijan
S.S.R. – Politics and government – Case studies. I. Title.
II. Series.
JN6549.E9W55   1992
324.2′04 – dc20   91–57   CIP

ISBN 0 521 39288 8 hardback

GE

To Nancy

Contents

Tables

Preface

Students of the Soviet system have long struggled to find and fit together the pieces comprising the Soviet political puzzle. Although less evident in the period of openness and radical reform, scholars have labored simply to determine the broad contours of that puzzle. Core pieces have often remained obscure. This book concentrates on one puzzle within the broader Soviet context: political patronage. Widely acknowledged as central to Soviet political life, patronage relations have received almost no systematic attention. My interest in Soviet patronage networks emerged in the twilight of the Khrushchev period, when Western observers were surprised by the top leader's sudden ouster. Scholars struggled to trace the emergence of the Brezhnev regime and the development of a new policy program. Initially I was interested in identifying broad norms of patronage politics, especially as they related to regime formation and power consolidation. Later, in the wake of Gorbachevian reforms, I became more interested in exploring the impact of political and institutional changes on deeply rooted elite behavioral norms. Throughout, I wanted to illuminate broad proclivities that transcended one regime and that were evident in both national and subnational Soviet politics. It was my good fortune that an academic year stay in the USSR yielded not only national, but extensive republic-level, data so that I could consider hypotheses in a comparative light.

Many people have provided encouragement and support during the stages of my work on patronage. I have profited immeasurably from intellectual exchanges with friends and colleagues during graduate school at the University of Michigan, research visits to the USSR, and my years as an assistant professor at Michigan State University and the University of Arizona. Bill Zimmerman, who chaired my dissertation, provided the intellectual challenge and support that I needed to move forward with my ideas on patronage and Soviet elite politics. Ellen Mickiewicz not only provided me with a formal introduction to Soviet politics, but helped me to define patronage politics as a primary research focus. Zvi Gitelman and Al Meyer enabled me to consider patronage in a broader comparative context, challenging me to rework my assumptions about the modern bureaucracy. George Breslauer helped me to refine my thinking not only about Soviet elite politics, but about patronage and its relevance to the Soviet system. Roman Szporluk helped me to better understand the politics of Soviet republics, sensitizing me to the value of long-term, careful study of particular organizational and regional settings.

Along the way others have reacted to some or all of my chapters, and I have benefited from their suggestions. Bill Reisinger saw the manuscript through all of its revisions, and his thoughts played a critical role as a more finished book took shape. Ron Hill provided helpful comments – and much encouragement – after reading the entire manuscript in its final stage. Donna Bahry, Steve Burant, Charles Fairbanks, Jeffrey Hahn, Eric Hoffmann, and Ron Suny read parts of the book as it evolved through various conference papers, and their suggestions were critical as the revision process went forward. Several anonymous reviewers for Cambridge University Press offered thoughtful and suggestive comments that significantly strengthened the book's organization and content.

A 1982–83 research stay in the USSR, supported by the International Research and Exchanges Board, was critical to both data collection and initial analyses. My Soviet hosts in the Department of USSR History of the Soviet Period, Moscow State University, extended me every courtesy and enabled me to have a most fruitful year. Nikolai Naumov was especially supportive in orienting me to the norms of Soviet academic research life. I also benefited from the professionalism and assistance of many staff members of the INION (Institute of Scientific Information for the Social Sciences) Library in Moscow. A follow-up research trip to Moscow, Vilnius, and Tallinn, supported by the Midwest Universities Consortium for International Activities and Michigan State University, provided important interviews that helped me to anticipate Gorbachev period developments.

I should also like to make mention of my editor at Cambridge University Press, Michael Holdsworth, who was most encouraging and helpful as the manuscript moved through the review, revision, and production process. Rachel Quenk gave the entire manuscript a careful reading and provided invaluable help as the final draft emerged. The staff of James Madison College of Michigan State University and of the Department of Political Science of the University of Arizona provided much needed assistance; I would especially like to thank Becky Moore, Kelli Waldron, and Bonnie Weybourne. Van Maas provided tremendous moral support throughout my long odyssey with political patronage, and I am most grateful. Finally, my wife, Nancy Stiller, inspired and encouraged me as a book slowly emerged from a doctoral dissertation. Nancy constantly motivated me with a laugh and a smile, and her love and support made all the difference. More than anyone Nancy enabled me to see this project to its completion. It is with much love and gratitude that I dedicate this book to her.

Introduction

Patron–client relations have played an important role in the recruitment, mobility, and behavior of politicians throughout the over seven decades of Soviet power. Operating in a highly centralized institutional setting and guided by a set of norms that reflected the hierarchical nature of political relations, Soviet officials have relied upon clientelistic ties to advance their interests in an essentially insecure political environment. These informal networks of interconnected careers have been critical to the formation of governing coalitions, bridging individual, institutional, sectoral, and regional interests. They have been a major device for increasing and maintaining politicians' power and authority.

However, among the approaches to the study of the Soviet political elite and policy making, patronage has remained an enigmatic and confounding factor. Our limited knowledge about clientelistic norms has stemmed in part from a paucity of information regarding established rules and practices of Soviet elite mobility and regime formation. The lack of extensive biographical and attitudinal data for the national political elite, along with the near absence of systematic data for subnational officials, has obscured the identification of such relationships and their norms. These extra-legal informal political associations are, by their very nature, difficult to identify. The governing ethos of the Soviet Union has decried and denied them. Given these dilemmas, the scholarly work that has been done on patronage, elite mobility, and regime formation has generally been qualitative, time and context-specific, and often speculative. The policy-making implications of these ties and networks have remained essentially unexplored.

The traditional Soviet political system has been hierarchical and highly centralized. There have been no alternative sources of power outside the unified set of party and government hierarchies. Patronage and other manifestations of a *second polity* have been decisive in this system, providing the necessary slack for it to operate, albeit incrementally. Patronage has served as an adhesive binding individuals and groups together, bridging various organized interests. Coalitions of protégés who worked and ascended the system together, supplemented with relative newcomers and allies whose policy and career interests merged, provided the basis for governance. Contrary to the more common arguments characterizing political patronage as merely politics of blatant economic nepotism, these networks have provided coherence to the political process. Although lower-level networks could obstruct regime policies and system goals, the strong central government was organizationally capable of countering many of those elements, pressuring resistant networks, and appointing new and presumably more reliable replacements. Traditional Soviet political norms helped top national leaders to grapple with the challenges of subordinate networks while enabling them to consolidate their hold on the political process by developing their own clientele.

In certain fundamental ways, this traditional Soviet setting is not unlike that of other political systems. Political development brought with it the modern bureaucracy, which has continued to grow in size and complexity for at least a century. A major challenge before modern political leadership is to control and direct that apparatus, for such mastery is a primary prerequisite for governance. The building of coalitions, in part based upon patronage, but encompassing a diversity of interests and views, has been essential to that mastery in many societies. This has been especially true where there is a lack of organized independent interest groups or competing political parties. Where power is concentrated in a rigidly hierarchical decision-making system, and where there is no viable political opposition, the structural conditions for extra-legal patron–client relationships arise. A certain rationale and legitimacy for patronage networks emerges where explicit rules and norms forbidding such informal arrangements are lacking or poorly enforced. Patron–client networks come to constitute an informal system of checks and balances that permits groups of politicians to advance their interests. The distribution of power among contending groups restrains the hegemonic urges of any single group.

Patron–client relations also have helped politicians to govern in the traditional Soviet system. Coalitions of protégés and clients representing various interests and institutions have provided a leader – a *patron* – with the support to develop and undertake a policy program. In national level politics, patronage ties enhanced the ability of the Communist Party General Secretary to consolidate power, to build a governing coalition, and to fashion a comprehensive policy program. Unlike many other political systems, in which newly elected leaders form new administrations of executive personnel, the traditional Soviet system required more informal mechanisms to permit a leader to form his own administration. The process of personnel turnover, elevation of trusted protégés, and building of alliances with major interests, was drawn out. Yet the successful completion of this process was vital to the long-term career and policy interests of all top decision makers, regardless of their levels of authority. The Soviet system gave leaders at both the national and subnational levels significant discretion and initiative within their own bailiwicks. But those leaders needed the cooperation of others to see a directive or program through to its implementation.

Gorbachevian reforms are transforming the Soviet system and altering the norms by which politicians advance and behave. The institutional and political reforms of the Gorbachev period are changing strategies of elite recruitment, coalition building, and regime formation. The hierarchical and centralized power structure of the Soviet system is giving way to a more decentralized, open, and democratic political process. An expanding range of actors and interests now influences the political process, and senior officials are less able to direct the country's political life. Moreover, informal interest associations and popular fronts are giving rise to formal interest groups and political parties that can legally compete for power with the CPSU. All of these changes contribute to a more formal separation of powers among political actors. As a result, a new rationale for career building may emerge; the politically ambitious may need new strategies to assure career success. Patron–client relations may take on a different relevance to the policy process of the 1990s.

This study of elite mobility, regime formation, and governance in the Brezhnev and Gorbachev periods considers patronage as an approach to understanding the Soviet political process. I examine coalition building at both the national and regional levels through an analysis of aggregate career data for over two thousand politicians. The study assesses the manner and extent to which leaders in politically stable and less stable settings – spanning different national cultural contexts – have relied upon clientelistic networks to consolidate power and to govern. Analysis of Lithuanian and Azerbaidzhani republic politics confirms tendencies found at the national level. Examination of post-1985 Gorbachev period developments reveals a dynamic set of conditions that is changing the face of patronage in Soviet political reality.

1 The elite, patronage, and Soviet politics

For centuries patronage relations have molded the political life of countries and their elite. In feudal and industrial societies patronage relationships were integral to the anatomy of the society itself. However, even in more highly structured political systems we find that these relationships continue to influence critical aspects of political life. Few countries have been so influenced by patronage relations as historical Russia and the Soviet Union. While many observers of Soviet and Russian politics acknowledge the importance of patronage to elite recruitment and behavior, it has largely remained an uncharted area of study. The approach here systematically explores patronage not only as a means of elite recruitment and mobility, but more importantly as a mechanism which structures the formation and development of national and subnational regimes.

The pervasiveness of patronage relations in the public arena stems in large part from the very nature of the political arena. The arena within which a political elite operates is dynamic and insecure. It is structured by the varied formal and informal mechanisms that ordinarily guide and moderate the behavior of politicians as they compete and promote their own interests.

The state, through its administrative institutions and rules, sets the most important formal parameters within which an elite operates. The expanding hierarchy of institutions within the modern bureaucracy generates ever more specialized functions and fixed rules which all aspiring officials must face. Other institutions, including popular assemblies, guide the attempts of politicians to influence the myriad of professional civil servants responsible for the effective operation of that bureaucracy. Political parties and organized associations of politicians are significant in that they allow particular interests to secure control over the state and its bureaucracy. They provide a certain degree of attitudinal constraint among members and help regulate the efforts of a wide range of politicians to direct the policy agenda and process.

These state and nonstate institutions, through developed rules and norms, moderate – but do not obviate – the insecurity of the political domain in which the actors' interests merge or collide. Thus, individuals active in political life often must rely upon additional, informal mechanisms to enhance their positions and advance their interests.

Among such informal mechanisms are individualized, reciprocal, political relations that often culminate in networks. These serve to link individuals' interests and help them preserve or expand their positions. Such personalized, reciprocal, political connections are what we refer to as patronage relationships. They provide security and direction to members' career ambitions, helping politicians both to advance and to govern.[1]

The very nature of political leadership encourages the emergence of patronage relationships. Political leadership presupposes a power relationship among individuals within a group who are dependent upon one another to attain mutual goals.[2] Thus it assumes not only a power differential between the leader and the led, but also an exchange of sorts, a reciprocity linking the intentions and interests of all concerned.[3] The leader–follower linkage develops over time, involving a series of exchanges or transactions between leaders and followers in which leaders both give and receive. The duration and the extensiveness of the transactions help to define the strength of the bond between two individuals with differing political means and potentially differing intentions.

Leaders, or possible patrons among clients, are the decision makers who set basic goals and priorities. They act as mediators within their groups, as well as spokespersons outside of them. They devote most of their resources to securing control over the decision-making process, whatever its form, and they maintain that control in order to guide and influence policy outcomes.[4] Yet if this relationship is based on mutual exchange between the leaders and the led, just what is the form of currency? At the most basic level leaders set the parameters for adequate role behavior in the attainment of their group's goal(s). Leaders' continuing effectiveness is related to their group's ultimate success.[5] At the same time, status, recognition, and esteem afford leaders greater influence and contribute to their legitimacy as leaders. Individuals acting as leaders help to fulfill expectations, achieve group goals, and also provide rewards for others, which are in turn reciprocated in the form of heightened influence, status, and esteem. Although there is a distinct inequality between leader and led, the relationship is clearly interdependent.

Political patronage can be defined as an informal network of personal, political relationships which are at the same time both asymmetrical and interdependent. They are an informal mechanism that provides security and direction to the career ambitions of a nation's political elite.[6] The environment in which politicians operate is uncertain and hostile. It often entails a zero-sum contest among members of the elite. In this setting, a politician's first concern is to minimize losses, not maximize gains. A major means of minimizing losses and securing one's position is through the formulation of coalitions based upon reciprocal relationships. Relationships that already have been tested and developed over time.

A clientelism model of political group formation and behavior depicts a political system composed of such coalitions. Individuals with career aspirations often advance within a political system on the basis of their ties to politicians who possess power at higher levels of authority. The resultant networks, centered around a guiding leader or patron, are often system-wide and may operate at all levels of decision making. In such a system, patrons are able to strengthen their own politicial position by appointing those loyal to them, usually those who have already worked with them, to positions at lower levels. The loyalty of subordinates to patrons is derived from the political goods they receive in return, such as political power, prestige, and the promise of future advancement.[7] By promoting loyal subordinates within the political system, politicians are able to enhance their own power position as well as effect desired policy ends. Increasingly powerful patronage networks help individuals to rise to power as well as to maintain that power.

A syndrome of characteristics distinguishes the patron–client bond. First, there is usually some kind of pre-existing personal relationship based on some kind of past experience of interaction. The parties share some degree of loyalty and reliability towards one another. However, it should be understood that this loyalty is primarily dependent upon its utility in bringing each party's political ambitions to fruition. Loyalty could be reinforced by the intimacy of a personal relationship, by fear of coercion, or both. The patron and the client may also share political views, though this is certainly not always the case.

Second, because patrons and clients operate on different authority levels, the relationship is inherently asymmetrical. Such inequality is not only accepted by both parties, but is a critical motivating force for both patron and client to join in the relationship. This is not to say that the power differential is always beneficial, as it could very well produce tensions which might undercut the loyalty of network members and thus weaken the patron–client bond. Equalization of the two positions could also make for just as tenuous a relationship, for without a power differential the relationship would no longer be that of a patron and client, but that of allies. An alliance in which the power differential is minimal is quite vulnerable to the exigencies of a given moment, and may not stay equal or friendly for very long.

The last, and perhaps most important, characteristic to keep in mind is this idea of reciprocity, a mutual exchange of political goods. The transactional nature of the relationship joins the parties together in a commerce of support, ideas, and favors. As individuals help one another to climb the political ladder, the patron–client bond is increasingly enhanced, thus relationships are likely to grow stronger with age. Clearly we are speaking of a relationship of interdependence, that is, a relationship in which the influence and power of one individual depends to an extent upon the influence and loyalty of another.

Patronage is often characterized as a form of corruption that serves individuals' needs while undercutting the process of governance. A closer, systematic study will show that patronage relations serve not only to advance members within the expanding hierarchy of the bureaucracy, they also allow politicians to govern more effectively. The histories and cultural traditions of any country are critically important in determining the manner in which patronage relations emerge and operate.[8] In many traditional and predominantly rural Latin countries, the regional *cacique* (boss or patron) possesses the coercive means to serve as a "political middleman," bridging the power and resource gap between the national government and the locales.[9] The widespread mass deference to authority in contemporary democratic Japan permits patrons at all levels (e.g. party leaders, business executives, and union officials) to assume almost exclusive responsibility for many aspects of the country's civic and economic life.[10]

Given these differences, I cannot comprehensively assess all country-specific, historical, and cultural background factors as they influence patron–client relations. Rather, I will explore the institutional and political circumstances that condition the way in which politicians rely on informal patronage relationships while enhancing their power and positions. Regardless of national setting, the conflictual nature of political relations presupposes that the manner of power distribution among contending interests will determine the behavior patterns of political officials.[11] Understanding the political relevance of patronage to a country's politics requires a consideration of power distribution – among individuals and institutions, as well as interests.

Patronage relations have molded the political life of many countries and their elite, but few have been as influenced by it as the Soviet Union. Social, economic, and political conditions have encouraged the thriving of patronage networks in Russia as well as in many other nations now comprising the USSR. The tradition of a strong central autocrat, governing in tandem with powerful regional figures, has enabled clientelistic relations to flourish at various levels of political authority.[12] The advent of Soviet power did not obviate the tsarist legacy of reliance upon patronage connections in the recruitment and mobility of elites and in the formation of regimes. In fact, Soviet political adjustments actually reinforced the political importance of these informal networks of patronage relationships.

While many observers of Soviet and Russian politics acknowledge the importance of patronage to elite recruitment, few have systematically explored it. The present approach systematically explores patronage not only as a means of elite recruitment and mobility, but more importantly as a mechanism which structures the formation and functioning of national and subnational regimes. Strong patronage networks which bridge different institutions can help a governing elite to master the policy process. The centralized, hierarchical Soviet system provides much political discretion to those who can surmount it. But at the same time, competing networks – or institutionally well-ensconced subnational networks – can confound the process of coherent policy making. Powerful networks committed to policy changes can advance initiatives, just as those protective of the status quo can assume an obstructionist stance. In the Soviet system, political patronage can facilitate both continuity and change. Only the most profound reform of the Soviet political system, i.e., with a fundamental redistribution of power and emergent pluralism, would alter the centrality of political patronage to Soviet politics.

The Soviet setting

Political patronage in the Russian and Soviet setting can signify both *protektsiya*, or patronage, and *sviazi*, or reciprocal connections. While *protektsiya* has a distinctly political flavor, both terms represent networks of reciprocal favors. They transcend the political arena to encompass the social and economic dimensions of Soviet life. At the most basic level, *sviazi* help one to obtain material goods such as food and consumer products, arrange repairs for one's apartment, or secure advancement in the workplace. At a higher level of social responsibility, plant managers rely upon *sviazi* to achieve production goals, i.e., to obtain the necessary material resources to fulfill the plan. In certain regions of the country, e.g., Georgia and Central Asia, *sviazi* are important not just for meeting material needs, but for strengthening traditional clan and familial solidarity. They help to determine one's social position and influence, as well as the direction of one's social responsibility.[13]

In many instances, patronage cultivates what has been called the "second economy," i.e., semilegal or illegal activities directed toward private economic gain.[14] *Protektsiya* and *sviazi* can therefore signify forms of premodern corruption for purely material individual interests. They may represent extralegal means by which one gains leverage in dealing with a basic economic and social uncertainty. Far from challenging the existent social structures that cushion such uncertainty, *sviazi* and other elements of the "second economy" provide slack and flexibility to what would otherwise be an excessively brittle set of socioeconomic structures.

Is there a comparable *second polity* operating in the Soviet political realm, involving the decision-making elite?[15] I contend that there are comparable informal political mechanisms which are related to the formal decision-making structures but which can serve to integrate further those structures and permit them to function more effectively. For example, clientelistic ties serve as vehicles which unite politicians' interests and provide slack in a highly hierarchical and rigid decision-making process. Yet clientelistic networks constitute an informally accepted, extralegal arrangement signifying more than an essentially illegal second polity. In the modern bureaucratic context, political clientelism can provide political integration where subordinate client politicians are loyal to a patron superior and his program. Clientelism can permit central penetration of the locales, bridging national and regional politicians, as well as regional and local politicians. As a result, the career ambitions and interests of these politicians are linked. The policy consequences may vary, however, as patronage networks may actually permit central governance or else reinforce lower-level resistance.

The Soviet political system's lack of any formal means for a new leader to form a new administrative team encourages clientelistic networks. A new leader coming into power at any level of authority does not come in with a whole group of new appointees or allies, but is compelled to work with those already in power and with the predecessor's appointees. Consequently, he is forced to build a consensus of support before beginning to appoint his own people, form his own team, and put forward his own program. This requires time. Given that all officials are said to be part of one "grand team," with the presumed absence of factions and policy disagreements, there is no legitimate open course for the new leader to easily or automatically build his own administration.

How do new leaders fashion an administration? They do so on the basis of effective coalition building across various (institutional and sectoral) interests. This requires not only establishing good working relations with those already in power, but, over time, bringing in reliable new personnel. It is this political fact of life, the slow replacement of cadres and the introduction of new personnel – often one's own loyalists – which enables first secretaries to begin building their administrations. It must be done carefully and behind closed doors. Through their control over the specific cadres departments within the party apparatus, by way of the nomenklatura system, new leaders are able to recruit new personnel and form new teams. It is only when they arrive at an initial consensus with their peers and form their own teams that they are able to develop and present their own policy programs.

Ultimately, leaders must possess many skills and resources to be successful. They must be able to bridge various sectoral and regional interests. They must be able to work with incumbents and those of their own political generation, at the same time forging bonds with the younger generation. They must position themselves within the past tradition, while evincing policy positions that distinguish them from the problems of the past. In building new governing coalitions leaders will become centrists of sorts. They will, however, need to have a firm political base of support: a base stemming in large part from their own networks and other political associations.

In explaining why politicians gain from patronage ties and why patronage plays an important role in the Soviet political system, I focus on the nature of the traditional centralized Soviet political system and the set of hierarchical institutional structures comprising it. Although this system and set of structures may change in light of

Gorbachevian reforms, it is clear that its essential features have facilitated networks and clientelistic politics at least into the early 1990s. In the traditional Soviet system, political mobility means moving up the interlocked bureaucratic hierarchies, with promotion by performance determined by superiors, rather than by explicitly impersonal rules. In this setting there are no political mechanisms – such as competitive political parties – moderating the politics of personality and ambition. In the logic of this highly centralized political system pressures stemming from high-level rivalries always influence rivalries and mobility at lower levels.[16]

In the traditional Soviet system, there is little to prevent one individual from directly transferring political status and influence to another. In fact, there are no formal mechanisms constraining the ability of politicians to transfer political power (e.g., offices) directly to particular individuals. This is an important differentiation between Soviet and Western systems. In the latter, popularity in the electoral context is the basic currency of power: a commodity not easily shifted to another person.[17] At the same time, the composition of the elite selectorate in Western competitive electoral systems is much more varied, with actors outside the political bureaucracy assuming an important role in the mobility process. In the more rigidly hierarchical and centralized Soviet system, the basic currency of power is authority and status. These qualities can be more readily transferred from person to person through political appointments. This is especially true where the responsible selectorate is a relatively homogeneous central political elite, as found in Moscow. The hierarchy of institutions linking all decision-making organs helps to link in a more direct manner careers and rivalries across levels of authority. While horizontal ties may influence an individual's behavior, the preeminent political relationship in the highly hierarchical context is one of domination and subordination. Such a political relationship can and does foster patronage connections.

One cannot consider the political landscape of the USSR without acknowledging the significant effects of its rapid socioeconomic and political transformation. Given the nature of power relations, the system structure, and the economic vagaries of a still-developing country, Soviet politics are characterized by uncertainty. Such uncertainty describes Soviet politics in periods both of relative stability and instability. The stakes for competing politicians have changed over time – certainly since the Stalin period. The lack, however, of explicitly defined rules for personnel recruitment and the absence of formal mechanisms for evaluating politicians' behavior continue to make political life unpredictable for politicians. To this is added the impact of an essentially underdeveloped peasant political culture. In such underdeveloped peasant settings, limited resources are distributed on the basis of parochial ties. Stress is placed on personalized or clan connections. The transformation of such an underdeveloped social and political setting, while changing the nature of social relations, only reinforces the utility of personalized patronage ties. The implications of such personalized connections shift from material resource acquisition (corruption), to power consolidation and governance through patronage networks (coalition building). Against this background, and given the paucity of legal constraints, patronage has become a sort of functional equivalent to law.[18] Institutional, historical, cultural, and developmental factors all contribute to the continued salience of clientelism in elite political behavior.

While the enumerated factors and norms of democratic centralism encourage the formation of patronage networks, the official ethos necessarily condemns them. And this has important implications for the observable enigmatic nature of these relationships in the Soviet polity. Unlike the experience of Latin American and other settings where clientelistic networks flourish openly, these personalistic connections are publicly decried in the socialist state. Parochial political relations are contrary to the concept of a developed, ostensibly "democratic" political system. The equalizing of all social groups and the normalizing of relations through recruitment by merit are the explicitly emphasized guiding principles of a society describing itself as increasingly modern. But if patronage ties enhance the position of relatively disadvantaged groups, they presume inequality on an individual-by-individual and group-by-group basis. While they can play a functional role in the political domain, they must be disguised by other stated recruitment criteria. Similar to many manifestations of the second economy, such informal political relations are often tolerated or simply ignored. As such, they are often studied only in so far as they constitute a form of corruption. Indeed, patronage can be dysfunctional to the Soviet system.[19]

Clientelistic networks can undercut system performance and political effectiveness. The Russian and Soviet past reveals a strong tradition – indeed, what has been termed an "elaborate etiquette" – of corruption among officials.[20] The anti-corruption campaigns of the Gorbachev regime are but the most recent efforts to rein in obstructing lower-level networks.

Politicians can use patronage networks to build localized political machines, enabling them to undercut national directives while enriching themselves. A perusal of Soviet newspapers for any period reveals the ongoing nature of this corruption.[21] Moscow has pursued many strategies, including personnel rotation in lower-level organizations, to counteract the problem. The transfer or removal of a network leader sometimes leaves a vital, entrenched, and resistant network still in place. Often, a local network is "decapitated," with a new local boss forming a network that is more closely aligned with the national regime and its interests. By and large, national authorities have been more concerned with the country's integration and the application of central directives outward and downward. It is generally only when lower-level network activities blatantly obstruct regime and system goals that Moscow has attempted to deal with them.

The intentions and activities of informal networks of politicians are commonly viewed as corrupt in nature because, by definition, they violate basic rules of the Soviet politicial system. In fact, it is difficult to identify precisely what constitutes corrupt behavior, and, as A.J. Heidenheimer argues, one may adopt a number of broad approaches in defining it.[22] We are considering various types of informal transactional relations, often entailing obligations that are ambiguous and somewhat abstract. For the purposes of this study it makes more sense to conceive of the problem in this way: corrupt behavior entails activities which the Soviet leadership explicitly identifies as dysfunctional to the Soviet system. Although different national regimes approach these matters with contrasting interests and perspectives, they all differentiate between necessary and often routine departures from the rules, and extreme behavior that obstructs the operation of the political and economic systems. Soviet leaders have tacitly acknowledged the necessity of certain forms of corruption to the country's economic life.

Clusters of politicians engage in various transactional activities of a potentially dysfunctional nature and these activities can be grouped into three broad types. First, there are petty economic and political transactions which are pervasive throughout the Soviet Union, which cannot be accounted for, but which are often functional to system and regime needs. Among such activities are the minor benefits and gifts exchanged between parties, usually of a more overtly economic than political significance. These exchanges constitute a violation of the socialist state's ethos, but they have no political importance and have been of little concern to national authorities.

Second, there are actions by officials which represent more routine political corruption of limited scope and nature. These include favoritism in appointments, modifying plans to ensure their fulfilment, or misreporting activities to favor oneself or one's network members and community. Such actions constitute abuses of power and office. Certainly national regimes are concerned about them, especially when they disrupt important system-wide goals. However, these actions are less important taken individually than when considered collectively. Because the cost to the national authorities of disclosing these activities would be considerable, it is only when individual actions cumulate to assume a more pronounced threat to higher authorities that action is likely to be taken.

It is the third, and from our standpoint the most important, set of illegal actions that is of broader scope and dysfunctional to the system. Here, the activities of a lower-level official or a network directly, and profoundly, block or undercut central directives. Individuals or networks may flagrantly violate or ignore national policies. Such cases usually involve a history of multiple violations. In all likelihood the local or regional network is well-rooted in its community and strong enough to pursue ends diverging from those of Moscow. It is in such cases that national authorities are most likely to take firm action against putatively corrupt patronage politics.

All three of these dysfunctional forms are interrelated and overlapping, making it difficult for anyone – especially an outsider – to draw distinctions. The Soviet system actually needs a certain amount of the first and second types of illegal activities. But when the activities of individuals and networks are of a sufficient magnitude to threaten the governance of the USSR, it becomes imperative to deal with them. As will become evident, Mikhail Gorbachev's contemporary efforts to root out troublesome regional machines are but the latest examples of a long-standing Moscow tradition of purging dysfunctional patronage networks.

While the traditional view of political patronage has concentrated upon its potentially dysfunctional corruptive dimension, my interest is in studying political patronage as a mechanism facilitating coalition building, regime formation, and policy making in the Soviet system. The complex push and pull of high politics signifies that a wide range of factors will influence the behavior, attitudes, and career prospects of aspiring politicians. While important, patronage is but one of numerous potential explanatory factors, as the following section will indicate. Its explanatory power is greatest in helping to account for: (1) norms of elite recruitment and mobility; (2) attitudinal constraint among politicians; (3) processes of regime formation; and (4) means of regime maintenance. A cluster of attributes characterizes the politically mobile politician in the more contemporary Soviet setting, and politicians will want to maximize their background strengths to advance. Career connections, however, often prove determinative. As a hopeful, young, upwardly mobile, Moscow city politician confided to me, the advice and assistance of a higher-level official (*qua* patron) can be all-important in constructing one's career. Particular background experiences and attributes can be highlighted or secured to maximize one's prospects. Through linkage with a superior, one is socialized to the "rules of the game" and instructed in the appropriate conduct and attitudes. This type of common career relationship – multiplied by the thousands of politicians and networks operating in the system – becomes an important component in the formation and operation of ruling coalitions. It explains much of Soviet elite political reality.

Other approaches

There are several other approaches to the study of elite behavior within the existing body of literature that help qualify the claims of the clientelism model. One set of explanations explores elite performance in a complex managerial setting. This rational-technical approach considers the nature of the tasks confronting the policy maker, the influence of outside agencies, and the restrictions of the bureaucratic structure. This approach considers an individual's mobility to depend upon expertise and ability to help achieve the basic social mission of rapid economic development. It is presumed that in a more developed political setting, there is an overriding concern that technical expertise in management should ensure efficiency and continued growth. In this setting decision-making norms vary by policy area, so that rules and norms are no longer uniform across cases. There is a concomitant natural movement toward a real diffusion of political power.

In a political context dominated by issues of socioeconomic development, cleavages among decision makers are seen as involving matters of policy – at the most basic level, the investment of scarce resources – rather than simply as matters of personal and/or factional rivalry. In this alternative view, loyalty is significant only to the extent that it influences the level of policy fulfilment. Political behavior is seen as being more closely related to role and position rather than to past relationships with particular individuals.

The rational-technical approach is based on a presumed change in the structure of decision making within the Soviet political system. Rules governing the political system are said to have become more explicit and more formally defined. Jerry Hough identified a tendency towards greater "orderliness" in the system, with clearer distinctions drawn among various decision-making bodies, and greater autonomy given to various central-peripheral political organs. There also seems to be greater security for cadres, motivating them to think in terms of less extreme consequences for upward and downward mobility. Indeed, Khrushchev's de-Stalinization policies, and the "stability of cadres" policy of the Brezhnev era, were conducive to a growing sense of elite security.[23]

It is argued that this presumed change in political structure and elite behavior has resulted in the greater "rationalization" of Soviet politics. Modernization, i.e., greater economic growth and the improved performance of the political system, is regarded as the primary concern motivating political behavior. The nature of the reward structure for the elite is thus altered, as policy effectiveness is increasingly defined by real economic growth. Within this context, factional disputes and personality politics become less important. Individuals are recruited and advanced on the merits of expertise and performance, and their behavior judged on the basis of their contribution to broad mission accomplishment. Loyalty, reliability, and competence in carrying out assignments assume a secondary importance. Moreover, the diffusion of political power to a wider range of institutions implies that central apparat superiors will not be the only actors evaluating performance and making mobility decisions.

A second, corporatist approach stresses the role of inclusion and representation of interests in elite recruitment at the all-union policy-making level.[24] As an approach to elite studies, corporatism emphasizes both a balance of interests across functional, institutional, and regional distinctions, and a balance of influence among members of the leading coalition.[25] It becomes necessary to include a wider range of officials to offset the authority of the party general secretary or any small hegemonic group within the top elite.

Upon initial reflection, the corporatist notion of balancing elite interests appears to be in opposition to the clientelist model and its emphasis on power asymmetry among elites. Corporatism does suggest a more symmetrical interest representation within the ranks of a governing elite. Yet at the system level, the notion of balanced interests is compatible with the clientelist conception of elite politics as balancing interests across different and competing patronage networks. These networks arise out of different sectoral and regional settings, and the inclusion of their patrons in a governing coalition signifies at least the potential representation of diverse interests.

The corporatist approach stresses the building of effective governing coalitions not only by recruiting competing politicians, but also by developing an acceptable set of norms for facilitating policy compromise. This involves in part an acceptable division of labor and responsibility among officials. An acceptable delegation of responsibilities within a diverse elite assumes a more effective bargaining process which is said to be less contentious.

Both approaches correctly emphasize the relevance of expertise and performance to political elite recruitment and mobility. They fail, however, to account for the significance of other factors, focusing almost exclusively on the meritocratic element. Expertise continues to be a necessary, but not sufficient, criterion for political mobility in the Soviet system. The constrained Soviet political opportunity structure limits the pertinence of meritocratic factors.[26] There is a scarcity of political resources, with many aspirants competing for a limited number of political slots. Politically important nomenklatura positions – at both the provincial and higher levels – only number in the thousands, while there are tens of thousands of potential office holders. Mobility opportunities for those making political careers are highly structured and centralized. An aspiring politician must attempt to advance through a very limited number of recruitment channels. Compared to more open societies, lines of advancement are rigidly prescribed by the institutional structure. Access to those channels and the political process is hierarchically determined. Thus, at any given moment, the political opportunity structure is very much defined by the current power elite. In such a context, rational-technical criteria can be of importance, but the decisive factor would involve an aspirant's connections with the selectorate.

An examination of the sectoral and regional representation of politicians in the highest governing circles may well reveal a more recent regime inclination to include a wider range of interests, as the corporatist model suggests. Nevertheless, when a top decision maker, or group of decision makers, appoints a politician to an important national position, they choose from among a variety of candidates. Even on the basis of expertise alone, there is no one candidate clearly superior to all others on the basis of only "objective" criteria. There will be numerous candidates who are suitable on the grounds of expertise and experience, as well as appropriate sectoral or regional affiliation. As a result, the value of these attributes among the top candidates for a slot is equalized across contenders. It is highly unlikely that a single candidate will evince a level of expertise decisively superior to all competitors. Other factors, especially connections, will come into play in the final decisive stage of the selection process.

Why do connections assume such an importance? Connections are often the necessary condition for recruitment because they afford the best prospects for political reliability. In the final analysis this is paramount because, above all else, a politician is concerned with safeguarding his position of authority. A Yugoslav politician observed that in the socialist political setting, there are "negative criteria" that affect elite recruitment. He told me that politicians are obsessed with ensuring that they do not risk their positions by recruiting unpredictable subordinates.[27] A candidate has appeal not only for the positive skills and experience he brings to a job, but also for the reliability and predictability that he offers his superior. The superior, after all, is committed to the "economic mission" only to the extent that he can at least maintain, if not strengthen, his own political position in the process. This is rationality for a politician with ambitions. A skilled subordinate who helps realize the mission while undercutting his superior is no asset. Past performance, as well as any social prestige or qualifications that the potential appointee might have, are considered in recruitment. Preference is given, however, to the individual least likely to challenge the patron, least likely to compromise him or weaken his position, and most likely to advance the patron's interests without question.

In evaluating reliability and loyalty we should not cancel out the relevance of a potential appointee's expertise, because achievement of tasks influences one's evaluation by superiors. But the achievement of a mission requires the responsibilities and contributions of many individuals to be assimilated at different levels of authority. It also requires some mutual covering up, so that the taut plan can be fulfilled and various assignments met.[28] Indeed, the nature of the Soviet hierarchical political structure all but requires such covering up by a politician in order to be successful. Mutual covering up benefits the system in that it reinforces the very set of informal political relationships that must function if the overriding economic mission is to be realized.

It is inappropriate, then, to counterpose meritocratic and clientelistic criteria for recruitment, as has been done.[29] Rather, it is more useful to consider them together as necessary and sufficient conditions for advancement in centralized political contexts which have constrained political opportunity structures. Individually, neither expertise nor experience are necessary and sufficient requirements for political mobility. Combined with patronage connections, they represent a viable set of resources that guides career advancement prospects.

Contemporary reforms in the USSR may confirm a second rational-technical suggestion that a more "orderly" Soviet system is emerging as policy-making rules become more explicit and routinized. Certainly, there are more rules, and they are more explicitly developed.[30] Formally, there is evidence to suggest enhanced routinization of certain types of policy making, and a more explicit formulation of institutional responsibilities;[31] orderliness and normalization can only come after a fundamental restructuring of the Soviet system: perhaps we shall see such a system as Gorbachev's reform program develops over time. A basic resetting of elite rules of behavior would be mandatory, keeping notions of public accountability preeminent. Barring these developments, informal mechanisms such as patronage networks will continue to structure elite motivations and behavior.

At the heart of rational-technical and corporatist explanations of elite recruitment and policy making is an understanding of elite political power relations suggesting a certain balance between the authority of the top leader and other members of the ruling elite. While viewing the party general secretary (or contemporary USSR president) as "first among equals," his accountability to the national elite is stressed as a critical factor severely constraining his political options. The image is raised in the post-Stalin period of a general secretary chairing a Politburo "board meeting," striving to find consensus among divergent interests. This image is especially applied during the early phase of a leader's rule, as he consolidates his power. Accountability before the Politburo notwithstanding, the general secretary still sets the policy agenda, structures the flow of information to Politburo members, and "initiates" the decision-making process. The power and prestige of the general secretary's office provide him with much authority, and the degree of his authority only grows as he strengthens his political position.

G.W. Breslauer's study of the general secretary's authority indicates that level of authority varies relative to the "stage" of a leader's tenure (e.g., early power consolidation phase, when authority is minimal, and power maintenance phase, when authority is more enhanced). But it is fair to conclude from his exhaustive account of the 1953–80 period that at no time did any politician other than the party general secretary assume an initiating role in Soviet political life. Khrushchev and Brezhnev were always the leading figures within their respective regimes.[32] While Gorbachev has come under great pressure in overseeing political and economic change, that change was only initiated under his guidance.

The nature of the hierarchical political structure and the influence of the traditional Soviet political culture do not obviate the guiding role of the general secretary.[33] They encourage it. This is a fact of Soviet political reality that has held, not only since Stalin's consolidation of power, but throughout the entire post-Stalin era.

The experience of the Russian past

The influence of patronage in elite mobility and recruitment has been pervasive not only since the earliest days of the Bolshevik regime, when Lenin and other top leaders placed trusted associates in top national decision-making positions, but even in the tsarist era. Political elite mobility in the seventeenth, eighteenth and nineteenth centuries was based on familial ties and common bureaucratic or military contacts – the precursors of contemporary patronage ties. An increasingly bureaucratized political system – the center of national power – and a long-term tradition of essentially feudal center–periphery relations encouraged the development of patronage-type relations.[34]

In tsarist Russia, an individual's familial and friendship connections were often critical to his elevation into top central government bodies.[35] This was true not only for the organs closely associated with the Tsar, such as the Boyar Duma, but also for central bureaucracies, the chanceries, and (later) ministries. Members of families which were prominent and favored by the Tsar filled many of the important governmental posts. Certain families came to dominate Russian politics over the course of decades, oftentimes assuming a decisive role in promoting major policy decisions or reforms.[36]

Systematic analysis of the composition of top central political bodies in the eighteenth century reveals considerable continuity over time in the inclusion of members of these prominent families.[37] One finds comparable tendencies in the country's military elite.

As the Russian political system evolved to find power concentrated in the hands of the land (and serf) owning gentry and the royal family, patronage became increasingly important. At the national level, matters of high politics were left to a small core of officials with highly centralized decision-making powers. More mundane day-to-day issues and lower-level administrative tasks were left to others, including the landed and lower-level officials. It is important to remember that pre-Soviet Russia did not rely upon collegial forms of political organization (e.g., elected assemblies, town meetings). Rather, it relied upon political officials who were subordinate to the sovereign. Thus the growth of the Russian state and bureaucracy resulted in the bureaucratization of the entire society. No important part of the society fell outside that state bureaucracy's purview. Opportunities for advancement in the state bureaucracy were linked in part to training, and patronage connections were essential to the training prospects of junior officials. The power and authority the landed gentry held at the regional level proved critical to the stability of the autocratic system. As Seton-Watson noted, the nobles were "pocket autocrats" on their own estates, but they left central power to the monarch.[38]

Political reforms instituted by Peter the Great formalized a centralization of power that heightened the Tsar's (Emperor's) power and authority. The Table of Ranks system introduced in 1722 more explicitly specified the gradations of power and authority associated with different institutions and positions. Its fourteen-level scale provided regulations governing the recruitment and mobility of all officials. It provided the Tsar and the central authorities with much greater power to assert their will over the state as well as the landed gentry.

This uniform ranking system formalized a tradition of hierarchy and precedence in elite mobility, and facilitated the continued reliance upon informal connections in the elevation of personnel. The Russian system of *chinoproizvodstvo* (the processing of ranks), stemming among other things from the Petrine Table of Ranks, ensured that the political stakes were quite high for those operating in the system. It not only determined the acquisition of positions, but established an individual's political status in the system. This highly developed system of regulated upward mobility of officials through ranks and the extent of its impact anticipated what would follow in the Soviet period nomenklatura system.[39]

While ultimate power rested with the Tsar, the political realities of a large, diverse, and modernizing society required that some authority and political status descend to others, generally court favorites, often through membership in high-level consultative bodies. Quasi-legislative advisory bodies were created to link the monarch and autocracy to important elements of the elite. The members of the State Council, for instance, established by Alexander I, were drawn from leading figures of the nobility and officialdom. Such bodies did little to constrain the activities of the autocrat, but they did represent yet another institutional vehicle enabling the autocrat to direct the behavior and upward mobility of aspiring officials.[40]

The expansive empire was linked to the center through appointed representatives of the Tsar in the provinces, the *voyevody*. First created by the Moscow city state in the seventeenth century, these tsarist prefects were often trusted associates of the monarch. From the earliest days, favoritism played a key role in their recruitment. Over time, these prefects were increasingly better educated and more experienced in the affairs of the locales, but patronage ties were still essential to their recruitment.

The complex role of these central representatives was evident from the beginning, foreshadowing a comparable complexity for the provincial party leaders of the Soviet period. They served as viceroys of the Tsar while also functioning as representatives of central bureaucracies and their interests (especially the Ministry of Internal Affairs). They were accountable to both. While representing the central authorities to locally entrenched groups and interests, they often articulated local concerns to the imperial government.

Catherine the Great's provincial administrative reforms resulted in the emergence of a more comprehensive and unified system of administration in the empire's periphery. Yet her provincial governors (*gubernatory*) operated in a still fragmentary system made up of a range of lower-level administrative actors. The 1802 creation of central ministries by Alexander I enhanced the influence of the imperial government over these prefects. The emperors, however, were reluctant to create a completely united ministerial system, leaving the provincial governors with at least a moderate degree of discretionary power.[41]

The growth of the Russian empire, modernization of Russian

society, and development of the Russian economy, necessitated the growth in size and power of the state bureaucracy. These changes also necessitated the evolution of a more sophisticated and diverse political elite. It is fair to conclude that the socialization and training process for the Russian elite became more advanced as the country moved through the latter eighteenth and nineteenth centuries. Experience, expertise, and loyalty all affected one's mobility prospects, yet there was no explicitly identified or consistently applied code of behaviour for aspirants. Even granting an era of increased professionalism, analysis of an aggregate population of mid-nineteenth century Russian officials reveals that the best predictor of who served in the state bureaucracy was that one's father had previously served in that same bureaucracy.[42] While Peter and his successors placed increasing emphasis upon aspirants' training and expertise, these "credentials" of professionalism generally needed to be matched by appropriate ascriptive qualities such as family connections, social background, and wealth.[43] Those desirous of reaching the top of the bureaucracy and the policy-making process still required powerful informal ties to superiors, including the Tsar.

The early years of Soviet power

The emergence of a Marxist-Leninist regime in Russia did not vitiate the importance of patronage in elite mobility and regime formation. To the contrary, the behavioral norms and revolutionary conditions of the previously clandestine Bolsheviks enhanced the critical role of these informal arrangements in the country's political life. The institutional arrangements that emerged under Soviet leaders further reinforced the political salience of patronage networks.

The Bolsheviks assumed power in November 1917 and immediately set about transforming the massive bureaucracy and set of procedures they had inherited from the tsarist regime. But their political organizations were not unlike those of their predecessors. Power was quickly centralized and the policy process continued to be bureaucratized and hierarchical in nature.

The early operational norms of the new Bolshevik elite stemmed in large part from its revolutionary experience, when power was shared informally among a number of leading political actors. The first months of Soviet power were dynamic. The Bolshevik Party was busy consolidating its position while at the same time attempting to work with Soviets which included threatening political rivals. Real authority within the party rested with only a handful of leaders, though norms of competitive selection of top leaders and open discussion of the policy agenda characterized the fledgling regime's first years. Informal networks, centered around leading national politicians, linked the various interests which comprised the party. While unified in its general orientation, the party experienced wide ranging debates among the members and leaders of those networks. As a result there was a considerable turnover in the composition of the ruling party Central Committee (CC), as members were frequently voted into and out of its ranks.

During this period, the selection of top-level personnel was left to a small cohort of party officials, with Yakov Sverdlov – a close ally of Lenin's with connections to many regional party organizations – assuming a critical role. His oversight of these issues was natural, given his extensive underground experience, his universally acknowledged organizational skills, and his wide ranging personal connections. His was an informal position, and he operated with a small staff.[44] Sverdlov relied upon many of his revolutionary period acquaintances and their protégés to fill open slots within the central apparatus and in the periphery.

During the early years of Soviet power, placements of top cadres involved not only family relations and spouses, but also protégés and friends from the prerevolutionary days. Among these were Lenin's wife, Nadezhda Krupskaya, his sister Anna and her husband (who became Commissar of the Railways), and the wives of other top Bolsheviks including Dzerzhinsky, Kamenev, Sverdlov, Trotsky, and Zinoviev. Lenin's secretaries and confidants from the Geneva period were selected for such important positions as the head of the Chancery and the Secretary of the Sovnarkhom. Often a politician filled his new bailiwick with trusted associates, as Lunacharsky did in packing the Education Commissariat with his protégés. Many such protégés offered considerable education and professional experience and proved to be politically competent. But it was their personal attachments and past associations with top Bolshevik leaders that were critical in their mobility.[45] Loyalty and reliability were key recruitment criteria as the Bolsheviks asserted their authority over an often antagonistic bureaucracy and tried to counter the attacks of domestic and foreign adversaries.

Meanwhile, at the regional and local levels, cliques formed around provincial and local party secretaries who served as patrons. These leaders, dispatched from the capital, were generally unknown to the local powers. They relied on Moscow's support to alter the local distribution of power and consolidate their positions. By the early 1920s, regional and local patrons with established ties to the all-union leadership were linked to factional struggles at the highest levels. This political infighting involving patronage networks thus included not only subnational issues and personalities, but also influences that stemmed from national politics.[46]

The mounting challenges to the new Bolshevik government altered these informal recruitment practices and encouraged the bureaucratization of the party and its membership. During the X Party Congress in 1921, when the party and state were still under siege from within and without, centralizing tendencies in personnel recruitment and policy making were more formally established.[47] Intra-party debates and challenges to the core leadership threatened the position of the regime and the implementation of its program. There was an incisive need to reinforce the central apparatus. A resolution, "on party unity," was passed by the Congress to halt factionalism among party members.[48] New procedures were adopted for determining the composition of top party bodies. Where previously delegates had voted for individual candidates – with the results not predetermined – delegates now voted for preselected slates of official candidates already drawn up by the top leadership. Top leaders now possessed greater latitude in ousting opponents and bringing in protégés and allies.

Meanwhile, organizational and personnel questions were increasingly left up to a small core of officials. After Sverdlov's death in 1919, the VIII Party Congress created several smaller bodies to guide and coordinate the mounting political, organizational, and personnel affairs of an expanding apparatus. A political bureau (Politburo), and organizational bureau (Orgburo), and a Secretariat were formed out of the Central Committee (CC) to oversee these matters. The members of these three bodies constituted the core decision-making elite of the regime, their political status having far transcended the previous "first among equals" status of top leaders. At the same time, CC departments were established to deal with various organizational matters. These departments grew rapidly, the total number of individuals working in them surpassing 750 by 1925.[49] Control over this central apparatus became essential to a politician's mastery of the policy process.

Even before Lenin's death in early 1924, the party apparatus had assumed a role quite different from that expected by many Bolsheviks. The bureaucratization of the intra-party mobility process helped shift the locus of decision making from the traditionally more representative CC to its smaller bodies, and especially its Politburo. Rather than serve the membership and the lower-level party organs, the apparatus – as directed by a small cohort of top officials – set policy and directed the activities of members.[50] Party leaders became adept at balancing the system-legitimating ethos of mass involvement with the political reality of concentrated power.

The victory of the apparatus was already complete by the early 1920s. The elevation of Joseph Stalin and several of his protégés to top supervisory functions in the apparatus assured its further power consolidation. Several of Stalin's associates (particularly Kaganovich and Molotov) assumed organizational positions that were critical to Stalin's ascent of power in the second half of the decade. The Stalin network was able rapidly to equate its interests with those of the expanding party apparatus, allowing the network to quickly expand its power. Soon no other politician or group of politicians possessed the ability to limit either that bureaucracy or the patronage network well positioned within it.

Stalin's mastery of the apparatus and recruitment process

Successful political power brokers diversify their bases of support while securing control over the elite recruitment process. This was certainly true of Stalin, whose mastery over the levers of political power ultimately stemmed from his dominant position within the party apparatus and his oversight of the recruitment process. His organizational preeminence was achieved primarily for two important reasons. First, within an amazingly short period of time, Stalin was able to build up a large patronage network and place trusted associates in critical positions in the apparatus. That network had its origins in the prerevolutionary and revolutionary periods, and was already considerable by the time of Stalin's appointment as party General Secretary in April 1922. Second, Stalin was at the same time able to have his interests and those of his network identified with the interests of the apparatus and the broader Bolshevik Party. He accomplished this through careful posturing and the skillful building of alliances with various actors and organizations, though his rapidly consolidated power was critical in enabling him to structure the political agenda.[51]

Stalin's final ascent to the pinnacle of power began with his appointment as the party's first General Secretary, simultaneously holding memberships in all of the top party organs (Politburo, Orgburo, and Secretariat). Promoted to this position because of his universally acknowledged acumen as an organizer and committee worker, he now held a set of positions which enabled him to coordinate and direct the activities of the party apparatus. He was assisted by two deputies, Viacheslav Molotov and Valerian Kuibyshev – both effective apparatchiki and both loyal protégés. His control over the Secretariat was especially important because it represented the power of appointment for both the party and state apparatuses. The Stalin network was in the position to set the agendas, change the rules, and influence the types of functions performed by top party bodies. The Secretariat soon became a permanent body, with an ongoing set of responsibilities, while the Orgburo and Politburo came to meet only periodically, with their members institutionally based elsewhere.

Throughout all this, Stalin was not without powerful opponents. Their bases of power, however, were much more limited than his. Trotsky, Zinoviev, and Kamenev, for instance, possessed higher levels of personal authority and more prominent revolutionary legacies, but these proved to be less important factors in acquiring political power. As Commissar of War, Trotsky's base of support was set in the Red Army. A number of his protégés were Komsomol leaders, as well as top planners and state officials. He also enjoyed influence over Ukraine, via his trusted associate, Christian Rakovsky. Zinoviev's and Kamenev's bases of support were geographically concentrated in the Moscow and Leningrad city party organizations, respectively.

Stalin's base was more widely diffuse. He was able to draw upon many connections forged in the revolutionary and civil war days, connections made in Tbilisi, Baku, and Tsaritsyn.[52] Among the more important of these earlier protégés were Ordzhonikidze, Voroshilov, and Budenny. As has been noted, Stalin's political might resided in the central party apparatus. In addition, he was institutionally positioned to influence government officials. From March 1919 until his April 1922 appointment as General Secretary, he headed the Workers' and Peasants' Inspectorate (*Rabkrin*): a position described as "a commissariat above all commissariats."[53] From the *Rabkrin* Stalin oversaw the composition and work of numerous governmental organs. As head of the Commissariat of Nationalities (appointed in

1917), Stalin also exercised control over many non-Russian regions: a role he continued to assume in the mid-1920s after he was selected (in 1922) to head a Politburo approved commission for regulating relations between the Russian and other republics. A number of his associates were also members of that commission, enabling Stalin to influence the advance of regional cadres. Kaganovich's supervision of the Secretariat's Organizational Section signified that the Stalin network would influence the appointment of clients to regional bureaus responsible for lower-level party affairs.[54]

Stalin used these important organizational settings to remove an impressive array of formidable adversaries.[55] In 1925 he was able to wrest control of the Moscow city organization away from Kamenev, and in early 1926 he was able to secure control over the Leningrad city organization from Zinoviev. Nikolai Uglanov replaced Kamenev's ally, I.A. Zelensky, as Moscow party Secretary, and Sergei Kirov, the Baku party Secretary and associate of Stalin, replaced Zinoviev in Leningrad. With Kliment Voroshilov's appointment as War Commissar after Frunze's death (1925), the circumstances were right for purging all remnants of Trotsky's influence within the Red Army.

Meanwhile, within the Politburo, Stalin protégés slowly moved into full and candidate member positions (e.g., Molotov, Voroshilov, Kaganovich, Rudzutak, and Mikoyan). The power of Stalin's network continued to grow, and by dividing organizational functions among his top protégés, Stalin was able to safeguard his leadership position. The presence of protégés heading CC sections (e.g., Kaganovich, Bauman, and Stetsky) was conducive to the ouster of Old Bolsheviks and their associates at lower levels of the central apparatus. By the end of 1926, the most important of Stalin's rivals had been routed.

Patronage and Stalin's maintenance of power

With his major rivals ousted and a large patronage network fully in place within the party apparatus, Stalin was already cultivating a second group of associates who would be given more and more responsibility while the Soviet leader "revitalized" his own network and reasserted his political will. These aspirants were from peasant or worker backgrounds. They did not have extensive revolutionary experience and often had only minimal education (usually of a technical nature). But they did have political experience within lower-level party organizations. Some of them were the clients of

Stalin's own protégés, members of an extended Stalin network. These politicians were moving up in the apparatus, often having had experience in local and regional settings as well as administrative experience in the central bureaucracy. Some served in the CC apparat (e.g., Khrushchev, Kozlov, Patolichev, Ponomarenko, and Suslov). Some had careers based in heavy industry management (e.g., Bulganin, Pervukhin, Saburov, and Yefremov), and in the security forces (e.g., Abakumov, Bagirov, Beria, and Serov). In background and expertise this was a diverse group. What they had in common, however, was the merging of their career ambitions with those of their patron, Stalin.

Examining what could rightly be characterized as a political machine, one should differentiate between members of Stalin's immediate coterie, and others who were linked to Stalin through the members of that coterie. For purposes of conceptual clarity, I am differentiating between "protégés", i.e., politicians with past common experience with the Soviet leader who experienced career mobility under Stalin, and "clients", i.e., politicians who experienced career mobility under Stalin, but whose common work experiences and immediate patronage connections were with Stalin's protégés and not with Stalin personally. Such politicians as Kaganovich, Molotov, Ordzhonikidze, Yenukidze, and Andreyev were contemporaries of Stalin, having worked directly with him and having experienced upward mobility with him. Others, for instance Khrushchev, Malenkov, and Zhdanov, experienced rapid career mobility under the General Secretary, but their initial entry into the top echelon was through Stalin's associates. Kaganovich played an especially important role in this regard, first sponsoring many of those who would dominate Soviet politics after Stalin's death.[56] Stalin was more than willing to sponsor new clients who were brought before him by loyal network members.

A major political dilemma for the Stalin regime was expanding Moscow's direct control over the diverse locales. The Bolshevik regime had been busy during the 1920s simply establishing Soviet power in the countryside. A center–periphery struggle continued throughout the 1930s, as Moscow attempted to cope with cadres' disciplinary problems and party disorganization. A major source of problems was that the regional party leaders possessed considerable discretionary powers in their own bailiwicks. Stalin attempted to replace unreliable provincial leaders with trusted associates, but even during the purge period of the mid-1930s many regional leaders exhibited considerable resilience. Some, while criticized by national leaders, were still reelected at their annual regional party conferences. Only pointed central pressure from Moscow, in the midst of national purges, brought down the well-ensconced regional leaders.[57]

Once his power was fully consolidated, Stalin became less active as a patron for protégés beyond the members of his own personal secretariat (e.g., Poskrebyshev). Rather, he chose to sponsor the clients of others. For the remainder of Stalin's leadership patronage networks were important at the level immediately beneath him: the level of the Secretariat, Politburo, and CC, where politicians such as Beria, Khrushchev, and Malenkov were quite busy developing their own networks.[58]

During the early 1930s, Stalin's patronage network was thriving, extensive in size and diverse in composition. The strength and confidence of that network was revealed in the diversity of policy positions publicly articulated by its members. Kaganovich and Molotov, for example, were quite vociferous in their support of the radical domestic program being promoted by the General Secretary. Others, among them Kalinin, Kirov, and Voroshilov, were much more low-key, even expressing some reservations about the speed with which that program was being implemented. Public debates took up the appropriateness of the liquidation of Stalin's opponents who at one time had been party leaders. One might have predicted these differences, given the dynamism of the early 1930s, the reconstitution of the elite, and the energy being devoted to the transformation of the country. This changed, however, with the December 1934 death of Kirov, as Stalin revealed his own willingness to sacrifice network members, both to remove potential rivals and to reassert his dominance over the network and state.

Stalin would use terror to "revitalize" the ranks of his own supporters, to assure the reliability not only of his protégés but of other politicians. Regular turnover of personnel – both trusted associates and others – became a norm of the Stalin era. Many of Stalin's prominent protégés did not survive the decade.[59] Stalin used the frequent movement of personnel and purging of officials to deal with the problem of rival patronage factions operating in other, especially lower-level, settings. The purges of the ranks of the elite, far from representing any diminution in the influence of the Stalin network, constituted an important personnel policy that was actually conducive to its expansion.

Stalin cleverly used periodic reorganizations of the policy-making process to shift potentially entrenched cadres about while making that process more amenable to his power needs. The reorganizations of the central party apparatus in 1930, 1934, 1939, and 1948 all entailed extensive reassignment of personnel. Altering the sizes of influential bodies (e.g., the 1952 enlargement of the Politburo and Secretariat) enabled Stalin to diminish the influence of more senior associates while enhancing the power of inexperienced aspirants. In the latter phase of his rule, especially after World War II, the selective rotation of personnel and the splitting of administrative functions among competing groups of politicians – including patronage network members – helped Stalin safeguard his position. In his last years, he was more than willing to play off such protégés as Malenkov, Zhdanov, and Khrushchev, who were competing as his potential successors.

Political clientelism proved to be a quintessential characteristic of the Stalin era and one of the most durable features of the Stalinist political legacy. Stalin's ascent to power was the direct result of his ability to place protégés in the party organization. The appointments of trusted protégés who oversaw the details of cadres advancement enabled Stalin to assume dominance within all of the top party and state bodies.[60] The development of his protégés' networks only enhanced that dominance, as those networks further connected intermediate-level organizations and the periphery to the center.[61]

Certainly, both fear and ambition motivated aspiring officials to commit themselves to Stalin's priorities and program. The presumed loyalty of subordinates was multifaceted and hardly uniform. Some (e.g., Ordzhonikidze) were long-term associates who had worked closely with Stalin over many years. Their loyalty was personal and intense, transcending the power dynamics of any one period in Stalin's rule. Others (e.g., Molotov) were political creations of Stalin, always subordinate and always aware of their dependence upon him. Most were rapidly mobilized loyalists who served short-term ends for Stalin. Their loyalty was surely rooted in a fear and awareness that they were very subordinate and fully dependent on an already powerful Soviet leader. Thus the Stalin network – similar to other patronage networks – consisted of unequal and diverse patron–client bonds. Ambition, coercion, and the logic of a central-ized hierarchical system all enabled Stalin to build a powerful entourage of supporters.

Stalin publicly criticized party leaders for dragging protégés with them when they transferred from one region to another, but such personalistic networks provided an alternative, extra-institutional mechanism for linking groups of the elite.[62] They formed an initial basis for what was to become the Soviet Union's second polity. Indeed, it was in the Stalin period that political clientelism became the critical mechanism integrating various organs and binding individuals and groups of the elite at all policy-making levels.

The post-Stalin period

The centralized structure of the political system and elite behavioral norms secured the role of patronage networks in the rise of Khrushchev and the governing coalition that succeeded Stalin. The politics of the 1953–57 power consolidation period were dominated by the maneuvering of top leaders and their clientele.[63]

Stalin's death meant the absence of an all-powerful politician and significantly affected the relative standing and career prospects of all his protégés and associates. Once-dominant network patrons now emerged as relative equals with a variety of party and state leaders. Kaganovich and Molotov – the most influential senior lieutenants of Stalin – had sponsored many of those composing the governing coalition. Now they were but two members of a collective leadership and would soon be eclipsed by their former protégés.

After 1957 and the ouster of these and other members of the anti-party group, Khrushchev was better able to advance associates from his earlier years of service in Ukraine and in the Moscow oblast.[64] In addition, as party First Secretary he possessed considerable influence over the recruitment process to sponsor many aspiring politicians.[65] Within the party Politburo (Presidium), trusted protégés helped to offset the influence of a sizeable group of officials not beholden to the First Secretary (e.g., Kosygin, Kozlov, Kuusinen, Podgorny, Shvernik, and Suslov). By the time of the November 1962 CC Plenum the membership of the Secretariat was being reshaped, as associates of Khrushchev, as well as associates of several other influential Politburo members, were added to its ranks.[66] The First Secretary's control over the periphery was realized not only through organizational changes, but also through a recruitment program that favored the dispatch of former Ukrainian and Moscow associates to regional secretaryships.[67]

During most of his rule as First Secretary, Khrushchev headed a large, extended patronage network consisting of both long-time protégés and more recent clients.[68] Many of his public supporters were tied to him through long-time associates. Leonid Brezhnev, for instance, had a sizeable patronage following, as did another Khrushchev protégé, Nikolai Podgorny. By the late 1950s, and especially after the defeat of the "Anti-Party Group," the turnover of personnel enhanced the ability of several top Khrushchev protégés to strengthen their own clientelist networks.[69] Yet these very networks helped to bolster the positions of their patrons, making them less dependent upon the First Secretary. Compared to his predecessor, Khrushchev possessed neither the immense personal authority nor the coercive might to easily advance his interests and political agenda without their support. Many of the politicians whom Khrushchev sponsored during his own tenure as party leader (e.g., short-term clients such as Leonid Il'ichev or his son-in-law Aleksei Adzhubei) did not have a political base of support separate from his own. These clients did enhance Khrushchev's position, but only when joined with well-positioned protégés such as Brezhnev and Podgorny.

Similar to Stalin, Khrushchev also used institutional reorganizations and the rotation of personnel to strengthen his position and advance his program. He possessed the discretionary power to affect institutional reforms that shifted policy-making authority from resistant state ministries to the party apparatus and to new party and state organs often guided by his protégés and allies. He initiated the 1957 Sovnarkhozy reform and the 1962 bifurcation of the regional party organizations in an attempt to weaken the positions of incumbents and to advance favored officials.[70] In 1956 he created a CC Bureau for the Russian Republic to enhance his influence over personnel matters in the country's most powerful republic. As head of the national party organization and formal Bureau chair, Khrushchev was in an institutionally strong position to influence personnel recruitment.[71] Through all these efforts Khrushchev intended to shift political authority to the very institutions over which he enjoyed more direct influence, either through formal institutions or informally through loyal associates.

Throughout the latter part of Khrushchev's tenure, cadres at the highest level were relatively secure, especially within the Presidium (Politburo). To advance his policy agenda, Khrushchev had to nurture and balance different sets of interests within an elite comprised of a good number of protégés. Ultimately, he failed where Stalin had succeeded in that he did not establish a set of mechanisms conducive to the regular rotation of personnel. In fact, the institutional reorganizations he initiated alienated many elements within the elite, including many of his own allies and protégés. At the subnational level, his efforts to rotate personnel sowed dissension among many of his own loyalists. A series of questionable economic initiatives and major policy setbacks only further weakened his political standing. In October 1964 the party leader learned he did not possess the requisite organizational might or personal authority to control his increasingly skeptical supporters, who would press for his ouster.

Khrushchev's downfall is a lesson in the importance and complexities of maintaining a large network of protégés and allies. Within five years of his succession, Khrushchev's organizational position allowed him to initiate a series of significant policy reforms. His extended network reached not only into the central party apparatus, but into important republics. But the unity and viability of his extended network – and the governing coalition he guided – were predicated upon the success of his program and the maintenance of his own authority. His lack of success undermined his authority and weakened his network bonds. Political alliances became more tenuous as ties with Khrushchev became less advantageous to the advancement of protégés' career interests. Powerful in their own right, Khrushchev's protégés found greater utility in working with their patron's rivals. Khrushchev's fate reveals there are limits to the power of network patrons and underscores the reciprocity of patronage relationships. Protégés and clients do provide the necessary resources for a patron to maintain political power, but they should never be taken for granted.

The Stalinist legacy and the lessons of the Khrushchev period greatly influenced the behavior and expectations of the more recent Soviet political elite. Many Brezhnev-era officials had risen through the sponsorship of Khrushchev, and they relied upon patronage connections to further enhance their own positions. Members of Brezhnev's so-called "Dnepropetrovsk group" were among others who assumed critical roles in top party and state positions. As we will see, they helped form the nucleus for a large coalition that governed the USSR for nearly two decades. The viability of that coalition hinged on many factors, including Brezhnev's style of consensus decision making, his network's ability to bridge interests and generations, and an impressive level of regime and system performance that continued at least during the first half of the regime. In the wake of Brezhnev's death, succeeding general secretaries protected their positions and advanced their interests by recruiting trusted protégés and sponsoring clients to important organizational posts. Other top officials have adopted the same strategy. The recent promotion of *perestroika* and dramatic political reform is the first evidence of fundamental change in elite mobility patterns and regime norms. Increased power sharing within an even less integrated group of politicians and institutions challenges the dominance of the second polity. The logic of Gorbachevian political reform questions the utility of patronage networks in the organization and conduct of Soviet political life. But patronage relations are deeply ingrained in the political traditions that shaped the contemporary Soviet Union, and as such, only the most profound deconcentration of power – combined with a formalized political pluralism – could offset them.

Four Soviet case studies

Soviet elite politics is a nebulous and often impenetrable subject. Its examination requires the application of a systematic mode of analysis. Previous studies of the Soviet elite and high politics have often entailed less than rigorous examination of particular politicians, with generalizations arrived at on the basis of small populations and often circumstantial evidence. Such Kremlinological studies have been helpful in highlighting the particularities of different regimes and individual politicians, but the applicability of their findings to whole classes of the Soviet elite is questionable. A more desirable approach is to employ large populations of politicians to identify the broad contours of the governing elite as well as to explore behavioral tendencies. Because a social-scientific approach to elite studies is not dependent upon the potentially unique experience of any one individual or small group of individuals, it is likely to develop propositions that have system-wide relevance.

This study uses aggregate biographical and career data to explore leadership change, elite mobility, and the formation of governing political coalitions during the Brezhnev (1964–82) and initial Gorbachev (1985–90) periods. These populations of politicians and their institutional contexts represent different national-cultural settings, divergent degrees of political stability, and different levels of policy-making authority. The role and utility of patronage to the politics of the centralized and hierarchical Soviet-type political system can be more effectively examined across divergent populations and settings.

Primary attention is given to the recruitment, mobility, and behavioral norms of the diverse group of national politicians. Examination of the national political elite permits not only an evaluation of top policy makers and the country's governing coalition, but an analysis of norms and trends within a divergent, predominantly Slavic and Russian context. While this group of officials spans the spectrum of Soviet sectoral and institutional interests, it is composed of individuals who direct, and therefore link, the various hierarchies of institutions operating in all regions of the country. There is sufficient background and career information on these politicians to explore numerous patronage networks and not simply that of the top party leader. Certain of these officials assume, in relative terms, much higher public profiles. They make speeches and publish articles touching upon a range of issues comprising the Soviet policy agenda. As a result, we can link political attitudes and behavior back to coalition formation and clientelism. Patterns and norms for both the Brezhnev and Gorbachev regimes will be analyzed. While greater attention is given to the eighteen-year Brezhnev period, examination of Gorbachev's first five years in power permits us to consider how institutional reforms and policy changes have influenced the politics of patronage and networks.

A Lithuanian study considers the politics of a European Baltic republic. The political leadership in this republic has been stable and, until recently, reliable in Moscow's eyes. The Lithuanian ruling elite adequately coped with a nationalism and religiosity that represented significant challenges to the Soviet regime. While Lithuania is *de jure* a republic, its *de facto* political status has more properly corresponded to that of Russian Republic (RSFSR) provinces (oblasts).[72] The republic party CC membership and its first secretary, similar to the leaderships of any provincial party committee (obkom), are directly accountable to the center for all subordinate political units. The party leader standing atop the Lithuanian political apparatus must represent Moscow's interests and attempt to assure domestic stability and economic productivity while balancing off nativist needs and attitudes. This is an important concern because Lithuania's political leadership has not been as penetrated by Russian and Slavic personnel as have many other Baltic and non-Russian republic leaderships. I systematically explore leadership recruitment and regime formation in Lithuania, identifying norms of power consolidation and regime building as well as the approaches by which a regime is maintained. The substantive focus is on patronage and its role in explaining these processes at a subnational level.

The study of Azerbaidzhan focuses on a traditionally less reliable party leadership whose performance has been judged to be generally poor by Moscow.[73] In contrast to Lithuania, the Azerbaidzhani party organization underwent a number of significant leadership changes in the postwar period. Azerbaidzhan has had a much less stable political leadership, though until recently this non-Slavic Caucasian population was more quiescent than that of the Baltic region. Its economic performance generally has been weak, and the republic rife with corruption. The time period examined was one of instability and forced change by Moscow, when a corrupt ineffective party boss was replaced with a rising KGB official whose task was the extensive transformation of the top hierarchy. The latter's efforts resulted in the reinvigoration of the Azerbaidzhani economy, and in the transformation of the ruling elite and the formation of a new stabilized coalition of politicians. But that leader's subsequent political legacy would prove to be suspect in the later 1980s, as succeeding regimes came under increasing pressure to address ongoing corruption and economic problems.

Considered in tandem with the Lithuanian case, the Azerbaidzhani analysis permits us to determine whether there are broader, cross-regional norms for elite recruitment and mobility in the USSR. We can assess whether or not there is a rhythm to power consolidation and regime formation. Both studies enable us to consider whether a particular organizational strategy is required for lower-level politicians to form an administration. As we examine these two very different settings, we can determine to what extent regional leaders have some discretion in carrying out Moscow's mandate in their own domains of responsibility.

An essential factor in examining Lithuania and Azerbaidzhan, as well as in considering the Brezhnev and Gorbachev national leaderships, is that leadership successions occurred during time periods for which aggregated career data were collected. Each case permits an investigation of coalition formation and change where most of the political actors can be identified. In each case, biographical and career data were available for the leadership group ruling before the succession and for the newcomer group which formed the succeeding coalition.[74]

The overarching intent of these studies is to evaluate the explanatory power of patronage networks, both to political elite mobility and behavior, and to regime formation and governance. Examination of a large population of officials who comprised the Brezhnev regime enables us to explore norms of the traditional, centralized and hierarchical, Soviet system. A comparable look at the first five years of the Gorbachev regime allows us to consider the continuing relevance of those norms, especially in the context of a significant reform program.

An empirical analysis of mobility patterns reveals the extent to which such networks are relied upon for promotion. We examine the patronage tie as a necessary and sufficient condition for recruitment and mobility. Many factors, including those highlighted by merito-cratic and corporatist theories, can play a role in the career advance of the ambitious. However, I hypothesize that the Soviet system has not broken away from the traditional Russian pattern of reliance upon patronage connections in personnel selection. This volume examines the extent to which this is true, not only in the Russian lands, but in other areas of the USSR. Observing the mobility patterns of the Gorbachev period enables us to assess how institutional reforms can moderate traditional patronage norms.

I also examine the role of patronage in elite coalition building and regime formation. Patronage networks can join together diverse actors and interests. Analyses of both the Brezhnev and Gorbachev regimes reveals how these networks fit into broader governing coalitions. In particular, I consider how leaders put together a team and form an administration. In the absence of formal rules dictating the process of regime formation, leaders can use loyalists, and those with whom those leaders and loyalists are allied, to construct that regime. Can we identify a rhythm to the process of regime formation in the Soviet system? And has such a rhythm been affected by the reforms of the late 1980s?

A special interest informing this analysis is the relationship between patronage politics and mastery of the policy process. How do networks, in the absence of other mechanisms, join the interests and constituencies of politicians? The perception that patron–client ties are made up of party hacks, ill-prepared, inexperienced, and totally insensitive to "rational" policy concerns is antiquated. The post-Stalin period has entailed the recruitment of experienced, trained politicians who still possess career ties with top leaders. These protégés themselves often form entourages, with the resultant networks helping to link important institutions in a complex and unwieldly policy-making arena. While no one element can predict the long-term viability of a regime or its program, a syndrome of factors contribute. Many factors, for instance, the effectiveness of a leader's style, or the objective circumstances with which he and a regime must contend, are context-specific; yet the imperatives of the political system mandate at least some control over the policy process. Network building is the single best way to secure such control. We cannot easily assess the effectiveness of a policy program, but we can find at least minimal evidence of a leader's and a regime's ability to govern in how a governing coalition is maintained and how a program is formulated and applied.

Two other aspects of system governance also merit attention. First, do patronage networks socialize members and encourage some level of attitudinal constraint among them? Such attitudinal constraint would further facilitate not only regime formation and maintenance, but also the development of a broader policy program. There are policy differences among Soviet politicians who are subject to numerous and conflicting pressures. The career and political interdependence among network members should encourage some level of policy consensus. Tracing the recruitment decisions surrounding leaders ("patrons"), exploring their policy programs, and identifying how others treat that program will help us to understand how governing regimes function.

In addition, I consider the importance of the patron or policy initiator in structuring the relevant policy agenda within his bailiwick. By patron I am referring to the CPSU general secretary, as well as to the republic-level first secretary, and the first secretary of provincial and regional-level party organizations. While all of these officials operate within certain limitations – whether set by the bureaucracy, superiors, or relatives peers – they do enjoy significant discretion within their own regions or administrative jurisdictions. To what extent do patronage politics reinforce or enhance such discretion, both in policy matters and cadres selection?

At the national level, it is necessary to examine the special position and role of the general secretary in elite mobility and the policy process. Until the dynamic years of Gorbachev, there had been a tendency for Western scholars to question the real authority of the post-Stalin period general secretary. This seemed natural in the wake of Stalin's stern grip on the Soviet polity. Khrushchev's fate only served to reinforce the image of a politically restrained party head. Nevertheless, many rushed too far in viewing the general secretary simply as a political manager. Political power stems from the way relationships are structured among individuals. By virtue of his office alone, the general secretary enjoys a wide range of political privileges; this is true regardless of the personal skills and professional strengths he brings to that office. His organizational position alone assures him of great discretion in cadres selection, and his management of top-level decision making ensures he will at the very least structure the policy agenda.

While examining patterns and norms characterizing Soviet politics of the 1960s, 1970s, and 1980s, I cannot remain indifferent to reforms of the early 1990s that could radically alter the Soviet political landscape. In assessing elite politics of the Gorbachev period, this study considers the conditions that may alter the politics of networks and patron–client relations. Indeed, as will become evident, the period 1985–90 may have entailed fundamental changes in norms of recruitment and regime formation and a moderating of patronage politics. The redistribution of power among institutional actors, an emergent pluralism, and the enhanced accountability of executives before subordinates and the public all portend important changes in the operation of the Soviet polity. In identifying the norms of traditional Soviet network politics, we may uncover the conditions that will be necessary for their decline.

2 Networks and coalition building in the Brezhnev period

The formation and power consolidation of a Soviet political regime is a long and complex drama in which actors compete for a role within the institutional hierarchy. In the wake of the October 1964 succession Leonid Brezhnev and other politicians maneuvered to build a new governing coalition. In the absence of explicit and formal rules, informal and extralegal arrangements were critical to the unfolding process of a new regime's emergence and consolidation.

The dynamics of the Soviet political system ensure that mastery of the political process does not automatically follow leadership turnover. A political succession is only the first step. The system needs a powerful chief executive who can shore up all his power, who can build alliances with other politicians and interests, and who can address the policy agenda.

A new Soviet leader will ultimately desire to differentiate himself and his regime from that of his predecessor, but this will require time. The new leader, after all, was likely to have been an important member of the past regime. Any desire for distancing – as through policy innovation – requires the new leader to consolidate his position, bringing in a new "team" of politicians while forging working relations with important incumbents. Unlike Western liberal democracies, there are no rules and no tradition mandating automatic replacement of personnel in the policy-making apparatus. In the Soviet system, the new leader must strengthen his position by easing out weaker and hostile incumbents, promoting reliable subordinates, and forming alliances with powerful incumbent politicians. There are no autonomous institutions outside the purview of the central party apparatus, but if the general secretary is to govern he must harness the cooperation of the highest policy-making organs. If the protégés and allies of the top leader do not regulate the power of the central party and state apparatus, that leader's authority will be undermined. Some have suggested that there is a "honeymoon" period for new Soviet leaders, with the new regime permitted greater discretion in policy making.[1] While skeptical that such a honeymoon period exists, I consider the early period of rule to be a time when a new leader is busy with personnel changes that will be conducive to his fuller consolidation of power. In all likelihood, a new leader's policy options open up only after his initial period of consolidation, when the governing regime is fully in place.[2]

Critical to the formation of an effective national regime and the eventual development of a comprehensive policy program is the creation of a governing coalition composed largely of the top leader's protégés, allies, and trusted subordinates. It is this kind of national level recruitment and coalition building that is the focus of this chapter's examination of the Brezhnev era. I will concentrate on the transfer and replacement of personnel in the important organs of the Central Committee apparatus directly overseen by the general secretary, key ministries and state committees, and significant regional party organizations. Both policy-making and policy-implementing bodies are examined. Beyond the rotation and replacement of officials, I examine the selective recruitment of trusted Brezhnev loyalists: politicians associated with or sponsored by the general secretary and his top protégés.

Leonid Brezhnev's succession was the critical first event in a series of cadres changes which occurred during the second half of the 1960s. This series of personnel changes would not necessarily be evident from an examination of only the top party organs, the Presidium (later Politburo), and the Secretariat. Change at the highest levels of political authority came slowly. The leadership was unified in rejecting Khrushchev and parts of his policy program, but it neither needed nor desired major personnel changes. In fact, Khrushchev's policy of heightened personnel turnover was explicitly rejected in favor of the more gradual Brezhnev "stability of cadres" policy. But during the Brezhnev regime's five-year period of consolidation, an important turnover of officials was quietly taking place. The top elite was transformed, with all major party and state organs affected. A more unified governing coalition emerged, with implications for politics at the republic and regional levels. By the time of the XXIV Party Congress in 1971, when the Brezhnev regime's comprehensive domestic and foreign policy thrust was presented, well over half of the leading officials in all top organizations had been replaced or transferred. A leadership succession at the highest political level of

Table 2.1 *Leadership turnover in leading party and state organizations, October 1964–December 1971*

Positions (N)	Oct.–Dec. 1964	1965	1966	1967	1968	1969	1970	1971	Turnover 1964–69[a] %	Turnover 1964–71[a] %
Politburo (20)[b]	2(1)	1(2)	1(2)	(1)				2(1)	40	45
Secretariat (10)		3	2		1				60	60
CPSU CC Departments (21)		9	2	1	1	1	8		67	67
USSR Council of Ministers (85)	1	45	2	7	3	1	8	1	69	75
Republic party and state leaders (44)[c]	2	3	3	2	2	5	6	4	39	57
First secretaries of RSFSR and Ukraine oblasts, krais and ASSRs (99)	4	10	9	11	8	5	9	8	46	58
First secretaries of other republics' oblasts, krais and ASSRs (64)	7	15	7	8	8	2	11	10	59	84

[a] In those cases where an organization had more than one leadership change, only one change was noted in calculating the total turnover percentage for the time period. Thus, a 100 percent turnover rate signified that every organization within a given category experienced a leadership change. The percentages given underestimate the actual number of personnel changes, because some organizations had two leadership changes during the 1964–71 period. The columns noting changes by year record all such individual changes.

[b] The membership figures for the Politburo and Secretariat are averages for the 1964–71 period. The average number of full and candidate members in the Politburo was 13 and 7 respectively. The figures in parentheses are Politburo candidate members.

[c] The total number includes the party first secretaries, council of ministers chairmen and supreme soviet chairmen for the 15 republics. The total is 44 because the RSFSR does not have a party first secretary.

authority had resulted in a significant alteration of the political elite below (Table 2.1).

It is against the backdrop of this important national leadership succession that we consider patronage and regime formation. Patronage networks provided a critical basis for the national coalition that governed the USSR during the 1964–82 period. A significant number of politicians who had served with Brezhnev in varying capacities and in different institutional and regional settings before his October 1964 succession assumed top positions within leading party and state organs. Others who earned Brezhnev's regard during his tenure as party leader were sponsored into important organizational slots. Yet Brezhnev's effectiveness as a national leader depended on more than the selective recruitment of protégés and clients into these policy and supervisory positions. He had to forge alliances that would bridge a number of important rival politicians and their patronage networks. Non-Brezhnev factions flourished throughout his eighteen-year tenure. While the genuinely threatening factions were eliminated during the early period of Brezhnev's rule, others assumed important roles in the development of a governing coalition. These allied networks lent a normalcy to the Soviet polity as personnel recruitment, turnover, and tenure practices were stabilized. When unified under a powerful party leader, these networks helped to merge various interests into a more coherent whole.

The governing team that emerged was consensus-oriented and represented a wide range of institutional and regional interests. It is no coincidence that the Brezhnev period exhibited corporatist tendencies, both in its formation and in the authoritarian welfare-state content of its policy program. Patterns of top-level elite recruitment also reflected a heightened sensitivity to meritocratic factors. The ranks of the national policy-making elite were not only more stable and diverse, they contained a more qualified set of officials.

At the center of the political system was the large Brezhnev patronage network. It rested on numerous long-term career associations, but grew to include aspiring politicians sponsored by Brezhnev and his top lieutenants. While not without opponents, this network undergirded the governing coalition. Because Brezhnev and his allies dominated the political process, they were able to formulate a policy program that shaped the Soviet domestic and foreign policy agendas for twenty years.[3]

The Brezhnev era political elite

The national political elite of the Brezhnev period was a diverse population of officials, many of whom possessed career connections to top-level policy makers. Of the total 939 Central Committee (CC) and Central Auditing Commission (CAC) members who served between October 1964 and November 1982, 244 are identified as associates of Politburo and Secretariat patrons (Table 2.2).[4] Based solely upon career advancement and geographic and institutional proximity to Politburo and Secretariat patrons (as augmented by World War II and education experience), fully one-quarter of the total national elite population was linked by patronage relationships to the top leadership of the Brezhnev period.

The one-quarter of the CC/CAC membership identified as belonging to major patronage networks represents a considerable proportion of the total national elite population. After all, the patronage measures applied tend to identify only longer-term political relationships. Cases of sponsorship in which an aspiring official experiences rapid mobility during a brief time period are undercounted. Institutionally camouflaged relationships may also be undercounted here. It is probable, for example, that associates of a long-serving central party official such as Mikhail Suslov are undercounted by my research approach.[5] Politicians can develop large networks, with the degree of their political power and authority dictating network size. Yet there are natural limits to the size of any politician's coterie of genuine protégés. The 244 identified protégés and clients represent the nuclei of the dominant patronage networks of the 1960s and 1970s. While we cannot determine the extent of these networks beyond the members identified here, it is reasonable to conclude that the 244 do not represent their maximum size.

The members of this national elite population who are not identified as associates of top leaders constitute a very heterogeneous group, not only in career backgrounds but in institutional affiliations, nationality, and national prominence. Because the CC is a representative party organ that taps all the politically relevant hierarchies, various types of politically prominent persons are included as members. Not all of them possess significant political power. An examination of the careers of these "nonclient" members reveals their different functions as members of top national political bodies. A significant number made careers in the party apparatus, moving into positions of all-union responsibility after working in the politi-

Table 2.2 *Identified clients and nonclients in the CC and CAC, and their political longevity (average number of CC/CAC elections)*

	N	%	Average number of elections
Clients	**244**	**26**	**2.9**
Brezhnev network	113	12	2.9
Other networks	131	14	2.9
Nonclients	**695**	**74**	**2.5**
Party apparatchiki	193	22	2.8
Administrators	132	14	2.9
National functionaries	72	8	2.6
Scientists	21	2	2.7
Military	60	6	2.2
1964–66 CC/CAC members	93	10	—
Heroes	13	1	3.9
Tokens	111	12	1.5
Total N[a]	939	100	2.6

[a]The total CC/CAC membership is used here. Politburo and Secretariat members are treated as potential patrons, not as potential protégés or clients of one another.

cal periphery or in specific sectoral hierarchies. Other careers are of a more symbolic nature and do not include serious policy-making functions. This population of "nonclients" can be disaggregated according to the primary functions of the individuals within the national decision-making apparatus: (1) party apparatchiki; (2) state administrators; (3) representatives of national minorities; (4) scientists; (5) military personnel; (6) Soviet "heroes"; and (7) token representatives of the working class and peasantry. In accounting for all members of this population base, an eighth group merits notation, as a number of CC/CAC members did not survive the 1964–66 transition period. While these officials did not evince career ties to Brezhnev regime leaders, many were protégés of Khrushchev or other top-level politicians associated with him. In some cases, their career connections to the deposed leader served as the pretext for their ouster. Others who were not reelected at the XXIII Party Congress in 1966 were physically infirm or simply less viable political entities and are not included in the subsequent analyses.

The seven types of "nonclients" encompass separate but distinguishable functional roles in the policy-making and policy-implementing structures. Based on my examination of their career précis, their national elite status is likely only derived from their status as representatives of important elements within Soviet society and the Soviet establishment, not from their relative political power. Their presence and diversity corroborate Gehlen and McBride's contention that the CPSU CC "has become a composite of the representatives of key functional groups and is the principal medium, either through individual members or as a collective, through which the members of the Politburo regularly exchange information with the elites of major interests in the system."[6]

Among the most important of those who are not linked to the dominant patronage networks of the Brezhnev period are apparatchiki whose careers have been built almost exclusively in the party organization. These officials are genuine career politicians who have served at various levels of authority in the party apparatus. Some moved from local and intermediate-level party organizations in the periphery to influential organizational positions in the republics or Moscow. Others worked almost exclusively within the national party apparatus, moving into senior positions meriting inclusion within the CC itself. All are party professionals, as opposed to "nonclient" administrators whose careers are predominantly in state agencies or specialized sectors. These administrators serve most of their professional lives within one sector or organization, and often come to lead all-union ministries and state committees. They are officials who, at best, infrequently work within party organs.

These "nonclient" apparatchiki and administrators include nearly half of all officials for whom I fail to identify patronage connections. A number of them headed important regional party organizations,[7] as well as important ministries and state committees.[8] Many rose to power on the coat-tails of departed top-level politicians, remaining in national elite positions for a considerable time period. While they once rose through patronage connections, they became an influential group in top-level political bargaining. Their national prominence in the Brezhnev period, however, did not depend upon the political standing of contemporary senior officials. Rather, they possessed the tenure and institutional bases necessary to elite status.

Other "nonclients" were representatives of various interests: national minorities, the technical intelligentsia, and the military. Again, some of these officials may have been cultivated by top-level politicians, but this information is not accessible. The remaining "nonclients" were symbolic members representing the broader society. They were included to lend legitimacy to the top leadership.

The political clout of these "nonclients" varied considerably. It is difficult to determine their influence without systematically examining their behavior. I have attempted to tap one dimension of influence through considering politicians' institutional affiliations and role. Another way to assess the relative political strength of these politicians is to consider their relative longevity within the CC/CAC. To what extent were individuals able to retain their membership and concomitant elite status over time? Assuming that longevity contributes not only to the stability of one's position but to one's status and influence, might such "nonclient" representatives have heightened their power by "outlasting" the more ambitious – but potentially more vulnerable – politicians?

An examination of the political longevity of members of most "nonclient" groups reveals that on average they were not members of the CC/CAC for a long time (consult Table 2.2). In fact, a significant proportion of the personnel turnover that took place between one CPSU Congress and the next involved "nonclients." The identified clients and the "nonclient" apparatchiki and administrators were, on average, elected to several convocations of the CC/CAC (2.9, 2.8, and 2.9 respectively). Remembering that the time gap between party congresses is five years, these figures translate into longevity rates of nearly fifteen years. These officials constitute a most formidable group. Token representatives, not surprisingly, were short-term members. They were elected, on average, to between one and two convocations. Ethnic representatives experienced greater CC longevity, though not as great as that of the apparatchiki and administrators. The relatively limited longevity of the military representatives is striking, as it is the lowest for any group of politicians whose institutional affiliation would suggest some influence (2.2 elections). Although this military group has constant representation in the highest party bodies, its membership tends to change more frequently than that of other groups. The military's relative lack of seniority in the CC/CAC reveals that its top officials were not among the more powerful within the policy-making elite. While they have constituted a stable 8 percent of the total CC membership since 1961, this high turnover rate indicates they did not acquire the longer-term political clout enjoyed by political counterparts in the central party apparat. Constant turnover of personnel is an effective technique by which the party can control the military elite.[9]

These data show that relatively few of the "nonclients" were serious politicians possessing real influence within the all-union policy-making process. The identified protégés and clients of system patrons constituted a high proportion of the decisive national elite. Thus, at least half of the dominant national-level officials were network members. The longevity of their membership in the central party organs demonstrates the political clout they enjoyed. The core group within this ruling elite – the Brezhnev group and the so-called "Dnepropetrovsk mafia" – on average were members of these top party bodies for approximately twenty years. Even the extended Brezhnev network, including the clients of his own protégés (e.g., the clients of Kirilenko, Shcherbitsky, and Kunaev), were members on average for nearly fifteen years. This degree of longevity is matched by the average for members of other clientelistic networks. As we shall see, the political strength of client–politicians is even more evident when we consider their institutional affiliations. By the early 1970s, with the departures of several powerful Politburo members and with their own increasing seniority, these politicians were the dominating power group within the central party apparatus.

Patrons, clients, and networks

The nearly 250 officials with career ties to Politburo members and CPSU secretaries advanced in a wide variety of institutional and regional settings. The sizes of these patronage entourages varied considerably, as is evident in Table 2.3.[10] Protégés and clients are identified for nearly all of these system patrons, with the entourage sizes ranging from forty-eight for Brezhnev (including ten Politburo and Secretariat members), down to none for Kuznetsov, Rusakov, and Tikhonov (with the latter two identified as part of the Brezhnev entourage). As expected, politicians who made their careers in the party apparatus, moving from region to region as they rose in the party hierarchy, assembled larger entourages. This group of politicians included Kirilenko (Sverdlovsk and Ukraine), Kunaev (Kazakhstan), Mazurov (Belorussia), Podgorny (Ukraine), and Shcherbitsky (Ukraine). Those who made careers in the party apparatus, but had power bases only in Moscow and not across more easily measured regions, had somewhat smaller – though not insignificant – clientelistic networks. Mikhail Suslov's entourage is a good example. Because Suslov served in Moscow for over forty years, it is difficult to identify clientelistic ties for those serving

Table 2.3 *Size of Politburo and Secretariat members' patronage networks among CC/CAC members, 1964–1982*[a]

Patron	N	Patron	N	Patron	N
Aliev	3	Kosygin	9	Rusakov	
Andropov	2	Kulakov	1	Shcherbitsky	16
Brezhnev	48(10)	Kunaev	12	Shelepin	12
Chernenko	2	Kuznetsov		Shelest	5
Demichev	6	Masherov	5	Shevardnadze	2
Dolgikh	3	Mazurov	9(2)	Solomentsev	1
Gorbachev	2	Mzhavanadze	2	Suslov	8(2)
Grechko	5	Pel'she	7	Tikhonov	
Grishin	2	Podgorny	13(1)	Ustinov	9
Gromyko	4	Polyansky	5	Voronov	3
Kapitonov	11(2)	Ponomarev	2	Zimyanin	1
Katushev	4	Rashidov	6		
Kirilenko	12(1)	Riabov	1		
Kisilev	1	Romanov	10		

[a]The numbers in parentheses indicate the number of Politburo and Secretariat members who have been identified as protégés or clients of that politician. The identified protégés of Brezhnev within the Politburo and Secretariat are Chernenko, Grechko, Kirilenko, Kunaev, Shcherbitsky, Tikhonov, and Ustinov. Brezhnev's identified clients are Aliev, Katushev, and Rusakov. The identified protégés of Kapitonov are Demichev and Grishin; the identified protégé of Kirilenko is Riabov; those of Mazurov are Masherov and Zimyanin; that of Podgorny is Titov; and those of Suslov are Pel'she and Ponomarev.

under him and for those in the regional party organizations for which he was responsible. My decision rules for identifying patron–client ties focus on regional transfers and identifiable promotions supervised by particular politicians. In spite of this measurement problem, ten politicians were clearly identified as Suslov's protégés and clients. The fact that two of Suslov's protégés were Politburo members indicates the political strength of his clientelistic group.

My clientelism measures more effectively tap the Aleksandr Shelepin group. Shelepin, who had served in Moscow for twenty years before Khrushchev's ouster, advanced through several institutions, pulling protégés and clients with him as his career progressed. The study identified twelve politicians who served in Moscow, in the Komsomol, in the Central Trade Unions organization, and in the KGB as his associates.

A number of politicians who have made their political careers in hierarchies outside that of the CPSU apparatus also exhibited fairly sizeable patronage networks. Those system patrons who served in Moscow and in their areas of expertise over a lengthy time period, such as Aleksei Kosygin and Dmitry Ustinov, had relatively large identifiable entourages. Their careers tended to be in specific ministries and can be traced through the available career data. Others, such as Marshal Grechko, Dmitry Polyansky, and Gennady Voronov, whose political careers at the national level were of a shorter duration, had smaller networks.

The relative sizes of these entourages roughly parallel the degree of power and authority their national patron-politicians possess. Most observers of Soviet politics would agree that during the 1960s and 1970s – in addition to the General Secretary himself – Kirilenko, Kosygin, Podgorny, Shelepin, and Suslov were the leading figures in the governing coalition; their relative positions may have changed (Shelepin, for instance, departed in 1975), but the level of their power and influence was always quite high. Their political clout and the duration of their national elite status enhanced their opportunities to promote associates and cultivate clients. But the organizational strength of these and other, especially regionally based, politicians also depended upon their associations with larger client networks: networks which linked the careers of those politicians powerful enough to secure membership in the Politburo and Secretariat. It is due to these network connections, as vehicles bringing together several Politburo and Secretariat politicians, that these individuals had such large coteries.

Throughout Soviet history, clusters of politicians have come together, spanning disparate regions, institutions, and positions of political prominence. While members of these clusters head their own entourages, their careers and those of their subordinates can intertwine to form a larger "network." I use the term "network," rather than "faction" or "coalition," to suggest that these inter-relationships transcend specific policy positions or institutional affiliations and extend beyond one single politician's own career. A "network" as defined here includes several relatively equal politicians and their coteries, though one politician could assume a sort of "first among equals" role. Such networks are distinct in that they represent broad coalitions of politicians and provide "constraint" to the political motivations of their members. While my decision rules identified only dyadic career ties (see the appendix, pp. 242–47), many of these individuals' careers suggested multiple linkages, and ties with patrons who themselves had interconnected careers.

The available data and the identified patronage entourages lay the groundwork for determining important networks at the all-union level. Within the Politburo and Secretariat of the Brezhnev period I identify five important networks of politicians which influenced national elite politics: (1) the Brezhnev network, at the heart of which was the so-called "Dnepropetrovsk mafia"; (2) the Suslov–Pel'she–Ponomarev group, headed by the long-time party *eminence grise*, Suslov; (3) a Khar'kov (Ukrainian) group, headed by Nikolai Podgorny and including Vitaly Titov and Piotr Shelest; (4) a Belorussian group, forged during World War II and led by Kirill Mazurov, while including Piotr Masherov and Mikhail Zimyanin; and (5) a Moscow-based group, headed by Ivan Kapitonov and including Viktor Grishin and Piotr Demichev. These five networks were identified using the same indicators applied to identify specific patron–client dyads. The careers of the Politburo and Secretariat members within each of these networks are linked together, with one member assuming a leading role among the other protégés. Brezhnev, for example, took the guiding role within his own group, always being the first to advance to higher authority levels.[11] The same pattern is true for the other groups, as Suslov, Podgorny, Mazurov, and Kapitonov preceded the other top members of these networks in advancing into leading republic and national positions. The careers of the top members of each network were interconnected. The institutional and regional affiliations of their numerous clients were also interconnected. Discernible networks of politicians bridged a number of authority levels as well as various institutional and regional interests.

The Brezhnev patronage network is at the center of this study. It was the most influential system-wide network from the latter 1960s to the early 1980s, encompassing a wide range of politicians. Some had worked with Brezhnev before 1964; others had careers that began to flourish under Brezhnev. Many had the influence to cultivate their own patronage factions, and in some cases they outlasted Brezhnev, influencing Soviet politics into the later 1980s. At the core of this "extended Brezhnev network" was Brezhnev's own career faction. Over thirty CC/CAC members were identified as members of a Brezhnev-led Dnepropetrovsk group.[12] The strength of the Brezhnev faction which included this group is indicated not only by the close career ties among its leading members (i.e., Brezhnev,

Table 2.4 *Membership of Brezhnev network in leading party and state bodies, 1964–1981*[a]

	1964	1966	1971	1976	1981
Politburo (20)[b]	1	1(3)	3(1)	5(1)	6(1)
Secretariat (11)		2	3	4	3
CC department heads (23)	1	7	10	8	8
Council of Ministers (100)	6	12	16	21	20
Republic leaders[c] (44)	6	7	12	12	9
Obkom first secretaries (123)	15	18	20	23	21

[a]The average membership sizes of the given bodies are noted after each institutional actor.
[b]For the Politburo row, numbers in parentheses represent candidate members who were Brezhnev network members.
[c]The heading "republic leaders" refers to the first secretaries, chairmen of the councils of ministers, and chairmen of the supreme soviets of the 15 union republics. The total is 44 for all 15 republics, since the RSFSR did not have a party first secretary.

Kirilenko, Shcherbitsky, and Tikhonov), but by the cross-career linkages among members of their various clientele. In examining the size, growth, and political strength of the extended Brezhnev network we illuminate the workings of an entourage and leading patronage network that dominated two decades of Soviet politics.

The Brezhnev network

The consolidation of power by General Secretary Brezhnev in the period after his 1964 succession entailed not only the turnover of personnel in various bureaucracies but the promotion of trusted faction members into top party and state positions (Table 2.4). The recruitment of protégés began almost immediately upon Brezhnev's selection as party leader, and it continued throughout his tenure. As Brezhnev's political strength increased, so did that of his top protégés, allowing them to form their own entourages (Table 2.5). As extensions of the core Brezhnev entourage, these groups of politicians bridged national and regional bureaucracies, thus helping the Brezhnev coalition to govern.

From the earliest days of his administration, Brezhnev's faction members became integral components of the central party apparatus, especially in heading CC departments. As of October 1964, only

Table 2.5 *Membership of Brezhnev's protégés' networks in leading party and state bodies, 1964–1981*

	1964	1966	1971	1976	1981
CC department heads (23)	1	1	2	3	3
Council of Ministers (100)	1	3	5	8	7
In CC apparatus	1	3	3	2	2
In Council of Ministers Apparatus	7	7	8	7	4
Republic leaders (44)	1	2	3	3	4
In Republic CC or Council of Ministers Apparatus	4	6	7	9	8
Obkom first secretaries (123)	9	11	14	15	16
In military command positions	5	5	5	5	5

one Brezhnev protégé, Andrei Kirilenko, was to be found in the Politburo. By the XXIII Party Congress in 1966, several other Brezhnev protégés had moved into the Politburo as candidate members.[13] It was only at the XXIV Congress in 1971, when Brezhnev was firmly in control of the party apparatus, that protégés joined him and Kirilenko as full members.[14] As Brezhnev and his faction enhanced their positions within the elite (and certain rival factions were being weakened), additional coterie members found their way to Politburo membership.[15] By the time of Brezhnev's last Party Congress in 1981, over one-third of the Politburo's members were politicians with past career connections to the General Secretary.

Members of the Brezhnev group also advanced into the party Secretariat, beginning as early as March 1965. Dmitry Ustinov became a CPSU Secretary in 1965 (responsible for questions of armaments production), while Kirilenko was advanced into the Secretariat in April 1966 (overseeing internal political questions and party work). The subsequent appointment of Konstantin Chernenko as a Secretary for administration only represented a further consolidation of Brezhnev's position within the party apparatus.[16]

While all of these protégés' portfolios were important in the supervising of policy, the party work and cadres appointments were critical. Andrei Kirilenko and Ivan Kapitonov, the Secretaries responsible for these portfolios, assumed important profiles in the post-1964 regime. The close Brezhnev–Kirilenko patronage tie bespeaks the Brezhnev group's influence in overseeing party work. However, the role of Kapitonov, not identified here as a Brezhnev protégé, was not negligible.[17] Kapitonov was allied with Brezhnev, having been politically resurrected by the General Secretary almost immediately after Khrushchev's ouster. He benefited from a number of important career advances within the first years of Brezhnev's rule. His position within the Secretariat and CC apparatus made him a key gatekeeper monitoring promotions within the top national party organs. His own Moscow-based patronage network flourished during the later 1960s and 1970s, as Brezhnev's extended network expanded its base of power. Kapitonov's resurrection and subsequent organizational clout reflect Brezhnev's leadership style as a consensus-builder willing to make accommodations with other political interests. Brezhnev augmented the elevation of his own associates with alliances to other patronage factions.

Brezhnev faction members were also recruited into important CC apparat positions. By the end of 1965 – just a year into the new regime – Brezhnev associates were heading a number of key CC departments, including the Administrative Affairs Department, the General Department, the Science and Higher Educational Institutions, and the Light and Food Industries Departments. As the personnel turnover within the central party apparatus continued, additional Brezhnev protégés moved into other top slots within the CC hierarchy (e.g., heading the Administrative Organs, Construction, and Liaison with Warsaw Pact Countries and Liaison with Communist and Workers' Parties Departments). This recruitment of trusted associates was a critical aid to Brezhnev's authority-building efforts for these CC organs were the "command posts" from which policy directives were issued and their implementation reviewed.

The promotions of long-time protégés expanded Brezhnev's own considerable power as party General Secretary. The additional recruitment of (1) younger, new clients of the General Secretary, and (2) associates of trusted politicians such as Kirilenko, Ustinov, and Chernenko, further strengthened the power base of the extended Brezhnev network. The expansion of that extended network's party organizational position included the rapid promotion of a young regional party leader, Konstantin Katushev, to a CPSU secretaryship (April 1968), and the advancement of one of Brezhnev's aides, Konstantin Rusakov (from heading a CC department to a secretaryship a decade later, in May 1977). Similarly, in the 1970s, a number of protégés of Kirilenko, Ustinov, Chernenko, and other Brezhnev loyalists, also moved into top CC organizational slots.

The influence of Brezhnev protégés as CC department heads was only enhanced as they served under secretaries such as Kirilenko and

Ustinov. Meanwhile, network members assumed important ministerial roles within the corresponding governmental apparatus and in agencies that were counterparts to those network-guided CC departments. Thus the priority military–industrial sector was fully dominated by Brezhnev network members. Brezhnev, Kirilenko, and Ustinov protégés led most of the important industrial and military ministries (e.g., the Ministries of Defense, Defense Industry, Construction, Machine Building, and General Machine Building). At the same time, Kirilenko and Ustinov oversaw this broad area as CPSU Secretaries. Other network members such as N.I. Savinkin (a Brezhnev protégé) and I.D. Serbin (an Ustinov protégé), were heading up the CC departments responsible for policy in this general area (guiding the Administrative Organs and the Defense Industry Departments, respectively). A similar situation occurred in the light and food industry sector in which Brezhnev's associates and protégés headed party policy making and governmental policy-implementing agencies.

The appointment of network members to important secretariat and ministerial positions underscores the might the Brezhnev group and extended Brezhnev network held within the central apparatus. Important policy consequences follow from these recruitment patterns. The promotion of trusted subordinates into positions on both sides of the decision-making process – policy making and policy implementing – was conducive to the fulfilment of policy initiatives. The situation increased the likelihood that Brezhnev's policies would actually be formulated and carried out. From our vantage point outside the Soviet policy process it is difficult to pinpoint just where specific policies originate. It is usually unclear who is responsible for particular directives and who is actually seeing them through. Yet as Franklyn Griffiths noted, "tendencies of articulation" are manifested that involve specific sets of policy concerns and specific institutions.[18] We can identify complexes of party and state institutions responsible for specific sectors of the economy and for broad policy areas. Politicians with long-term career ties to Brezhnev and to his closest protégés assumed leading positions in several of these complexes. It is no coincidence that this pattern held in the very domains in which important Brezhnev initiatives were offered. A more detailed discussion of the actual Brezhnev policy program is provided in chapter 3, but suffice it to note that major Brezhnev initiatives involved the defense, agriculture, and light industry areas. And it was in these three areas that reliable members of the extended Brezhnev network assumed positions of responsibility on both sides of the policy process: in the policy-initiating CC apparat, and in the policy-implementing Council of Ministers.

Brezhnev's institutional powers as General Secretary were extensive and conferred more than a *primus inter pares* role within the decision-making process. But as the head of a large patronage network he was able to expand that influential power base to encompass a wider range of political institutions. His power was thus unrivaled from the mid-1960s up to his death in late 1982. As a result of Brezhnev's factional strength and institutional prerogatives, loyal entourage members were promoted into top governmental organs, including the Council of Ministers Presidium. By the height of Brezhnev's authority in the mid-1970s, nearly half of the members of the Presidium were Brezhnev protégés. A number of his trusted associates and other extended network members were Vice Chairmen serving immediately beneath rival Chairman Aleksei Kosygin: Nikolai Tikhonov (Kosygin's eventual successor), I.V. Arkhipov, I.T. Novikov, V.N. Novikov, and L.V. Smirnov. These politicians were all of Brezhnev's generation; several of them were part of the "Dnepropetrovsk mafia." Their high-level supervisory positions within the government made them responsible for important policy areas, some of which were critical to the broader Brezhnev program (e.g., foreign trade relations, defense technology, machine building, and construction). These protégés represented an important extension of the Brezhnev faction's influence into a potentially less reliable policy-implementing hierarchy: a hierarchy not only organizationally separated from Brezhnev's institutional home turf, but also headed by one of Brezhnev's rivals (Table 2.6).[19]

The inroads made by this extended network into the governmental apparatus varied by sector and institution.[20] Two appear to have been targeted for placement of trusted associates. As already noted, a number of Brezhnev's associates, as well as those of Ustinov and Kirilenko, assumed important roles within the important military-industrial complex. These politicians built careers in this sector, as did important members of their factions. Meanwhile, several of Brezhnev's most trusted associates, including relatives, were placed in the top internal security organs. The Dnepropetrovsk group dominated the internal security organs throughout his administration. Yury Andropov was virtually surrounded by Brezhnev cronies throughout his fifteen-year tenure as KGB chief. Andropov worked with the Brezhnev network, but was not a member of it. His first

Table 2.6 *Institutional affiliation of members of the Brezhnev network,*
December 31, 1969

Network	Entire Brezhnev clients N(%)	Brezhnev group N(%)	Dnepropetrovsk protégés N(%)	Clients of Brezhnev N(%)
Secretariat	3 (3)	3 (6)	1 (3)	
Central Committee Apparatus	17 (14)	12 (22)	3 (9)	5 (8)
Council of Ministers Apparatus	26 (22)	16 (29)	12 (38)	11 (17)
Republic organs (including RSFSR)	19 (16)	7 (13)	3 (9)	11 (17)
Oblast and city organs	38 (32)	8 (15)	8 (25)	30 (45)
Military	11 (8)	6 (11)	1 (3)	5 (8)
Other[a]	6 (5)	2 (4)	4 (13)	4 (6)
Total[b]	120(100)	54(100)	32(100)	66(100)

[a]This includes officials in the all-union Komsomol and trade union
organizations.
[b]These population sizes vary from those noted in earlier tables because a
number of these politicians had died or retired in the period between
October 1964 and December 1969.

deputy chairman, S.K. Tsvigun, however, was a close protégé of the
General Secretary and served with Brezhnev in Dnepropetrovsk
(latter 1940s) as well as in Moldavia (early 1950s). Tsvigun's presence
within the KGB continued throughout Andropov's entire tenure.
Another Dnepropetrovsk crony, G.K. Tsinev, was deputy chairman
of the KGB from 1970 until 1982, when he became first deputy
chairman. Meanwhile, Brezhnev clients headed the other security
organ, the Ministry of Internal Affairs. N.A. Shchelokov served as
minister from 1966 to December 1982 (removed only a month after
Brezhnev's death), while another Dnepropetrovsk client, V.S. Papu-
tin, served as the first deputy minister until his death in December
1979. Even V.M. Chebrikov, touted in the 1980s as an Andropov–
Gorbachev protégé, had connections with the Dnepropetrovsk group
that dated from the 1940s and 1950s.

The already-powerful Brezhnev network was bolstered by political
connections that extended into several important regional party
organizations. The General Secretary's extensive experience in

regional politics had ranged across both Slavic and non-Slavic party organizations, including not only the Dnepropetrovsk city and province, but also the industrialized Ukraine, Moldavia, and Kazakhstan. His connections with leading protégés had been forged during their common service in subordinate party bodies. The Brezhnev-led network included politicians from a number of non-Russian republics who were sponsored by such top-level protégés as Shcherbitsky, Chernenko, and Kunaev, and the long-time Moldavian party boss Ivan Bodiul.[21] All told, these republic and regional politicians accounted for approximately forty, or roughly one-third, of the total members of the identified Brezhnev network. Influential RSFSR regional party organizations (e.g., Sverdlovsk and Gorky) were linked to the network through those Politburo members who headed regionally based factions (e.g., Kirilenko and Katushev respectively).

The regional-level members of the extended Brezhnev network possessed only limited influence at the all-union level. There was a hierarchy within the network itself in which Russian protégés at the national level possessed greater authority. While the three non-Russian regional patrons in this network – Aliev, Kunaev, and Shcherbitsky – had a large entourage of protégés, most of their associates were influential only within their own regional settings. Beyond their inclusion in the CC, they generally did not possess the institutional bases of support that could afford them expanded power. Of the thirty-one officials with career connections to Brezhnev's non-Russian protégés, only four ever advanced to hold positions of national responsibility. As a result, only the non-Russians directly working with Brezhnev – those who were his protégés – had any real opportunity to advance into top national positions. In contrast, nearly all identified protégés of Kirilenko, Ustinov, and Katushev came to hold important posts in Moscow. These officials were ethnic Russians or other Slavs. Many of them began their careers in the periphery, even serving there during the early years of the Brezhnev regime; but, through the help of their powerful patrons, they were able to advance, often finding their way to Moscow.

The extended Brezhnev network grew stronger through the course of the General Secretary's tenure (Table 2.7). A significant number of Brezhnev's protégés were already CC members when he was elected the top party leader in October 1964. Approximately twenty more were elevated to membership in that body during his eighteen-year

Table 2.7 *Membership of the Brezhnev and other major national networks in the CC/CAC, 1964–1981*

	1964	1966	1971	1976	1981
Brezhnev network	27	40	45	49	45
Brezhnev's protégés' networks	11	19	36	46	50
Total extended Brezhnev network	**38**	**59**	**81**	**95**	**95**
Kapitonov–Demichev–Grishin network	4	10	12	17	16
Suslov–Pel'she–Ponomarev network	5	8	10	12	11
Mazurov–Masherov–Zimyanin network	6	9	9	11	10
Podgorny–Shelest network	8	15	14	10	7
Shelepin network	4	8	6	3	3
Kosygin network	4	7	9	8	5
Total CC/CAC membership	393[a]	439	477	511	545

[a] A total of 395 CC/CAC members were elected at the XXII Party Congress in 1961. Two of these members died before the October 1964 CC Plenum, which is the starting point for this analysis.

tenure.[22] Brezhnev's extended network grew rapidly as associates of his own Politburo protégés moved into these top party organs. Their numbers rose from eleven in late 1964 to 50 by 1981.

Overall, the network maintained its power and high profile within the central party apparatus through the 1970s and into the early 1980s. The XXV Party Congress in 1976 represented something of a high point in the network's authority, both in the number of members and in their positions of responsibility in the highest bodies. The year 1976 was also critical because it marked a shift in the network's composition in favor of Brezhnev protégés' clients (in 1981, there were forty-five of Brezhnev's own clients to fifty of his protégés' clients). The network was aging, elderly associates were retiring or dying. Between 1976 and 1981, the number of Brezhnev protégés and clients in the CC declined from forty-nine to forty-five. As the network aged, the associates of senior Brezhnev lieutenants were in an ever better position to advance. The General Secretary, having stood atop the party apparatus for over a dozen years, increasingly had to rely upon the judgment of others in advancing officials. While many of those recruited to top nomenklatura posts had career connections that made them members of an extended network, they were generally more directly tied to protégés than to the General Secretary himself. Some had worked more directly with the General Secretary in the pre-1964 period: fourteen of the total sixty-five associates of Brezhnev protégés held identifiable career linkages to Brezhnev. But the career and authority gap separating them from Brezhnev constituted a political distance. Being less directly connected to the General Secretary, they were less responsible for his policy problems and were in a better position to distance themselves from him after his death. As the Brezhnev regime moved toward a leadership succession, the cleavages that arose among contending senior protégés (e.g., Chernenko and Kirilenko) increasingly divided those parts of the overall network. Because of these rifts, the network was not able to survive the departure of its patron.

In tracing the evolution of the extended Brezhnev network, important contrasts must be drawn between those members closely tied to the General Secretary and other members who were linked to him only through intermediaries. Brezhnev's institutional discretionary powers as national party leader facilitated the growth in power and authority of trusted protégés such as Kirilenko, Ustinov, and Chernenko. It was no accident that Brezhnev faction members such as Chernenko and Ustinov moved into critical organizational slots. Ustinov, for instance, was promoted over a number of influential uniformed military professionals to become the USSR Minister of Defense in 1975. His selection represented the appointment of a party apparatchik to the top military position: a decision not universally supported by the professional military. This promotion, however, not only reaffirmed the party's oversight over the military, but also reinforced the organizational linkage between the General Secretary, his faction, and the military sector. Brezhnev's extended network grew to include more and more members of his protégés' factions, yet this growth represented Brezhnev's increasing reliance upon subordinates who were less directly tied to him. The authority of the office of General Secretary, combined with the power of the extended network, made such subordinates reliable. But the linkage of political interests between such extended network subordinates and the "grand patron" of the network was more tenuous.

The Brezhnev network constituted a broad coalition of politicians and interests which was in an organizational position to structure the policy agenda. Trusted subordinates guided those state organizations critical to the realization of the Brezhnev program. Meanwhile, members of this network linked a number of important regional party organizations, both within the RSFSR and outside it, to the regime in Moscow. It was in the central party apparatus that the power of the Brezhnev network proved decisive. In general, network members headed the CC departments responsible for cadres matters, party work, and important sectors of the economy. By the mid-1970s, the Politburo members and CPSU secretaries supervising these departments were all Brezhnev protégés. From an organizational standpoint, the Brezhnev-led network of patronage factions was the dominant element in the national leadership. It provided an effective nucleus for a governing coalition. By selectively dispatching its members into top organizational slots, this network helped to make the diverse bureaucracies of the Soviet political system more pliable.

Other political networks

The Brezhnev network formed the core of the governing coalition during nearly two decades, but it did not operate within a vacuum. Other institutional and regional networks headed by powerful officials also influenced the Soviet policy process. Among the most prominent network leaders were Mikhail Suslov, Aleksei Kosygin, and Nikolai Podgorny. They assumed leading roles in the post-Khrushchev period and their political strength was very much reflected in the networks of associates serving with them. It is likely that the strength of their networks was critical to their staying power. They were genuine rivals to Brezhnev.

Others have considered the careers of some of these Politburo patrons, analyzing their leadership skills and the political struggles in which they were engaged.[23] Any examination of the patronage networks of these politicians, however, constitutes a different cut at the Soviet political landscape of the period. An analysis of the size, location, and composition of these politicians' entourages will help us understand the balance of interests among the Soviet political elite. While each of these networks is formed around key top-level politicians, they are all geographically and institutionally focused. Accordingly, an examination of these major networks permits us to consider the different influences brought to bear on national politics.

The prevalence of patronage politics is demonstrated by the fact that networks are found in diverse political settings. Besides the Brezhnev network, other Politburo members' networks arose with strong bases of support in the CC apparat, the Moscow party organization, the Ukrainian and Belorussian party organizations, within the all-union governmental apparat, and within the all-union

Table 2.8 *Institutional affiliation of members of other patronage networks, December 31, 1969 (percent)*

	Kapitonov–Demichev–Grishin N(%)	Suslov–Pel'she–Ponomarev N(%)	Mazurov–Masherov–Zimyanin N(%)	Podgorny–Titov–Shelest N(%)	Kosygin N(%)	Shelepin N(%)	Entire Brezhnev network N(%)
Secretariat							3 (3)
Central Committee apparatus	6 (33)	5 (32)	3 (20)	1 (6)	1 (11)		17 (14)
Council of Ministers apparatus	1 (6)	1 (6)	1 (7)	4 (22)	8 (89)	3 (33)	26 (22)
Republic organs (including RSFSR)	2 (11)	8 (50)	7 (47)	4 (22)		3 (33)	19 (16)
Oblast and city organs	9 (50)	1 (6)	4 (26)	9 (50)		1 (11)	38 (32)
Military							11 (8)
Other[a]		1 (6)				2 (23)	6 (5)
Total	18(100)	16(100)	15(100)	18(100)	9(100)	9(100)	120(100)

[a]Includes officials of the Academy of Sciences, the all-union Komsomol, and the all-union trade union organizations.

Komsomol. Members of these other networks gained all-union elite status as their patrons advanced (see Table 2.7).

Several networks of this period were based in the central apparatuses in Moscow. An important network was centered around three high-level officials – Ivan Kapitonov, Piotr Demichev, and Viktor Grishin. This network was composed primarily of politicians who had advanced in the Moscow city and oblast party organizations in the 1940s and 1950s. The three network patrons had assumed important roles in the Moscow party organizations, serving together as they were elevated to all-union political prominence.

Kapitonov appears as "first among equals," although he is the only one of the three who was never elected to the Politburo. He moved up in the Moscow city party organization, becoming a Secretary and then Second Secretary of the Moscow Obkom in 1951–52. He subsequently worked as the First Secretary of the Moscow city organization, and then headed the Moscow Obkom from 1954 to 1959. During this period, both Demichev and Grishin advanced. Demichev served under Kapitonov in the early 1950s, while Grishin followed him as Moscow Obkom Second Secretary in 1952. The element of reciprocity is apparent in the relations among these three politicians, for the two once-junior members helped to resurrect Kapitonov in the mid-1960s, when he returned to Moscow as the CPSU Secretary for cadres assignments. At that time, both Demichev and Grishin were in either the Secretariat or the Politburo.

The entourages of all three of these politicians are closely interconnected, making it difficult to link individuals with only one patron.[24] This fact only underscores the importance of multiple linkages to a functioning network. Most of this network's clients had also served in either the Moscow city or oblast party organizations, though a number of them had been promoted to leadership positions in other regional party organizations. Several advanced into the RSFSR party and state apparatuses.[25] Others advanced into positions of responsibility for the country's economy.[26]

The Kapitonov–Demichev–Grishin network was good-sized, spanning a range of levels of responsibility and important substantive interests (Table 2.8). Kapitonov's own institutional base in the Organizational–Party Work Department (OPWD) contributed substantially to the network's prominence. Responsible for cadres selection, this was arguably the most important CC department. It oversaw the selection of both CC apparatus workers and top regional and republic party cadres. It also supervised the selection of central trade union and Komsomol personnel and sanctioned the appointments of military, police, and diplomatic personnel.[27] The network's power was augmented by the authority of its patrons, many of whom occupied positions at the highest levels of the party hierarchy for a considerable time period. Kapitonov headed the OPWD and was a party Secretary for nearly eighteen years.[28] By the early 1980s, Demichev and Grishin were senior Politburo and Secretariat members. Together, they and their clients were a formidable group.

Mikhail Suslov, the long-time party ideologue, led another important network composed of several other Politburo and Secretariat members as well as sixteen identified CC clients. This network was probably forged in the Moscow Institute of Red Professors where a number of its top members studied or worked in the late 1920s and early-to-mid 1930s. Suslov, Pel'she, and Ponomarev all attended the Red Professors' Institute, as did at least one of their identified protégés, long-time Estonian party boss I.G. Kebin. The network included individuals at the all-union and republic levels, though most were working in Moscow by the 1960s. The results in Table 2.8 probably undercount the actual number of network members because two of the network patrons, Suslov and Ponomarev, held top-level positions in Moscow for a long time. Despite these identification problems, several important figures in the areas of ideology and communication can be linked to Suslov. Among other things, Suslov was responsible for overseeing party organs, including *Pravda* and *Kommunist*. Many editors of these newspapers had career ties to him.[29]

Both Suslov and Pel'she worked in the Baltic republics and developed political connections there in the postwar period. Given this experience, they were designated the national leaders overseeing the politics of the Baltic republics during the Brezhnev period.[30] Baltic politicians moved to the political center on the "coat-tails" of these Politburo patrons.[31]

Suslov and Ponomarev associates also advanced in the CC International Department. Boris Ponomarev was an understudy of Suslov, having been a party Secretary and the Department Head since 1961. A Comintern Official in the 1930s, Ponomarev helped two of his associates in the International Department advance into the CC itself during the 1970s.[32]

Both the Kapitonov and Suslov networks were based in the central party apparatus and were composed primarily of Russians. Organizationally, these networks were well situated to influence national

policy in important areas (e.g., questions of ideology, cadres promotion, foreign policy, and intra-bloc relations). Their patrons had
consolidated positions and built up followings over a lengthy time
period. From what we know, these politicians never challenged for
the top party position, but rather were content to stake out turfs
within the central apparat. Unlike Kapitonov and Suslov, however,
another network patron, Aleksandr Shelepin, did challenge for the
top position.[33] He was able to fashion a sizeable entourage involving
all-union officials, though it did not last long.

Shelepin's entourage was similar to the Kapitonov and Suslov
networks in its diversity and representation in top national organizations. Shelepin had risen quickly in the party hierarchy and had
held responsible positions in a number of important institutions. His
credentials at the time of the 1964 leadership succession were
impressive: he had recently headed the KGB and at the time was a
national party Secretary. His relatively large and diverse clientele
was drawn from the variety of institutions with which he had been
connected. But by the end of the 1960s, Shelepin's influence was
already quite limited. The evidence shows that Shelepin had reached
his peak of political influence by 1966, and that by the end of 1967 he
and his clients were in retreat. This was a dramatic turnaround as
Shelepin, already a party Secretary for three years, had become a full
member of the Politburo at the November 1964 CC Plenum. By 1968,
a good number of his clients were already being demoted. Some
were "retired" into ambassadorial positions.[34] Others were either
shifted into insignificant domestic governmental slots or simply
ousted.[35] By the end of 1969, no Shelepin clients were serving in the
CC apparatus. By the XXV Party Congress, nearly all of Shelepin's
associates had been removed from the CC membership. Clients of
honorably departed patrons could survive their patron's ouster, but
Shelepin's associates possessed neither the political seniority nor the
independent institutional base of support to withstand their patron's
fall.

In addition to the networks based in the all-union apparatus,
several important regional networks also influenced Soviet national
politics during the Brezhnev period. Traditionally, a significant
ethnic contingent within the top all-union elite has come from
Ukraine. The importance of the Ukrainian republic, second only to
the RSFSR in all-union politics, promised its politicians a prominent
position, but, as Slavic ethnic rivals to the Russians, this group could
not maintain its position within the ranks of the top elite. Those

Ukrainian politicians with any staying power, such as long-time Ukrainian party First Secretary Vladimir Shcherbitsky, generally associated themselves with Russian-led networks like Brezhnev's. The evolution of the Khar'kov network guided by Nikolai Podgorny, Vitaly Titov, and Piotr Shelest is more typical of the fate of Ukrainian networks in national politics.

Podgorny's Khar'kov network was among the largest of the Brezhnev period. Its size reflected both Podgorny's important role in Ukraine during the 1950s and early 1960s, as well as his status as Brezhnev's major political rival. Podgorny developed this network not only while he was moving up in the Ukrainian party apparatus, but also during his career as Ukrainian party boss (1957 to 1963) and CPSU secretary (1963 to 1965). The network was based in the Khar'kov party organization, and Podgorny's alliance with the Donetsk party organization (through A.P. Liashko, V.M. Tsibul'ko, and A.A. Titarenko) only further consolidated the network's position within Ukraine.[36] But Podgorny's transfer from the CPSU Secretariat to the USSR Supreme Soviet in 1965 represented a "kick upstairs" and an immediate slip in real political power. Although his Ukrainian associates headed important regional party organizations in the republic, they experienced difficulty in advancing to all-union positions of responsibility. An investigation of the Khar'kov party organization and publication of a CPSU CC declaration on its deficiencies in 1965 severely weakened this elite cohort.[37] Highly placed protégés only moved downward during the Brezhnev period. Titov, who had headed the Party Organs Department and had been promoted as a party Secretary in 1962, was quickly demoted in 1965 from the CPSU Secretariat and transferred to head the troubled Kazakh party organization.[38] Podgorny's successor in Ukraine, Piotr Shelest, was ultimately ousted in favor of Brezhnev's long-time protégé, Shcherbitsky.[39] Shelest's position in the all-union party hierarchy was never an especially important one, although his position had merited a brief membership in the Politburo.[40]

Those Podgorny associates who became CC members had moved up from Khar'kov and Kiev in the 1940s, 1950s, and early 1960s. Some advanced to Moscow with Podgorny.[41] Most remained institutionally based in Ukraine, serving either in republic apparatuses or as regional party first secretaries. Nearly all were "retired" either when Shelest was ousted or when Podgorny was removed in 1977.[42]

One other major network representing a regional party organization and ethnic group was the "Belorussian partisan group" led by

Politburo member Kirill Mazurov. This network formed during World War II, when a number of its leading members served together in the partisan movement.[43] After the war, Mazurov moved up in the Belorussian party organization, taking members of his coterie and the Belorussian partisan group with him. These officials served in both the Minsk and the republic party organizations. This group dominated Belorussian politics for several decades, both through Mazurov and his protégé and successor Piotr Masherov. It did not relinquish its hold until 1980, following the death of Masherov, when an outsider – Tikhon Kisilev – was transferred from Moscow back to Minsk to head the Belorussian party organization.[44]

As in the case of Podgorny's Ukrainian network, the careers of most members of this network were limited to republic or regional organizational slots. One network member, Vasily Shauro, became head of the CC Culture Department in 1965. Mikhail Zimyanin, who participated in the partisan movement with Mazurov and Masherov, also moved to all-union prominence. He served in all-union governmental and diplomatic positions until he was appointed chief editor of *Pravda* in 1965. In March 1976 he became the party Secretary responsible for ideology and propaganda: a position he retained through the duration of the Brezhnev regime.

The Belorussian network assumed an important balancing role within the all-union political elite. Top politicians in this group tended to align themselves with politicians outside the Brezhnev network.[45] Mazurov served under Kosygin in the Council of Ministers for thirteen years and he supported Kosygin's policy positions (and also when they collided with those of Brezhnev). Zimyanin served under Suslov in the 1960s and 1970s; the promotions he received probably were due in part to Suslov. While I have not identified a patronage tie between these two politicians, it is fair to assume that Suslov and Zimyanin worked closely together for at least a decade and a half. Suslov oversaw the broad areas of ideology and propaganda in which Zimyanin's career was made.

A politician who was influential in national politics and who headed a sizeable group was Aleksei Kosygin. As Chairman of the USSR Council of Ministers, Kosygin assumed an influential role in the Brezhnev regime. He was in a position of both relative strength and weakness in national elite politics: he was able to recruit clients, but only within the governmental apparatus and in specific economic sectors. His entourage was not as diverse as those of Brezhnev, Podgorny, and Suslov. Kosygin had made a career within the governmental apparatus in the areas of economic planning, textiles, and light industry. The composition of his entourage reflects this career past. Most of his clients served in the light and food industries and in the state planning organ, Gosplan. Several clients who were top members of the Council of Ministers, including V.A. Kirillin and M.A. Lesechko, advanced into its Presidium soon after Kosygin did. Both Kirillin and Lesechko served under Kosygin as deputy chairmen. They, along with another Kosygin protégé, N.K. Baibakov, oversaw the 1960s reforms associated with Kosygin. In addition, several ministers, including S.F. Antonov (Meatpacking and Dairy Industry), A.A. Ishkov (Fish Industry), and N.N. Tarasov (Light Industry), moved up under Kosygin and held portfolios during most or all of his tenure. The organizational roles and public positions of these and other Kosygin clients probably helped him in undertaking certain policy initiatives.[46] Yet the size and location of his entourage show that while Kosygin enjoyed discretion within his own institutional domain, his organizational strength did not extend into the highest party organs.[47]

A number of system-level patrons not discussed here were regional leaders who were not identified as members of broader networks.[48] Others were national-level leaders whose prominence was either very short-lived or restricted to narrow institutions.[49] Several, with relatively small identified entourages, were independent political actors, though their careers suggest links with important officials and networks. Yury Andropov's career, for instance, was associated with Brezhnev. He enjoyed mobility under Brezhnev and he had personal connections which included individuals who were linked to the Brezhnev group.[50] Party Secretary and Politburo candidate member Mikhail Solomentsev likewise enjoyed mobility under Brezhnev. Two politicians who had career ties to Solomentsev were also members of Brezhnev's network.[51] Politburo candidate member Vladimir Dolgikh also experienced mobility under Brezhnev, having come from the same region and having worked with Brezhnev's close protégé, Konstantin Chernenko. All three of these politicians had ties to Brezhnev and his group, but all three remained independent actors.

Examination of these other patronage networks points to the overall strength of the sizeable Brezhnev network. That core patronage network, combined with the attached entourages of Brezhnev protégés, was formidable in both its size and its institutional location. Yet the presence of these rival networks also reveals that there were real organizational limits on the power of the General Secretary's group. The networks identified and explored here were, by and large, institutionally or geographically based and did not have the organizational or geographic range of the Brezhnev group. But their sizes and organizational locations did make them forces to contend with in the policy process. Individually, none proved to be diverse enough and strong enough to challenge the increasing strength of the Brezhnev group. Taken together, however, they represented a genuine constraint. Thus, in the constellation of Soviet national politics, the patronage networks of the party boss and other politicians constituted an informal system of political checks and balances. The General Secretary possessed considerable authority and policy discretion, but the limits of his own and his network's power required some receptivity to the interests of other influential political actors. As will become evident in chapter 3, Brezhnev's effectiveness as a national leader stemmed largely from his ability to build and maintain a governing coalition that bridged many of these actors, their networks, and their interests.

Patronage and recruitment to national office

As we have seen, organizations at the national level are linked through the patron–client connections of the cadres who head them. These networks occur in different institutional settings and are made up of both horizontal (patron–patron) and vertical (patron–client and patron–protégé) connections. Politicians with career connections to senior national patrons are recruited into many of the most impor-tant national party and state positions. Patron–client networks help to link the political center and the periphery. Junior members in the entourages of politburo patrons often assume important positions in regional party organizations. The personnel turnover of the 1964–69 period made it possible for many aspiring politicians to move into positions of regional responsibility.

Tracing the upward mobility of network members reveals that many eventually held important top-level slots, though the national organizations in which they worked are not easily ranked in terms of political importance. But it is possible to evaluate systematically the importance of patronage connections by examining the career mobil-ity of officials serving in the periphery. Many aspiring politicians advanced through service in regional party organizations. These regional settings vary in their importance and influence in national politics. Do officials with connections to top-level national politicians tend to serve in the more important regional organizations? Often the national leaders themselves once served in key regional posts, forging connections which enhanced the mobility prospects of others in those settings. In other cases, officials from prominent regions are better able to capture the attention of the political center. In both cases, the presence of patronage ties strengthens the linkage between the center and the locale.

Fortunately, the available data permit these regional party organizations to be ranked according to their political importance. They can be ranked by the number of delegates that each sends to the CPSU congress.[52] According to the rules of the CPSU Mandate Commission, each delegate elected to an all-union party Congress represents a predetermined number of party members. The stenographic records published for each CPSU congress list all delegates elected and their regional organizational affiliations. The figures for the approximately 5,000 delegates attending a congress can be summed to provide a ranking of all regional party organizations.[53]

I have totaled the delegate representation figures for the 1976 XXV Party Congress. This Congress was the high point of the Brezhnev period, falling at the midpoint of the post-power consolidation phase of the Brezhnev regime (i.e., 1969–82). At this point the important patronage networks of the period (e.g., those of Kosygin, Mazurov, Podgorny, Shelepin, Suslov, and of course, Brezhnev) were already in place.[54]

According to the mandate rules of the 1976 Party Congress, one delegate was selected for every 3,000 CPSU members.[55] A total of 4,998 delegates represented 145 republic and regional party organizations. These figures were summed and the resultant rank ordering of the 145 subnational party organizations was used to measure the political importance of regions.

In examining leadership change and mobility of clients in subordinate regional settings, I find a positive relationship between the placement of clients and the importance of regional party organizations. In the aggregate, there is not a statistically significant relationship between leadership change and rank positions of organizations for the very reason that changes were taking place at all levels during the Brezhnev regime's five-year period of power consolidation. Over half of all regional party organizations underwent leadership changes. Many of these, however, were the top regional party organizations. Of the twenty-five most important regions, 60 percent experienced leadership changes during this period.[56]

By the end of the power consolidation phase, protégés and clients of Politburo patrons headed many of these organizations. In some cases, protégés and clients were already in power as of October 1964. Thus, the lack of a leadership change did not necessarily mean that a region was not linked to the new Moscow leadership. Application of a trichotomous variable, with entourage members separated from non-entourage new leaders and non-entourage incumbents, reveals a relationship between the importance of a region and its leadership's link to Politburo patrons.[57] As the new national regime consolidated its own position, its networks secured their own positions by elevating trusted lieutenants into important intermediate-level slots. The most important regional party organizations were generally linked to the national leadership through patron–client connections. Less important party organizations, on the other hand, tended to be headed by new leaders lacking career connections to top national figures. Meanwhile, those incumbent regional party bosses who lacked ties to the new top leadership but who survived the personnel turnover of the consolidation period tended to head those party organizations in between these extremes. The lack of such political ties did not obviate the fact that these incumbents possessed resources that made them valuable to the new national regime.[58]

Through the 1970s, the personnel linkages between Politburo and Secretariat politicians and regional party leaderships were only enhanced. As regional posts opened due to retirements, death, and personnel turnover, associates of national leaders continued to advance to top regional positions. By the end of 1976, in the wake of Brezhnev's triumphant XXV Party Congress, over two-thirds of the top twenty-five party organizations were headed by identified protégés and clients.[59] An analysis of variance test including all regional party organizations reveals a statistically significant relationship between the political importance of regions and the presence of regional party first secretaries with career ties to mentors in Moscow.[60]

Patronage networks helped bridge the political distance between Moscow and the periphery. The political tails of high-level national officials extended into the country's political periphery. Ambitious, upwardly mobile politicians were best served by associating themselves with influential politicians to move into all-union prominence. Aspiring officials with network connections were the most likely candidates for important regional leadership positions. They were also the most likely regional party representatives to gain all-union elite status through CC membership and the most likely to advance to national positions.

Patronage and political survival

The data demonstrate the enhanced mobility prospects patronage relationships offer aspiring junior politicians. The data also reveal the heightened political control powerful officials gain through the advancement of trusted subordinates. The basic assumption under-lying the analysis is the interdependence of influence and prestige between patrons and clients. The focus thus far has been on upward mobility, with clients following patrons up the career ladder. Given the constraints of the limited political opportunity structure, junior "connected" politicians often advance rapidly. Their "rising star" patrons provide them with opportunities to amass power as they build their careers. It follows that maintenance of their positions is dependent upon the political fortunes of their patrons. Not only the promotion but also the demotion of patrons should have severe consequences for the future mobility opportunities and political fate of clients. One logically hypothesizes that the removal or demotion of patrons will bode ill for those politically dependent upon them.

During the Brezhnev period a number of important, nationally prominent, patrons exited the political scene, leaving sizeable net-works in their absence. An examination of the fates of these networks results in a less straightforward, but relevant, explanation for members' future career prospects. We find that clients' careers are threatened by the departure of a patron, but that they can survive.

Of the thirty-nine Politburo and Secretariat patrons, thirteen departed from the political scene during the eighteen-year Brezhnev period. Six of these politicians left the pinnacle of power without taint, either dying while still in power or honorably retiring.[61] The other seven were demoted and disgraced.[62] The differences in circumstances that conditioned a politician's removal from power are important because they define his or her own legacy. That legacy has significant implications for the political survival of associates.

Of the sixty-seven associates identified for the thirteen Brezhnev era system patrons who departed the national leadership ranks, thirty-five retained their elite status in the wake of the patron's departure.[63] Although the patron's departure did not mean the automatic departure of clients, it did have consequences for those dependent upon him. When patrons died leaving the political scene with honor, clients tended to retain their elite status (twenty of twenty-seven, or 74 percent). When patrons departed in disgrace clients were not so successful in holding on to their positions (only fifteen of forty, or 40 percent). But the fact that 40 percent of the clients of ousted patrons did hold on to power suggests that other factors were also at work moderating their political fates.

In addition to their patronage connections, clients have institutional affiliations and career track records that influence the probability of their political survival. I hypothesize that a party apparatchik, who may enjoy rapid upward mobility within the hierarchy, has similar rapid downward mobility prospects, especially when facing the loss of a powerful patron. I also hypothesize that professional experience – within a specialized sector and transcending party organizational politics – cushions a politician's position. Politicians with experience and expertise beyond party organizational work have skills that make them valuable to the political system, translating into greater job security in the bureaucracy and greater longevity as governmental representatives (i.e., administrators) in the Central Committee. These politicians are in a better position to carve out bureaucratic niches that make them less dependent upon Politburo and Secretariat patrons. They are less vulnerable to the vagaries of high-level elite conflict.

Analysis of the career fates of Brezhnev-era politicians reveals that those with expertise ("administrators") have better survival prospects than the party apparatchiki, though the differences are not statistically significant (42 percent of administrators retained to 31 percent of apparatchiki).[64] A politician's longevity within the ranks of the political elite, however, does prove to be an important factor in his or her survival. Table 2.9 measures longevity in terms of number of elections to the CC/CAC. It demonstrates that clients who had been at the top for a considerable time period were able to survive the departure of a disgraced patron (67 percent survived). Clients who were relative newcomers to the top did not (only one of nineteen, or approximately 5 percent, survived).[65] These results indicate that apparatchiki with minimal tenure tended to have the poorest prospects for survival. Officials with significant tenure based outside of the CPSU apparatus had the best prospects for survival. These politicians had built and solidified their own bases of support

Table 2.9 *Mobility of clients of ousted Politburo patrons, by institutional affiliation and political longevity*

	Party apparatchik				Administrator			
	1 or 2 elections		3 or more elections		1 or 2 elections		3 or more elections	
	N	%	N	%	N	%	N	%
Retained	1	10	4	67	0	0	10	67
Ousted	9	90	2	33	9	100	5	33
Total N	10	100	6	100	9	100	15	100

Where for party apparatchiki (columns 1 and 2): Chi Square = 3.28; D.F. = 1; Significance Level = 0.07; Fisher's Exact Probability = 0.04.

Where for Administrators (columns 3 and 4): Chi Square = 7.73; D.F. = 1; Significance Level = 0.005; Fisher's Exact Probability = 0.002.

and, consequently, were less dependent upon their political mentors.

Junior politicians can also strengthen their political positions and survive the vagaries of high-level politics by developing career connections with several patrons. The careers of Soviet leaders have often revealed multiple patronage connections.[66] Out of the total population of identified protégés and clients in this study, thirty-one had ties with two system patrons. It is very likely that such multiple-patron connections occur more frequently than these figures show. The limitations of the available biographical data and the measures of clientelism employed here make it difficult to identify all cases. This subgroup of the total population represents an unusual set of politicians who were apparently able to build their careers through successive linkages with several prominent leaders. Career connections with superiors were forged in midstream, after these junior politicians had already begun their ascent of the nomenklatura ladder. What is striking about these identified protégés and clients is that most were apparatchiki whose careers spanned a number of different hierarchies. Eighty percent of the thirty-one protégés and clients with multiple clientelistic connections served in several identifiable hierarchies. The typical career began within regional Komsomol organs, followed by service in regional party organs before moving to republic-level or national positions of political responsibility. These politicians were politically resilient, with their average length of CC/CAC membership being eighteen years – far above the average for their peers. Even those associated with fallen Politburo patrons could survive their superiors' ousters.[67]

Certain of these "multi-patron" clients possessed administrative or technical expertise that made them valuable to competing Politburo members. The multifaceted administrator, V.Y. Dymshits, forged connections with both Brezhnev and Kosygin, which not only helped him rise to power but also contributed to his longevity in office. His ties to Brezhnev extended back to the 1940s, when both had worked in the Zaporozh'e province. He rose quickly in the USSR ministries, working closely with Kosygin for over twenty years in the Council of Ministers. His varied background (which included administrative positions in the areas of metallurgy, construction, energy, and supply) and organizational skills made him a valuable member of the Council of Ministers' Presidium for over two decades. Others with particular specialties served in sectors that linked their careers with those of several system patrons who advanced in those sectors (e.g., those politicians who served with Brezhnev, Kirilenko, and Ustinov and who were associated with the military–industrial sector). Some of these politicians moved up primarily through one network (e.g., the Moscow or Ukrainian networks), while others made careers which included several networks, or the entourages of several unrelated Politburo patrons. All these patronage arrangements heightened the prospect for competent politicians to survive the departure of powerful patrons and the vicissitudes of national elite politics.

Patronage and governance in the Brezhnev period

Patron–client relations underlay the political networks that dominated Soviet politics of the Brezhnev period. These networks contained most of the important Politburo members and party secretaries, and included a significant number of Central Committee and Central Auditing Commission members. They spanned party and state institutions, and helped link Moscow and the expansive periphery. For network patrons, these linkages represented a means of influencing institutions and politicians. For protégés and potential clients, they were avenues by which aspiring politicians could advance into policy positions. Although the interdependence of network members' careers suggested very real political risks for clients – especially those who rose quickly in the party apparatus – the potential payoffs for career advancement were tremendous.

Over the course of the Brezhnev period, as would prove true under his successors, new mobile politicians developed increasing levels of expertise and skill (at least as measured by such ascriptive attributes as level of education attained).[68] Those elevated into top nomenklatura positions evinced considerable previous administrative and organizational experience, in many cases, across a wide range of institutional settings. Even though these successful politicians had apparent rational-technical skills, they still relied on long-term career ties to powerful national politicians. Networks flourished through the decades of the 1960s, 1970s, and early 1980s.

Brezhnev's success in forming a governing team depended on many factors, but patron–client networks were among the most important. The coterie of politicians who had moved up with the General Secretary since the 1930s was at the core of the Brezhnev administration. This group included not only the Dnepropetrovsk politicians, but other officials who had served in the political periphery with him. It also included politicians who had advanced with Brezhnev in Moscow during the 1950s and early 1960s. Yet Brezhnev's own entourage was but a part of a broader network which was at the heart of the national regime. This network included politicians who had not previously served with Brezhnev, but who worked directly with him after 1964 and who experienced mobility to the highest political levels. It included many officials whose political mobility was due to protégés of the General Secretary. Their authority grew as did that of Brezhnev during his tenure. This extended network represented many institutional and regional interests, and spanned several generations of politicians. As we shall see, it was augmented by alliances with other politicians and networks which, when combined, formed a national ruling coalition.

A critically important function of the Brezhnev network was its ability to connect policy-making, policy-implementing, and supervisory organs. These linkages, in areas critical to the Brezhnev policy program, represented real organizational control by this leading political group. Any evaluation of the political achievements of Brezhnev's regime must take note of the pervasiveness of his extended network across these organizational hierarchies. It is not coincidental that priority sectors (e.g., the military–industrial and agricultural) were dominated by Brezhnev protégés and allies.

Any assessment of Brezhnev's policy success must also include an acknowledgment of his effectiveness as a consensus builder across factions. If the history of this period shows a continuing growth in power and authority of the Brezhnev entourage and its extended network, it also demonstrates that other networks not only survived but thrived. Other patronage networks were also based in important organizations and regions, but these were settings not penetrated by the leading politicians and clients who collectively constituted the extended Brezhnev network. As a result, these "rival" networks were institutionally strong, meriting their inclusion in the broader governing coalition. In a sense, the corporatist contention that the Brezhnev coalition came to encompass many vested political interests is quite accurate. Numerous patronage networks of this period emerged out of particular sectoral or geographical settings. When associated with a patron – and when linked by that patron to Brezhnev and his dominant network – they constituted an impressive cross-section of major interests within the society. However, the critical predictor of an individual's advancement and inclusion within the top nomenklatura elite was career connection, not institutional affiliation. To maintain one's position within the governing elite it was necessary to work with the General Secretary and his network without threatening his and their interests. Rival groups, for instance those of Shelepin and Podgorny, that were directly competing with the Brezhnev network on the same turf did not fare well. Brezhnev and his group secured the necessary political muscle to eliminate them, but in order for Brezhnev to build his authority and govern effectively, he and his extended network had to make coalition arrangements with other viable and resilient elements within the national political elite. If patronage ties enhanced Brezhnev's position, they likewise bolstered the positions of other leading politicians. Rival patronage networks provided a certain check on the leadership position of Brezhnev, further encouraging him to engage in consensus building.

Cadres stability was a by-product of the Brezhnev coalition. The strong position of the General Secretary, his patronage faction, and the extended network he guided – enhanced by important linkages to other politicians and interests – ensured that stability. Policy consensus was an important product of this reality, with a comprehensive policy program emerging that was in the interest of the governing Soviet elite.

3 Patronage and the Brezhnev policy program

The nebulous character of patron–client relations makes it difficult to assess their policy consequences. Their pervasiveness is quite apparent, but, in a political system not easily opened to outside scrutiny, exploring their political implications is challenging. This chapter examines the Brezhnev policy program and investigates how network and non-network members reacted to it. That program, touching upon all important sectors and interests, was composed of numerous specific "planks" or issues about which most prominent officials spoke in public addresses. By tracing the evolution of this policy program, and by examining the degree to which officials supported its policies, we tap into one of the few sources of information on governance during the Brezhnev years. While the analyses confirm the importance of network and coalition building to governance, the relationship that is revealed is complex.

In a mono-party system where basic political differences are not acknowledged, patronage bridges the variable interests of a heterogeneous elite. Patronage ties impact upon the policy process because they "constrain" the behavior of clients and protégés. Those who are politically subordinate to the network patron are under pressure to support that patron and his broad policy program. We have already seen the potential for rapid upward and downward mobility connected with supportive or unsupportive subordinates. Within the centralized, hierarchical Soviet political setting, there are both positive and negative incentives for clients to support the initiatives of their patron.

Because the clients and protégés comprising a patronage network are diverse, their policy support will be manifested in numerous ways. After all, the national policy agenda is large, and the influences brought to bear on national-level politicians will pull them in different directions. Membership in a clientelistic network, however, links the political fates and policy concerns of members to foster support for the policy initiatives of the leader. Group cohesion and mobility prospects ultimately depend on both the viability and success of a patron and his policy program, and the loyalty of that patron's subordinates.

The absence of systematic information on the Soviet decision-making process precludes a direct investigation of policy formulation. Although we are not able to weigh individual politicians' inputs into the process, I have employed substitute measures for politicians' behavior based on publicly expressed orientations.[1] The available career and attitudinal data for the top Soviet political elite allow us to consider the relationship between career linkages and issue orientations, and for more than one patronage network.

We have comparable attitudinal data for a small group of Soviet officials, the members of the party Politburo and Secretariat. Although comprising no more than twenty-five members at any given time, this is a group for which we can identify at least the broad contours of individual policy positions. It is possible to go beyond the positions of the chief policy initiator, the General Secretary, and consider those of the major actors – supporters and rivals – with whom he had to contend.

There were forty-five such top-level decision makers during the entire Brezhnev period. As we have seen, a number of them guided important patronage networks in the 1960s and 1970s. These network leaders offered public discussions of the issue agenda, directing their comments toward the evolving set of policies and symbols that comprised the Brezhnev program. Their public discussion of the Brezhnev program is the substantive focus for systematically analyzing these leaders' views.

Soviet elite norms have traditionally constrained politicians' public discussion of policy matters, but Western studies of Soviet politics have long demonstrated that officials can and do engage in public policy debates.[2] Soviet politicians are circumspect in their public articulations, but they can and do openly advocate policy positions. It has been argued that politicians became even more assertive and willing to engage in such public discussions during the Brezhnev period.[3] As a result, there are a number of published statements by top officials that can be used to test hypotheses regarding patronage, coalition building, and policy.

The Brezhnev program and Supreme Soviet election speeches

The Brezhnev policy program was comprehensive and touched upon all aspects of Soviet life during the regime's eighteen-year evolution. I concentrate on the major planks of the program, tapping its diversity. Others have already examined the Brezhnev program and its legacy in detail.[4] My intention is to (a) identify policies and symbols associated with the Brezhnev program; (b) examine how top-level politicians spoke about and manipulated those policies and symbols; and (c) determine whether there was attitudinal constraint among network members.

My analysis assumes that the General Secretary is the decisive Soviet policy initiator. The national policy agenda strongly reflects his concerns and priorities. While the top party leader is compelled to consider a wide range of sectoral and institutional interests, his organizational position is decisive and assures his direct involvement. All politicians are aware that the General Secretary assumes a critical role in cadres' career futures. At the very least, his position is one of oversight, guaranteeing him veto power in personnel selection. Organizationally, he is in the best position to direct the national policy discussion. Providing such direction is his major role as party leader. While an individual's political proclivities and leadership style will help determine the form and content of his agenda, the authority of the office of the party General Secretary assures its occupant broad-ranging policy discretion.[5]

Other politicians are reluctant to challenge directly the discretionary policy-making position of a powerful top leader.[6] They are compelled to await his initiative or to react to his position, and they are likely to be assertive only when the General Secretary is not actively involved. Politicians may attempt to influence the substance of policy, but there are negative incentives for doing so even if it is done cautiously.

Politicians with career ties to a powerful patron are motivated to support that patron's policies. I hypothesize that Brezhnev's associates exhibited decisive support for the Brezhnev program as it developed. I expect their backing was the bedrock for Brezhnev's political position, and that it was stronger than that of others who lacked career connections to the General Secretary. I would expect to find greater support both in associates' espousal of a larger range of policy planks within the program, and in associates' overt linkage of policies and policy success with Brezhnev personally. I also expect strong support would have come from Brezhnev allies. Some of these politicians had career or institutional ties to the General Secretary. Others experienced significant career advances under him.

To test these contentions, I utilize an index encompassing specific policies and symbols that were integral parts of the Brezhnev program. Rather than focusing on one domain or set of issues, this index is designed to span the range of concerns advanced in that program. By including themes stressed by politicians as they confronted the agenda of issues before the country, I have used this index to gauge top politicians' support for the Brezhnev program.

In identifying the positions Soviet officials took on various issues, I am looking for the way in which high-level politicians characterized particular policies and themes. I am concerned with teasing out more general policy positions, noting what a politician considers to be top priority sectors, noting how that politician describes the international arena (in positive, mixed, or hostile terms), and determining whether that politician believes more resources should be committed to a given problem (e.g., the perennial agricultural question). Soviet leaders have advocated different strategies and have been willing, albeit cautiously, to stake out rather different issue positions. Their positions have different implications for the vested interests that composed the Soviet establishment. While most Soviet national-level officials took care not to be explicitly opposed to any of those vested interests, their characterizations put particular spins on their public utterances. Their stances can be determined by a thematic analysis of their public pronouncements, with a cautious comparison of relative descriptions and stated political priorities.

This analysis considers the major Brezhnev policy priorities. I focus on these policy priorities not only for reasons of analytical parsimony, but because the major Brezhnev planks were the themes drawing the most public comment from politicians during this eighteen-year period. There is a discernible consistency in the rationale and broad contours of the Brezhnev program, though manipulation of policies and symbols varied across time. Some changes in policy priorities during this period reflected the stages of growth that the regime went through, i.e., from (a) power consolidation to (b) full program presentation to (c) implementation and *post-hoc* rationalization.

In the early Brezhnev period, the rejection of the Khrushchev program and legacy helped to unify officials in their public presentations. By 1965, the policy program of the new regime began to take shape, and was fully presented by Brezhnev in 1971. We can periodize the Brezhnev regime to account for certain changes in policies and priorities and to predict periods of greater consensus and dissensus among politicians. Contrary to the common prediction that policy change will occur in a regime's early years, the dynamism and uncertainty of the immediate post-succession period encouraged competing politicians to be cautious as they carved out their niches in the national hierarchy.[7] Articulation of the new line and adherence to it came only after the initial five-year regime formation period. The longevity of the Brezhnev regime guaranteed that challenges to Brezhnev's comprehensive program and its planks would emerge. Policy problems were bound to surface – and they did – requiring a reconsideration of the political formula used. Near the midpoint of the Brezhnev period, there were reasons and incentives for officials to question the broad policy thrust and to anticipate alternatives.[8] However, a combination of factors, including policy successes, weaknesses of rivals, and the political strength and flexibility of Brezhnev and his network ensured the regime's survival.

As we shall see, the Brezhnev program was wide ranging. Generally speaking, the program represented a policy thrust of both guns and butter, with increased military spending, rising consumption, and growing overall investment. Among the top priorities of his regime was the policy of heavy investment in and mechanization of agriculture, which was said to be placed upon an "industrial footing." Brezhnev set the goals of massive investment of funds in agriculture early on in his administration, certainly within a year of his succession, and continued to emphasize it throughout.[9] The primacy of agriculture was set against the traditional priority of heavy industry and the related military complex. As in the past, the light and food industries were secondary.

These views of heavy industry and agriculture were basic to the overall Brezhnev policy approach. His program evolved over time, however, and later included positions and themes coopted from other – often rival – politicians. The evolution of the Brezhnev program is apparent when noting some of its more specific policies and symbols. For instance, the development of Siberia and the Soviet Far East assumed prominence in the later 1970s, as increasing attention was directed to fuel and energy resource exploitation. In the foreign policy domain, a Soviet "peace program" emerged, taking on a discernible form after the XXIV Party Congress in 1971, as the *rapprochement* with the West flowered.

These policy initiatives were at the center of the Brezhnev program, but a number of symbols can also be closely associated with his regime. Helpful in legitimating policy programs, these symbols were especially susceptible to manipulation by politicians in their public utterances. One symbol was the characterization of the domestic context of that time as one of "mature" (*zrelyi*) or "developed" (*razvitoi*) socialism.[10] These terms were said to describe the culmination of the first developmental stage on the path to communism. Brezhnev had invoked the term as early as his 1966 Supreme Soviet election speech, and frequently employed it thereafter.[11] The notion that the USSR had advanced into the developed socialist phase was linked with a number of Brezhnev initiatives. It was emphasized in the wake of the 1977 Soviet Constitution, another symbol associated with Brezhnev. References to mature socialism and to the new Constitution underscored a suggested regularization of Soviet life. The rhetoric suggested the appropriateness of the Brezhnev program and was intended to add legitimacy to Brezhnev's regime.[12]

While these policies and symbols cover many aspects of the Brezhnev program, one last factor must be noted: public criticism of governmental planning and administrative organs and the concomitant call for an enhanced watchdog role for party organs in ensuring government agencies' more effective functioning. The issue had been raised by Brezhnev at several CC plenums.[13] His criticisms were an indirect means of castigating Premier Aleksei Kosygin, who was a major rival through much of his tenure. Because of the discussion incited by Brezhnev's criticisms, Kosygin eventually felt compelled to respond publicly. Other Soviet politicians also publicly addressed this issue. References to the reform of planning and administrative organs – and the strengthened position of supervisory party bodies – had powerful connotations during the Brezhnev years.

A patronage model of Soviet politics predicts attitudinal constraint among network members. Such constraint was evinced for members of Brezhnev's entourage, as they provided consistent support for their patron's policy program. As Brezhnev's positions evolved, those of his protégés did likewise. Comparable consistent support for the Brezhnev program was not demonstrated by other politicians, even those identified as his allies. Allies supported a broader range of Brezhnev positions than did others, but they did not match the support offered by protégés. In fact, the stated positions of such allies shifted with the political fortunes of the General Secretary. As the General Secretary and his patronage network grew in power, officials allied themselves with him and increasingly supported his stances. Their positions were much more independent when the General Secretary was relatively weaker – during both the early and late periods of his regime.

The views of these top officials have been determined through an examination of four sets of Supreme Soviet election speeches delivered in 1966, 1970, 1975, and 1980. These four time points correspond with the periods of power consolidation (1966), of program formulation (1970), of regime maintenance (1975), and of impending regime change (1980), thus permitting an examination of the evolution of politicians' public attitudes as the regime itself evolved.

Election speeches have traditionally been presented in the national press in a common format, in similar length and detail, allowing for a more systematic comparison of attitudes. All speeches were delivered and subsequently reported within a concise time period of approximately one month. While they were delivered throughout the country in different electoral districts, they targeted comparable populations of Soviet voters. As a result, these speeches are especially conducive to a systematic comparison.

Although Soviet elections traditionally had no relevance to leadership selection and policy change, they have been important forums for leaders to set out the party's record. In assessing the past, politicians identify the key tasks facing the government and society, followed by a careful discussion of issues and invocation of symbols. The speakers address a potentially wide range of issues. The published speeches, however, involve a relatively limited space for issues to be developed. A concise and summary presentation of a politician's view of the regime's priorities is set out. Within the election campaign setting, the various leaders speak as "candidates" who are expected to address the issues of the day. Because election speeches present the more particular policy concerns and views of individual candidates, they are especially useful for systematic analysis. Speakers are not acting as representatives of the institutions they head or the sectoral interests with which they are connected, so the constraints upon a politician when speaking in his official guise to a specific audience are lessened.[14] As a result, the defense minister, the party Secretary for agriculture, and every other high-ranking official speaks as a nominated "potential" member of the Supreme Soviet.

One other aspect of election speeches that makes them useful in identifying elite attitudes is that they do not appear to be so subject to severe central editing. Major public presentations to CPSU congresses, to joint meetings of the Central Committee and Council of Ministers, and to other high-profile convocations are stringently edited. These presentations represent the view of the leadership and must reflect its collective will. This is not true of election speeches, where "candidates" speak for themselves in much less authoritative forums. It is therefore more appropriate to link specific issue positions to individual speakers based on their election speech comments. By applying an index of Brezhnev policies and symbols to four sets of election speeches it is possible to evaluate the influence of patronage on elite political behavior.

The policy discussion of the early years: the 1966 election speeches

Brezhnev policy priorities

The first two sets of election speeches examined here were delivered in 1966 and 1970, as the post-Khrushchev regime constituted itself. Emphasis was placed on collective leadership, with no one politician publicly dominating the policy discussion. Brezhnev assumed a leading role, as was evident at the XXIII Party Congress in 1966, but he did not assume a decisive role until the early 1970s.[15]

As we have noted, an initial overriding concern in Brezhnev's policy focus was to undo many of the discredited Khrushchev initiatives. The new regime anticipated a stabilization of the political process. The hoped-for return to incremental policy change was matched by regime efforts to accommodate a wide range of interests. Officials expressed concern over the enhanced stability of cadres within leading party and state organs.[16] The size of top party organs expanded during the initial phase of the new regime, and continued to grow throughout its tenure.

The substantive policy priorities of the new regime became evident rather quickly. CC plenums in March and September 1965 provided opportunities for the national leadership to address the state of the economy and the direction of policy in both agriculture and industry. It is fair to say that, since Khrushchev's ouster, Soviet leaders have not publicly dealt with the more technical aspects of the general economy. Khrushchev did so, especially in the agricultural sphere, but his efforts only created more difficulties for himself.[17] Given the Khrushchev legacy, leaders took care in how they publicly addressed these issues. Brezhnev, however, gave considerable attention to these issues, and he was able to assume a guiding role in the formulation of policy beginning with his March 1965 CC Plenum address. Brezhnev pressed for a major infusion of resources into the troubled agricultural sector while pointing to the desirability of maintaining a top priority for the group A industries. In September, Premier Aleksei Kosygin presented proposals for partial reform of industrial management and planning.[18] Some deconcentration was indicated to be optimal for continued industrial productivity growth. A push for planning recentralization rounded out the top policy priorities identified by the new leadership.[19]

How did top politicians react to this changing policy agenda? Were different positions staked out by groups of individuals comprising the new ruling coalition? To what extent was there attitudinal constraint among members of the top patronage networks as the policy program was hammered out? We can address these questions by identifying the perspectives of the top figures of the Soviet regime – Brezhnev, Kosygin, and Podgorny – subsequently noting how network members and other high-level officials reacted to those perspectives.

In his 1966 election speech, Brezhnev addressed a range of domestic and foreign policy concerns, giving special attention to the issues of raised productivity and the state of the Soviet economy. What was referred to as the "scientific and technical revolution" assumed a special importance in his approach to encouraging national economic growth. The March and September 1965 CC plenums had stressed this factor and promoted greater investment in scientific research and its application to economic tasks. Brezhnev identified the scientific-technical revolution as a "decisive factor in the development of society." It required not only the strengthening of the sciences, but their technical application to production, permitting the more extensive mechanization of industry and agriculture. His position was that combining science with production would maximize the use of the nation's resources.

Brezhnev's position assumed expanded investment in a number of areas, some traditionally meriting such support, and some not. The heavy industry sector continued to enjoy primacy, and its leading position was touted by the General Secretary as "an immutable principle of our economic policy." Characterized as the foundation of technical progress in all other branches of the economy, Brezhnev treated it as the primary base for strengthening the defense capacity of the USSR. But Brezhnev also emphasized the necessity of bringing growth rates of the light and food industries closer to that of heavy industry. He acknowledged that insufficient resources had been appropriated for the sector B industries, with the needs of the population not fully satisfied in the past. This line of argument had originally helped to legitimate the 1964 change of leadership.

In Brezhnev's estimation, many fundamental questions of Soviet economic development hinged on the state of agriculture. In his speech he stressed the interrelationship between industry and agriculture. Strengthening agriculture, as a policy theme, assumed an importance beyond the sector itself. It was a component of a broader policy thrust said to safeguard traditional priority areas.

In the 1966 election speech Brezhnev pressed for large-scale capital investment.[20] Especially important in his agenda was a land reclamation program. He called for the creation of a vast cultivated zone for the stable production of grain and other crops. Brezhnev's proposal for a developed agricultural sector also required a broader transformation of the rural setting. He intended to strengthen the rural social and economic infrastructure through wage increases and by providing a better and a wider selection of services. He indicated that material incentives would be enhanced for both state farm and collective farm workers, and that a strong effort would be made to lower the income gap between the two. Additional incentives to increase agricultural productivity would involve the improvement of the forms and methods of economic administration. The particulars were necessarily vague, but the gist of Brezhnev's comments was a desire to improve the planning and management of agriculture at all authority levels, ranging from the collective farm to national ministries.

These were the basic foci of Brezhnev's policy priorities as of mid-1966. Beyond these policies there were broader issues of economic management and foreign policy. Concerns over economic issues entailed efforts to perfect production planning and management across the board, not just in agriculture. Activities directed toward developing a new Soviet constitution provided a new opportunity to examine reform of the governmental apparatus.[21]

In the foreign policy realm, Brezhnev used his election speeches to

develop the image of the Soviet Union that came to characterize
Soviet policy into the 1970s, i.e., that the USSR was increasingly
strong and better able to develop relations of accommodation with
the West, though still engaged in a long-term struggle with it.
Brezhnev directly acknowledged the potentially divergent consequences of such a foreign policy for the Soviet Union. On the one
hand, he identified threats coming from the West in some detail,
using the old theme of vigilance at home to legitimate a variety of
domestic policies.[22] These threats justified an increased commitment
to the military: "In today's conditions our country is obliged to
devote even more effort and attention to strengthening its defensive
might," he declared in 1966. But he balanced these comments by
detailing positive improvements in Soviet relations with a number of
Western countries.

Brezhnev's articulated views anticipated the broader policy program ultimately adopted by the XXIV Party Congress in 1971. By that
point, they formed the basis of the broad consensus that would
emerge. Before the XXIV Congress, however, public discussion
among Soviet leaders reflected contrasting views of the best way to
cope with the economic and political legacy of the previous regime.

A rival perspective

A major policy alternative to the Brezhnev set of positions was
offered by the two other leading members of the post-Khrushchev
coalition, Kosygin and Podgorny, in their 1966 election speeches.
Briefly stated, their positions reflected a more specific concern with
strengthening the light and food industries while acknowledging the
ongoing priority of heavy industry. They proposed a less ambitious
agricultural investment program and some capping of defense
spending. Kosygin's and Podgorny's broad characterizations of the
state of the Soviet economy and the USSR's role in the world
supported their budgetary preferences.

Kosygin called for enhancing production by improving management, applying scientific and technical research to production, and
using labor and material resources more effectively. Kosygin also
promoted a "scientific approach" to decision making which involved
comparing options, acknowledging limits, and relying on data
beyond output quantities to evaluate performance. There was a need
for more "scientific" planning and management not only in heavy
industry, which Kosygin identified as a top priority sector, but also

in agriculture. In the case of agriculture, which as we know was assuming a central role in Brezhnev's policy package, Kosygin argued there were already sufficient food products to meet the population's needs. He noted that "the necessary reserve for the normal supply of foodstuffs has been created." There was a sufficient quantity of meat and dairy products, as well as vegetables, sugar, and bread. The problem with the agricultural area was not the supply, but the poor organization of supply which lessened the availability of produced goods. The means of supply and distribution needed to be changed, and this necessitated management reform at various levels of authority. The agriculture sector did not require a new major infusion of resources. It required reorganization.

Kosygin had identified a serious problem. To meet the population's demands for manufactured goods, resource investment would need to be heightened. Although investment in the light and food industries had doubled in the past years of the current five-year plan, Kosygin pressed for further increases. He called for a long-term commitment to closing the gap in growth rates for the heavy industry and the light and food industry sectors. In general, Kosygin was committed to providing more quality state services, especially in the areas of housing, education, and health. Contrary to other candidates who praised the advances achieved during the previous years of the current plan, he stressed the need for more investment. The industrial sector was strong enough to permit it. The state of international relations also permitted it, because the policy of peaceful coexistence was said to have solidified the Soviet Union's international position.

In addressing foreign policy concerns, Kosygin was careful not to explicitly link Soviet domestic policy changes with an altered international position. He simply noted that the Soviet Union and its allies were strong, and that the "main lesson" of Vietnam demonstrated that adversaries would no longer be able to act with impunity in the international arena. Unlike many other Politburo and Secretariat election candidates, Kosygin offered no specific comments regarding defense, although his was among the most lengthy speeches published. His emphasis was clearly not on the traditional military–heavy industry priorities. Kosygin's positions, outlined in his speech, differentiated him from the policy thrust advanced by Brezhnev.

In his 1966 election speech, Supreme Soviet Chairman Podgorny more explicitly identified the interrelationship between the state of international relations and the domestic Soviet economy. His position very much corresponded to that of Kosygin. He championed light industry and consumer interests, though he also pressed for more new investment in agriculture. Podgorny tacitly expressed concern about the state of heavy industry, noting the centrality of that sector to the country's defense capacity. The main task as he saw it was to ensure higher rates of growth especially for areas of mass consumption. This meant not only heightening the application of new technologies and enhancing labor productivity – traditional solutions to the production question – but also providing more and better incentives to workers. It would also be necessary to further increase wages and pensions, and to improve various services.[23]

Podgorny did support Brezhnev's call to commit more resources to agriculture. He identified the further "industrialization" of agriculture as "a task of the entire people." He characterized the heavy and light industry sectors as dependent for their strength on the enhancement of the agricultural sector. Podgorny voiced support for the doubling of capital investments in agriculture for the eighth five-year plan. He felt that agriculture should be on a similar priority level to that of heavy industry.

Podgorny argued that foreign policy developments permitted the investment policies that he was proposing. While he referred to US policy in Vietnam and manifestations of revanchism in the Federal Republic of Germany, he devoted more attention to the development of cooperative relations involving trade, science, and culture. He described the Soviet Union as having a heightened profile in the world community, noting that "without the Soviet Union, not one major international problem can be resolved now." As for Soviet security needs, increased resources should be made available only if future contingencies required them. Podgorny did not indicate any such immediate need.

The views of Brezhnev protégés

The differences between the position of Brezhnev and those of Kosygin and Podgorny reflected important parameters in the public policy discussion as the regime consolidated power. These were the leading members of the new coalition. Other top officials raised divergent sets of issues that, in part, reflected their differing institutional and sectoral affiliations. Broad economic and investment questions took on the local color of the economic needs of specific republics and sectors. Politicians representing administrative units composed of ethnic minorities, for instance, often more explicitly dealt with issues of ideological conformity and culture. Those speaking to constituencies that were primarily industrial highlighted issues of Soviet science and technology development. Most politicians, however, discussed the investment priorities identified by these top three politicians, even if their comments were guarded.

How did Brezhnev associates react to this discussion? Among the Politburo and Secretariat members in 1966 were four Brezhnev protégés: Andrei Kirilenko, Dinmukhamed Kunaev, Vladimir Shcherbitsky, and Dmitry Ustinov. Three of them moved into these top party bodies only after Brezhnev's succession in 1964, and all were junior members of the national leadership. While they represented divergent sectoral and regional interests, their election speeches provided strong support for the most important policy positions associated with the General Secretary. Specifically, their public stances demonstrated: (1) an affirmation of the traditional priority position for heavy industry (with related support for defense); (2) support for expanded agricultural investment and identification of agriculture as a top priority; (3) commitment to an improved standard of living but with no specified support for increased investment in group B industries; and (4) a characterization of the international arena as one facilitating increased East–West cooperation but also requiring a strengthened military (see Table 3.1).

Brezhnev's closest protégé, Kirilenko, was professionally tied to the heavy industry–military sectors, especially to the machine-building industry. Not surprisingly, he stressed the economic primacy of both, noting the importance of machine building for various branches of industry and the salience of both to the further strengthening of agriculture and light industry. He specifically called for the quickened development of a number of branches that became priorities of the Brezhnev regime: energy, machine-building, metallurgy, and oil and chemical industries. Kirilenko also emphasized the need for increasing investment in agriculture, which he characterized as "one of the most important branches of our economy upon which the normal provisioning of the population with foodstuffs and industry with resources depends." He felt that a massive ten-year land reclamation program was merited, though it would be highly dependent on other industrial branches. In Kirilenko's thinking, the state of international relations only further legitimated strengthening the military. While the international context did not preclude

Table 3.1 Policy positions of top leaders and their entourages, 1966 Supreme Soviet election speeches

	Kosygin	Podgorny	Belorussian group	Moscow group	Brezhnev	Shelepin	Suslov
Priority of heavy industry	Priority	Priority	Priority	Priority	Top priority	Top priority	Top priority
Investment in agriculture	Stabilize	Increase	Increase	Increase	Increase		Stabilize
Priority of consumer goods	Priority	Priority	Priority	Secondary	Secondary	Priority	Secondary
Characterization of international arena	Mixed	Mixed	Mixed	Mixed	Mixed	Hostile	Hostile

enhanced domestic spending, this Brezhnev protégé offered no plan to increase the regime's commitment to the light and food industries.

Ustinov, another Brezhnev associate and the new party secretary overseeing military industries, exhibited almost the same set of policy positions. His institutional affiliation did not keep him from expressing a strong explicit commitment to the Brezhnev agricultural policy. He argued that strengthening the agricultural sector would only heighten the power of the armed forces. Along with other Brezhnev protégés, Ustinov directly cited the need to lessen the gap in economic growth and the standard of living between the urban and rural settings. But Ustinov offered his support of the Brezhnev agricultural investment drive only with strong acknowledgment of the continuing primacy of his own, military–industrial sector. In his estimation, the strengthening of the group B industries and the raising of the standard of living were predicated on the continued growth of heavy industrial production.

The positions staked out by the other two Brezhnev protégés, Kazakh party leader Kunaev and Ukrainian Premier Shcherbitsky, were comparable. Their comments focused on their own republics, emphasizing the state of their economies. Both expressed strong support for the land reclamation and agricultural programs of the national regime.[24] Both gave attention to the further consolidation of the scientific and technical revolution, which was said to bolster the priority group A industries. As for light industry and the services sector, Kunaev and Shcherbitsky adopted the Brezhnev view, stating that problems in these areas stemmed not from insufficient resource allocations but from problems of organization and management. All four Brezhnev associates identified the need to refine state planning and improve management in strengthening the economy. Their concern was to fulfill the existing plan as opposed to designating even more funds.

Entourage members were in agreement in supporting the basic Brezhnev issue positions. They shared his priorities for investment, justifying them with similar characterizations of the domestic and foreign policy contexts. Divergences among them reflected their different emphases on and preoccupations with regional or organizational concerns. They did not represent major substantive differences.

Perspectives of other national leaders

We find a much greater diversity of issue orientations when we examine the views of other groups of national leaders. Podgorny's protégé Piotr Shelest assumed a very careful position which, while not contradicting the position of his patron, did not offer it much real support. As a junior member of the leadership, and with his patron already on the political defensive, this stance was not surprising. Shelest's discussion of the issues entailed no risk-taking and no novel treatment of the pressing issues before the national leadership. Similar to his Ukrainian rival (and Brezhnev protégé) Shcherbitsky, Shelest dwelt upon issues relevant to his own republic. The special complexities of Ukraine, with the ever-present threat of anti-Soviet nationalism, prompted Shelest to characterize foreign policy differently than did his patron. He failed to identify any positive feature of East–West relations, but rather emphasized the "cunning actions" of the US and West Germany that demanded "a constant strengthening of the armed forces of the Soviet Union."

While Kosygin and Podgorny offered what could be considered as quasi-reformist alternatives to the Brezhnev program, other politicians and their entourages assumed even more traditional positions than Brezhnev and his group. In fact the positions staked out by Brezhnev and his group fell closer to the middle on a crude policy continuum, with those of Kosygin and Podgorny at the one end, and those of Shelepin and Suslov at the other (Table 3.1). Others expressed views that fell somewhere in between, often closer to the Brezhnev positions.

Among those who adopted traditional political attitudes were Shelepin and Suslov. Shelepin, a formidable rival to Brezhnev during the regime's early years, also offered a guns and butter program promising increased investment in both the military–heavy industry and light and food industries sectors. His views were similar to those of Kosygin and Podgorny in emphasizing the need to raise the standard of living by strengthening those sectors directly responsible for it, but unlike Kosygin and Podgorny, Shelepin stressed the need to significantly increase defense spending. He characterized the world arena as containing an increasingly dangerous United States which was behaving "more and more recklessly." The US economy was said to be switching onto a "war footing" as it attempted to achieve its goals through "all means of economic, political, diplomatic, and ideological struggle" against the USSR and its allies. The upshot was a need to significantly strengthen the traditional priority sectors while also expanding the resource commitment to group B industries. He identified the usual sources for such resources, i.e., increased labor discipline and productivity, and the application of science and technology to production. Shelepin's program appeared to offer something for everyone, but with the intimation of "negative incentives," including discipline campaigns, to stimulate production.

Suslov and his entourage also assumed more traditional positions and a more rigid approach than Brezhnev. Both Suslov and his protégés Pel'she and Ponomarev consistently favored the traditional economic sectors and a strengthened military. They clearly supported the group A industries, paying less attention to agriculture. They described a tense state of international relations that necessitated increased expenditures on heavy industry and the military. While the Soviet Union was said to be in a much stronger global position, the world socialist camp needed to be further integrated, and the national defense "tirelessly perfected." Similar to Podgorny, Ponomarev commented that "at present there are no cardinal questions of world politics that can be solved without the Soviet Union." Ponomarev, however, drew different conclusions, arguing that existing circumstances merited additional security-related expenditures.

Other groups of officials expressed less traditional positions, advocating some shift in resources from the military–industrial complex to other sectors. The Belorussian contingent assumed a set of positions compatible with those of Kosygin and Podgorny. Both Mazurov and his protégé, Belorussian party leader Piotr Masherov, emphasized the light and food industries as economic priorities.[25] Mazurov, for instance, argued that demands by the population for more and better consumer goods had not been completely fulfilled: "We place before ourselves this task [fulfilling that demand], and we have the potential to resolve it in the not-too-distant future," he argued. The inflow of new allocations, the application of science and technological achievements, the use of new principles of economic management, and a less threatening international environment would improve the standard of living.[26] As for the agricultural sector, the Belorussians felt some increased investment was merited, but they emphasized themes of careful resource use and economy.[27]

The members of the Moscow party cohort assumed an intermediate position, similar to that taken by the Brezhnev group. All members of this group – Demichev, Grishin, and Kapitonov –

stressed the primacy of both heavy industry and agriculture, treating the light and food industries as tertiary concerns. While pressing for increased availability of higher quality goods and services, they emphasized the continuing need to maintain and expand the means of production. To this end, agriculture was important. Grishin, for example, commented that "the securing of resources of industry and of consumer goods for the population is dependent upon the successful development of agriculture." Various initiatives associated with the Brezhnev agricultural program were supported by these politicians, with explicit reference to efforts at reducing the gap in income and living standards between the city and countryside.

The Moscow cohort members generally did not address foreign policy and military concerns. They neither identified a military threat, nor pointed to positive aspects of East–West ties. Grishin did comment on the need to strengthen the military, but only Demichev spoke of any sort of external threat and it was of an ideological, and not a military, nature. Demichev had been the CPSU Secretary responsible for internal ideological matters since 1961; his comments reflected the impact of his own institutional affiliation. Overall, commonalities in the issue positions of these three politicians distinguished them as a group from other top leadership elements.

Agriculture and its representatives

Among the national politicians delivering election speeches were three leading officials of the agricultural sector. Comparison of their election speeches reveals very contrasting perspectives that reflect their career ties to particular senior Politburo members.

Fiodor Kulakov, who was then the party Secretary for agriculture, was linked with Brezhnev as an ally, if not a client. Among the agricultural representatives within the top hierarchy, he most strongly echoed Brezhnev's position, emphasizing new investment in agriculture, with a focus on land reclamation in the non-black earth zone. Kulakov's position required more expenditure across the board, not only for equipment and fertilizers, but also for the transformation of the rural population's standard of living. This translated, for instance, into guaranteed payments for collective farmers that would be on a level approximately equal to that for state farm workers. A strengthened rural infrastructure with more incentives for production was the basis for his approach to agriculture.

Dmitry Polyansky, a Deputy Chairman of the USSR Council of Ministers who had a strong interest and background in agriculture, assumed a different position, although he also favored some increased agricultural investment. He diverged from Brezhnev's position in stressing resource and labor efficiency over increased expenditures. He noted, for example, that much more could be obtained from the lands already reclaimed and not irrigated. He argued that already existent farms, both collective and state, needed more new equipment and that farming standards could be improved. Although he acknowledged that increased investment might be desirable, his primary focus was on the better use of already available resources and capabilities. Polyansky called for improved agricultural planning and management, but unlike Brezhnev, he did not feel that such improvement required the involvement of political actors outside the already established hierarchy. Anticipating Brezhnev's inclination toward heightened party involvement, Polyansky commented that "daily intervention from outside in the organization of production does not yield the needed results."

A third politician, Gennady Voronov, then the RSFSR Premier, also adopted a stance that was more compatible with Kosygin's policy perspective. Voronov argued that the agricultural sector could make do with the material resources and labor that it already had in abundance. His primary concern was the more skillful use of those resources. Organizational changes were necessary. There was a need for the unification of fragmented agricultural branches and production units.[28] He proposed the formation of geographically distinct agricultural complexes that would pool resources resulting in more efficient production. The application of scientific management techniques and new technologies would facilitate the integration and streamlining of agriculture, without dramatically expanded investments. Voronov argued that the resultant revitalization of the agricultural sector would help bolster consumer production, an end both he and Kosygin favored.

If the eighth five-year plan (1966–70) summed up the actual program adopted by the national leadership, it is clear there were no real losers but some very substantial winners in the ongoing policy dispute. The plan essentially provided something for everyone, as all major sectors received real increases in investment. This outcome was an initial victory for Brezhnev and his group because it signified a continuing commitment to traditionally favored sectors, at the same time strengthening the position of others, especially agricul-

Table 3.2 *Policy positions of top leaders and their entourages, 1970 Supreme Soviet election speeches*

	Kosygin	Podgorny	Belorussian group	Moscow group	Brezhnev	Shelepin	Suslov
Priority of heavy industry	Priority	Priority	Priority	Top priority	Top priority	Top priority	Top priority
Investment in agriculture	Stabilize	Increase	Increase	Increase	Increase	Increase	Increase
Priority of consumer goods	Priority	Priority	Priority	Secondary	Secondary	Secondary	Secondary
Characterization of international arena	Mixed	Mixed	Mixed	Mixed	Mixed	Hostile	Hostile

ture. It allowed him to carry on with new initiatives such as the detente policy with the West.

The General Secretary had the support of a number of protégés who were already members of top party organs. Entourage members, bridging some important sectors and regions, exhibited attitudinal consistency in supporting their patron. Their position was bolstered by others who were in the middle of the attitudinal spectrum – especially the Moscow group – so that the unfolding policy program also reflected the views of elements outside of the Brezhnev network. Brezhnev's set of positions, combined with that of his group, placed his network in a moderating position among the range of groups and interests. Their views arguably threatened no major interests while providing either stable or enhanced resource commitments to several important sectors. Patronage support and a set of central issue positions thus enabled the General Secretary both to bridge divergent interests and to move toward a more decisive leadership position.

Election speeches from 1970 to 1980: the power maintenance stage and support for Brezhnev policies

The arguments set out by the top national elite in the 1966 Supreme Soviet election speeches anticipated the broad policy positions that would be taken in subsequent years. Accordingly, my analysis of election speeches in the 1970 to 1980 period is more abbreviated and highlights the shifts in positions and degrees of policy agreement and disagreement among politicians.

By the time of the 1970 Supreme Soviet election, the political position of Brezhnev and his group had grown noticeably stronger. The 1970 speeches continued to reveal attitudinal constraint among Brezhnev network members, but the number of members had grown. Other politicians began to lean more towards the positions staked out by Brezhnev – a tendency that would continue through the 1975 election campaign, when the Brezhnev entourage would be dominant.

In their 1970 electoral addresses, Brezhnev and his protégés continued to support the basic policy thrust discussed in 1966 (Table 3.2). Thus in the agricultural sector, for example, Brezhnev's 1970 remarks reemphasized the need to create a material and technical base for the full development of the sector. The broad picture highlighted agricultural successes, but warned of the significant challenges to be faced if the momentum dropped.

Brezhnev protégés affirmed the correctness of the overall policy thrust, including the continuing priority given to agriculture. The strong career and institutional ties of most of these protégés to the heavy industry complex did not diminish their expressed support for their patron's agriculture policy.[29] Katushev described agriculture as "a key problem of the entire economy." Kirilenko assumed the same position and in the process restated the basic Brezhnev policy rationale: only the uninterrupted growth of agriculture and industry would permit the production of those very consumer goods and services that would ultimately satisfy popular demands. Regionally based protégés argued likewise, referring to their regions' special needs or circumstances.[30]

If any new argument was put forward by Brezhnev and his associates, it was a more detailed commitment to the further development of basic science. They argued that the solution to economic problems was to be found at the juncture between science and its technical application. Improving the performance of those supervising the economy was a matter of both research and management. Katushev, in particular, emphasized this concern. He explicitly linked the theme of science and technical progress to the USSR's economic growth potential. Katushev stressed the use of computers on a wide scale. Drawing support from Brezhnev's speech to the December 1969 CC Plenum, he argued that the gathering and processing of information was critical in improving the organization and management of the economy.

The Brezhnev group's policy positions remained midway in the spectrum of expressed attitudes. The same was true of Moscow group members. Demichev, Grishin, and Kapitonov provided a common set of commentaries in identifying priorities and characterizing the recent past. Their views on investment priorities were similar to those of Brezhnev and his coterie. Following up on Brezhnev's comments to the December 1969 Plenum, they also emphasized better planning and management in improving the economy. But they diverged from the Brezhnev line in the foreign policy domain, where they were less sanguine about prospects for significantly improved East–West ties. In this area, they had more in common with the conservative element, providing no justification for new Soviet overtures to the West.

Other groups' positions were moderating and moving closer to the center and Brezhnev. Among these were the more conservative elements in the leadership. Shelepin's agenda had moved toward the

Brezhnev domestic priorities as his political position weakened.[31] While pushing for increased allocations to a range of sectors, he focused on the external threats, calling for an enhanced defense. The Suslov group also exhibited support for the Brezhnev domestic priorities, though they did not place agriculture on the same priority level as the group A industries. Capital construction and better use of existent labor reserves were posited as the appropriate approaches to heightened productivity.

A broad consensus was emerging, bridging "middle of the road" politicians such as Demichev, Grishin, and Kapitonov, "tradition-alists" such as Suslov, and the Brezhnev entourage. The General Secretary assumed the guiding role. Champions of light industry and expanded services were on the defensive. Podgorny and his Ukrain-ian protégé Shelest had backed off from their previous strong stances on the light and food industries. Their expressed commitment to raising the standard of living was now vague. Their comments now constituted a reaction to the Brezhnev issue agenda. They spoke not of new expenditures but of the more careful use of resources already available.

Brezhnev's other major rival, Premier Kosygin, was also on the defensive, especially in regard to proposed economic reforms. In his 1970 electoral comments he did not reject the reforms, but instead urged patience, characterizing reform as "a complicated and dynamic process." Meanwhile, the Belorussians, Mazurov and Masherov, continued to support themes linked with Brezhnev rivals, including the management and planning reforms associated with Kosygin. They spoke of the need for creating economically accountable asso-ciations and the liquidation of multi-level management. Similarly to Podgorny, however, they now qualified their stress on the consumer goods and food industries by raising themes of increased effi-ciency.[32] The Belorussians' resistance to the Brezhnev domestic agenda centered upon the questions of resource allocation and economic organization.

Kosygin continued to downplay the priority of agriculture. His characterization of policy successes in the sector was a rosy picture and certainly did not legitimate major spending increases. In marked contrast, he showed other domestic areas to need an infusion of resources. One such area was education, which Kosygin described as "a problem of all of society."

Turning to the international arena, Kosygin extolled the Soviet defense effort and argued that it constrained the aggressiveness of adversaries. His characterization of global conditions was mixed, as was Brezhnev's. He did not recommend increased defense spending. In fact, on matters of expanded East–West ties, Kosygin, Podgorny, and the Belorussians were all of a similar view. Podgorny was most explicit, characterizing the improved East–West economic and political ties as solid and long term. His discussion of the importance of high-level personal contacts with other leaders suggested that positive payoffs could result from more active contact with the West.[33]

Kosygin, Podgorny, and the Belorussians held a number of common views, but collectively they did not offer an alternative political agenda. The consensus surrounding Brezhnev that now included the conservative and Moscow groups had put them on the defensive. Support for Brezhnev views was mounting. Agriculture was now generally accepted as a top priority. Light industry was clearly secondary. Heavy industry retained its favored status.

The position of the Brezhnev group was further strengthened by the public stances assumed by several relatively independent officials. Yury Andropov and Mikhail Solomentsev were advancing under Brezhnev, and their public statements reflected good working relationships with the guiding coalition.[34] In their election speeches both men developed themes associated with the General Secretary. They discussed the scientific–technical revolution, especially in raising the qualifications of personnel. Solomentsev clearly supported his own heavy industry sector as a domestic spending priority, commenting that the gap between the output of the means of production and the output of consumer goods was already being closed. Andropov spoke about peaceful coexistence. While he was not sanguine about the domestic policy payoffs of coexistence, he did indicate its usefulness in enhancing European stability.

Polyansky's modified position on agriculture also reflected the strengthened position of the Brezhnev group. As Kulakov continued to articulate Brezhnev's position, rival Polyansky moved closer to the General Secretary's line. Both politicians now contended that a strengthened agricultural sector required not only creating the material and technical base for enhanced productivity,[35] but also creating the necessary infrastructure that would make life and work in the countryside more appealing.[36] Polyansky argued that much could be done to overcome the lag between the light, food, and meat industries' development and the growing demands of the population.

RSFSR Premier Voronov's positions, however, continued to diverge from those of Brezhnev. Once again adopting a position compatible with Kosygin's, Voronov emphasized the need for resource conservation and better organization of agriculture. Throwing money at programs, to "fulfill the plan at any cost," was unnecessary and undesirable. Increasingly at odds with the governing consensus, Voronov would be ousted from the national leadership within a few years.[37]

By the time of the XXIV Party Congress, Brezhnev's political position was consolidated and his policy program fully laid out. Numerous personnel changes strengthened the Brezhnev group's position and weakened that of many rivals. Among the most notable developments were the promotions to full Politburo membership of Brezhnev supporters Grishin, Kulakov, and Kunaev. Rivals Shelest, Shelepin, Podgorny, and Voronov were under pressure, with clients dropped from CC membership. Around the time of the CPSU Congress important personnel changes in Ukraine strengthened the position of Brezhnev protégé Shcherbitsky at the expense of Shelest. Similar developments in Kazakhstan (i.e., the ouster of top Podgorny protégé and former CPSU Secretary V.N. Titov as republic party Second Secretary) and Georgia (i.e., the removal of party leader V.P. Mzhavanadze's Second Secretary) represented further gains for the Brezhnev group. While Voronov's clients were in retreat, Kulakov appointed his own associates to important national agricultural posts.

As the first decade of the regime's rule ended, important Brezhnev initiatives involved not only the development of agro-industrial complexes (late 1973), but also an extensive land reclamation program for the non-black earth zone (early 1974) and the expansion of the Siberian development project (1974). Commitments to expanded defense spending were forthcoming in the mid-1970s. The emergent program reflected a politically strong General Secretary, a growing patronage network, and an expanding set of alliances. As was evident in their public statements, protégés and allies were in marked support of the General Secretary.

Brezhnev dominance and the political discussion

Although Brezhnev and his extended network dominated the public policy discussion through the course of the 1970s, there were periods of challenge. Policy setbacks in the early-to-mid 1970s led the coalition to alter investment priorities and to coopt positions taken by others. Agricultural difficulties combined with the growing needs

Table 3.3 *Support for Brezhnev program, by patronage affiliation, 1975*

	Protégés N(%)	Allies N(%)	Others N(%)
Support	4(67)	1(17)	0 (0)
Lack of support	2(33)	5(83)	12(100)
			N = 24

Where support means at least two-thirds of the Brezhnev policy positions were supported by the politician. Chi Square = 10.863; D.F. = 2; Significance Level = 0.0044.

of light industry led to changes in the public political discussion.[38] Brezhnev coopted the arguments of Kosygin and Podgorny regarding the resource needs of the group B industries. Investment had increased during the early 1970s, but this represented only a short-term commitment, and Brezhnev had pulled back by 1975. In the foreign policy domain, Brezhnev adopted a line commensurate with earlier Kosygin and Podgorny arguments. The policy of peaceful coexistence was formally presented as a "Peace Program" in 1971, and became the focus of foreign policy. Brezhnev broadened his characterization of a coexistence policy in emphasizing positive domestic and foreign policy payoffs.

The number of Brezhnev associates in the leadership was still growing and, as in their earlier electoral speeches, they provided bedrock support for the General Secretary's overall program (Table 3.3). The protégés tended to articulate more identifiably Brezhnev positions; the average election speech included references to nearly four of the five major policy planks associated with him.[39] Those who were allied with Brezhnev and his group made fewer – but still a significant number – of references to Brezhnev positions (average of 2.7). The remaining politicians, who were neither members of, nor aligned with, the Brezhnev network were decidedly less supportive (1.6 references on average).

Brezhnev protégés often offered different characterizations of policy themes than non-protégés, underscoring their relative support for the broad program. Treatment of the Peace Program is illustrative. Most of the top politicians dealt with this major initiative, but their descriptions of past experiences and future probabilities – of potential costs and payoffs – differed. Members of the conservative Suslov group, for example, were all skeptical about the prospects for improved East–West relations. Ponomarev cited a number of events to indicate that "the nature of imperialism has remained unaltered." Pel'she, in recalling the events of the past half decade, commented that "peace is not in the harbor yet, it is only on the way there." In contrast, Brezhnev protégés focused on past successes, addressing issues of Soviet–American and Soviet–West European relations in praising the detente policy. Comparable commentaries were provided by the Moscow politicians; both Demichev and Grishin explicitly linked the growth of communism to a successful detente policy.

The policy discussions of a number of more independent political actors offered support limited to selected planks of the Brezhnev program. Foreign Minister Gromyko, who had been elevated into the Politburo just two years earlier, fêted Brezhnev in his 1975 speech: "Who is unaware of the outstanding role played by Leonid Il'ich Brezhnev in both foreign and domestic affairs? By his multifaceted activity he expresses the thoughts and wishes of our Party and the Soviet people . . . and also millions of people abroad." Gromyko, however, reserved his comments almost exclusively for foreign policy matters. Even granting that his formal position required him to concentrate on foreign policy questions, his positions on domestic policy were left unclear. He emphasized that an effective detente policy would help ensure the conditions for domestic policy success, but he offered no broader conclusion on the correctness of the Brezhnev program.

Similarly, Romanov and Dolgikh, two up-and-coming politicians, also supported portions of the overall Brezhnev program in their electoral comments. They were supportive of the group A industries and the military, as would be expected given their affiliations with those sectors. But they did not offer comparable support for the agricultural program, which was treated as a secondary priority. Neither provided explicit support for Brezhnev's Peace Program.

In their 1975 electoral remarks, Uzbek party leader Rashidov and USSR Minister of Agriculture Polyansky provided greater support for the Brezhnev program than in past election speeches. Rashidov's comments, however, continued to focus on the state of the Uzbek economy. Polyansky's stated positions more closely approximated the Brezhnev policy thrust. He discussed the imperatives of the agricultural sector in terms very much like those of the General Secretary. Neither Rashidov nor Polyansky was in a particularly strong position within the top leadership. Rashidov continued to be a candidate Politburo member based outside of Moscow while Polyansky, whose profile faded during the 1970s, was but a year away from his political retirement to Japan as Soviet Ambassador.

In 1975, as earlier, it was Kosygin and Podgorny who provided the fundamentally different view of the past decade and future agenda. For the most part, the Belorussians, Mazurov and Masherov, still shared their views, offering only minimal support for the Brezhnev program. All of these politicians provided some surface support for the Brezhnev thrust. Certain planks, such as Brezhnev's approach to agricultural development, now garnered their support. They praised a number of initiatives associated with the General Secretary (e.g., creation of agro-industrial complexes, the BAM project, the development of Siberia and the Soviet Far East). They also offered explicit support for the Peace Program, though as noted earlier, interest in this initiative had long been forthcoming from many of these national leaders. But the implications Kosygin and others drew from the Peace Program diverged from those of Brezhnev and his broad coalition. They concluded that the Peace Program hardly justified high spending in sector A industries. They proposed that the changed world arena permitted the expanded development of group B industries, helping the country to meet mass consumer needs. They felt that the standard of living, having already increased 25 percent over the previous few years, should continue to advance.

Mazurov and Masherov paid lip service to Brezhnev positions while supporting the alternative Kosygin line. Although they expressed the need for new "intensive methods of economic management" as Brezhnev had suggested, they, like Kosygin, did not refer to the role party organs would have to play in ensuring this. Like Kosygin, they asserted that the population's growing material needs were not being met. Mazurov supported the detente line, but he did not link it with Brezhnev. In general, these politicians had little to say regarding Brezhnev's role in either foreign or domestic policy formulations and successes. Their total neglect of Brezhnev's role ran counter to an identifiable tendency within the leadership to lionize Brezhnev's activities.

Overall, the 1975 election speeches revealed not only the continued strong position of Brezhnev, but the success of his and his network's efforts to withstand the policy setbacks of the previous few years. A continually growing number of protégés were publicly supportive of his policies. Formidable allies and important independent actors cautiously but publicly supported the broad contours of the program.

Brezhnev network members and allied politicians continued to express an essentially centrist policy position. They set the general direction of the policy discussion, though other politicians helped to set the broader parameters on some issues. Adversaries accented different priorities and concerns, but they did not counter a policy thrust that now included some of their own earlier views. They offered corrective comments to the program presented by the dominant group. Those leaders who earlier had threatened Brezhnev's political position had either been retired or were soon to be retired from the national leadership.[40] Brezhnev and his network, in firm control of personnel and organizational matters, now clearly commanded the policy discussion.

A mature regime with an impending succession

The XXV Party Congress in 1976 represented a high point for the Brezhnev regime. The policy difficulties of the previous few years had not diminished Brezhnev's authority. Organizationally, his position was further consolidated; in general his opponents' issue positions had been either coopted or discredited. There were influential national politicians who adopted public postures divergent from those of the Brezhnev network, but they never came to represent a unified opposition. By 1980, all of Brezhnev's major opponents were gone. The regime was a mature one, with the Brezhnev network firmly in charge. But Brezhnev himself was physically weak, and his extended network was so large and the interests of his coalition so diverse that centrifugal forces had begun to appear. It was disadvantageous to the maintenance of the governing coalition to include more than a sufficient number of members, i.e., a majority. Too many interests needed to be served, heightening the potential for cleavage. The specter of a weakened central leader only hastened the process of coalition decay.[41] In the 1980 election speeches, strains in the governing coalition were already obvious; there was movement away from the Brezhnev line.

Policy disputes among national leaders were more pointed in the 1980 election speeches, as politicians jockeyed for power (Table 3.4). Leading members of the Brezhnev group positioned themselves to assume Brezhnev's mantle,[42] but with the group patron still formally in charge, disagreements among group members were not publicly articulated. Carefully couched criticism came from outside the group as contending officials vied for power.

Table 3.4 *Support for Brezhnev program, by patronage affiliation, 1980*

	Protégés N(%)	Allies N(%)	Others N(%)
Support	7(87)	3(50)	0 (0)
Lack of support	1(13)	3(50)	12(100)
			N = 26

Where support means that at least two-thirds of the Brezhnev policy positions were supported by the politician. Chi Square = 15.966; D.F. = 2; Significance Level = 0.0003.

Brezhnev protégés focused their 1980 electoral comments on themes set out by the General Secretary at the November 1979 CC Plenum. Among the more important were: (1) the need to expand the country's energy resources; (2) the increased production of mineral fertilizers to bolster a troubled agricultural sector; (3) the improvement of the transportation system to enhance distribution and deal with bottlenecks; (4) the expanded development of the machine-building industry to supply the requisite equipment to both the rural and urban production settings; and (5) the charge that state planning and management agencies were greatly responsible for a growth slowdown. Protégés called for the opening of Siberia with its rich natural resources. They also supported efforts to further the network of major territorial production complexes, a Brezhnev priority.

Brezhnev's political success continued to be enhanced by his ability to associate himself with a strengthened light and food industry sector while maintaining priority support for heavy industry and agriculture. He characterized the expansion of light industry as a long-term concern, and described industry and agriculture as immediate priorities. Brezhnev protégés argued that the raising of the population's standard of living was a long-term process. They indicated there was already tangible evidence of the appropriateness of the Brezhnev line regarding the population's needs, citing the newly adopted Constitution to exemplify the gains of the previous decades. Kirilenko identified the Brezhnev Constitution as "the manifesto of developed socialism," while Chernenko said it was "a powerful means for the further development and deepening of socialist democracy."

Worsening relations with the West did not preclude protégés from supporting the detente policy. Chernenko's comment that "there is simply no sensible alternative" to the detente policy may have suggested a certain defensiveness on the part of those who had been responsible for that policy thrust. Yet all protégés – spanning the spectrum of institutional affiliations – explicitly supported the Peace Program.

As in the past, the Brezhnev entourage was joined by the Moscow group and a number of independent politicians. The Moscow group had been a key ally for over a decade, and it continued to align with the General Secretary on most of the major planks. Among the independent politicians, Solomentsev was perhaps the most supportive of the broad policy thrust. Others, however, were already distancing themselves. Andropov was basically noncommittal. Others expressed support for specific policies, but did not overtly support the general program.[43]

Those connected with Suslov and Kosygin on both ends of the policy spectrum also exhibited attitudinal consistency across members. They were, however, moving away from the Brezhnev program and suggesting rather different policy priorities.

The Suslov element reasserted the primacy of the military–industrial sector to the exclusion of both agriculture and the light and food industries. In the wake of problems with the West, they indirectly criticized the detente policy, concentrating on the negative trends that had arisen during the previous decade. Although they disagreed with Brezhnev positions, these politicians did not work in tandem with Kosygin and his interests. In fact, Suslov, Pel'she, and Ponomarev all criticized Kosygin's planning and management organs, arguing that their performance was actually undercutting economic growth.

For his part, Kosygin took note of the November 1979 Plenum criticisms of planning and management, but he placed the blame on specific sectors, most notably those associated with Brezhnev's interests, including the heavy industrial area (e.g., machine-building, metallurgy, railway transport, and construction). In acknowledging these problems he commented that "changing production conditions will constantly demand corresponding changes in the forms and methods of management and the forms and methods of planning in our country – both long-term and short-term ones." Once again, "scientific methods of management" were proposed to help make better use of wasted potential. As for foreign policy, Kosygin directly identified gains from detente – an initiative he had supported since the 1960s.

Table 3.5 *References to Brezhnev and leading party organs, 1975 and 1980 Supreme Soviet election speeches (as published in Pravda)*

	1975				1980			
	Brezhnev	(No. of lines Brezhnev)	Central Committee	Politburo	Brezhnev	(No. of lines Brezhnev)	Central Committee	Politburo
Protégés	4.5	(23.8)	5.2	2.0	9.0	(42.4)	5.4	1.4
Allies	4.8	(14.7)	5.5	2.0	7.0	(35.8)	6.0	0.7
Others	2.8	(5.4)	3.8	1.1	6.6	(23.4)	7.0	1.0
Average	4.0	(12.3)	4.6	1.5	7.4	(32.1)	6.3	1.1
				N = 24				N = 26

Table 3.6 *Support for Brezhnev and his detente policy, by patronage affiliation, 1980*

	Protégés N(%)	Allies N(%)	Others N(%)
Support detente and link with Brezhnev	7(87)	3(50)	1 (8)
Support detente and not link with Brezhnev	1(13)	3(50)	6(50)
No support for detente	—	—	5(42)
			N=26

On domestic issues, the Belorussian politicians, Masherov and Zimyanin, continued to share many common views with Kosygin. They still favored their past investment priorities, offering little support for Brezhnev's thinking on investment priorities. In the foreign policy realm, their position shifted to a more hardline and anti-detente focus. Emphasis was placed on problems in the international arena that undercut genuine *rapprochement* with the West.

One of the ways in which officials revealed their political proximity to Brezhnev was in their manipulations of his personality cult. Brezhnev's cult had burgeoned since the early 1970s. It was intended to enhance the position of the top leader, providing legitimacy to his initiatives. Brezhnev protégés were certainly motivated to further his cult, and they did so (Table 3.5). Protégés invoked his name frequently and provided detailed praise of his leadership and vision. Those allied with the General Secretary also cited him frequently in their policy discussions. By 1980, protégés were lavish in the extreme in their praise of Brezhnev: where other politicians balanced references to Brezhnev with praise of the leading party organs such as the Politburo and CC, protégés accentuated Brezhnev's political profile.

Such sycophantic behavior does not automatically translate into policy-making support. But effusive commentaries help to set a tone that can add momentum to a patron's initiatives. The conscious manipulation of the leader's name, like the careful treatment of specific policies and symbols, can help a politician advocate a particular concern. The case of Brezhnev's personality cult and the important detente policy is illustrative.

The detente policy had been a long-term initiative closely linked with the General Secretary. The manner in which politicians manipulated this issue and the role they described Brezhnev and top party organs playing in its development serve as a litmus test for evaluating their relative support for Brezhnev. As Table 3.6 indicates, most politicians were publicly supportive of detente, even given the international complexities of the late 1970s. Only among those politicians not linked to the Brezhnev network was there the suggestion of any lack of support. Those expressing overt support for the policy either attributed its success to particular party organs or to Brezhnev. Brezhnev protégés almost unanimously associated the detente policy with Brezhnev. Half of those identified as allies of Brezhnev and his entourage also linked this policy to him; but in 1980, at the height of the Brezhnev cult, only one of those not allied to Brezhnev referred to him in discussing detente. Even given Brezhnev's considerable power, top leaders provided divergent assessments of his political profile. Predictably, Brezhnev protégés were most expansive in their discussions.

In the last years of the regime, Brezhnev's top protégés continued to exhibit outward attitudinal constraint as fissures in the governing coalition were emerging. With their pasts grounded in the Brezhnev legacy, they could ill afford the rapid unravelling of his program. Other officials were distancing themselves from that program to varying degrees. More orthodox politicians supported some Brezhnev investment priorities, but diverged on other major planks. Others, who might be seen as potential reformers, strove for more of a balance of investments across the industrial, agricultural, and consumer sectors. The results of the detente initiative were treated differently by the range of Politburo and Secretariat members. Protégés more readily identified its beneficial legacy. Most others were less sanguine about its prospects.

Among the competing groups, only the Moscow cohort unambiguously supported the Brezhnev line. Many of these officials' careers had been resurrected after the difficulties of the Khrushchev years. They remained linked to the Brezhnev team even after the November 1982 succession. It is no coincidence that so many members of this network were retired or experienced precipitous career declines in the wake of Brezhnev's death.[44]

Until Brezhnev's demise, his program remained a consensual, middle-of-the road set of policy positions. As his regime moved toward its end, patronage network members assumed an ever more critical role in publicly defending the developed program; but, as other politicians began to distance themselves and stake out different positions, the policy struggles of the future became more and more apparent.

Patronage and the evolution of a national regime

Examination of both the Brezhnev patronage network and the policy discussion reveals that there are identifiable phases through which Soviet regimes evolve. The nature of these phases, and the relative manner in which political power is distributed among contending interests, influence the form and political consequences of patronage networks.

During the first phase – that of power consolidation and regime formation – the political context is fluid. There is a natural shake-down from the previous regime as power is redistributed among a range of competing actors. Lasting approximately five to seven years, this phase entails the emergence of a definitive leader who will increasingly dominate the political scene. That leader is also the patron of a clientelistic network, which serves as his initial and decisive base of support. His primary task is to expand that network, while bridging extra-network interests. This is the heart of the regime formation process. The unity and integrity of his network is mandatory. Its members must assume public policy stances fully supportive of the patron's position. As the General Secretary's power increases during the course of his tenure, his network members' support for him and his policies becomes more pronounced. But the key to becoming a system leader with staying power is effectively building broader political alliances that transcend that network.

During this initial phase, there will be opposition to the leader's emergent, increasingly favorable, power position. The consolidation of power by the top leader and his team, however, helps to narrow the range of issue positions articulated by top officials. It is highly unlikely that an opposition will be organized. The variety of perspectives among rivals obviates the unity of their positions. Diversity and opposition in the ranks of the ruling elite strongly motivate the national leader to build a consensus that includes at least a few of those rivals. The Brezhnev experience suggests that common power and policy interests will drive those consensus-building efforts. The national leader may coopt the policy positions of others, or he may merge them with his and his group's policy interests. By the end of this power consolidation and regime formation phase, the top leader will have built a solid patronage network – indeed, an extended network as described here – but its survival is predicated upon his working relations with other institutional actors.

In the second, regime maintenance phase, political power will be concentrated with the system patron, his network, and allied officials and their interests. There will be some diversity in perspectives across groups, but a dominant position will have been staked out and a broader policy program put into place. The emergence of such a program signifies the transition into this second phase.

Politicians who are on the fringes of the governing coalition represent an important constraint on the dominant leader and his team. Even though the most threatening rivals may have been removed from the scene, the Khrushchev legacy is a powerful reminder that other interests must at least be taken into account. Rival actors will also be motivated to maintain their power positions during this second phase, offering contrasting views where appropriate but not straying too far from the dominant policy line. After years of regime consolidation, these rivals will have learned to accommodate themselves to the governing coalition. In fact, they likely will work in tandem with it.

Cleavages do emerge within the patronage networks and within the governing coalition during the regime maintenance phase. This is especially true of an extended network that encompasses a diversity of politicians. My analysis of politicians' treatments of the major planks of the Brezhnev program only partially reveals this. Many factors affect the level of attitudinal constraint among network members, not the least of which is the political vitality of the system patron. A strong network patron should be able to enhance the unity of network members, as Brezhnev did during most of his tenure as party boss.

If the articulated views of the forty-five national officials are evaluated on a case by case basis, one finds important instances where institutional and sectoral connections moderate politicians' views. The vagueness of the public policy discussion and the reluctance of Soviet politicians to discuss issues more technically and in detail make it difficult adequately to tap specific views. Politicians' treatments of issues are affected by whether a given issue falls within or without their realm of political competence. In cases where the issues are intimately connected with officials' ongoing professional responsibilities, attitudes can be constrained by politicians' institutional roles. While clients generally exhibit greater support for a patron's views than nonclients, the impact of constituency pressure is more evident where such support involves their institutional home base. If the goals and interests of the patron's and clients' institutional bases correspond, there is no constraint on clients providing decisive support. Where institutional and patronage interests diverge, clients' publicly expressed orientations are sometimes moderated. Considered within their specialized sectors or institutions, clients are more supportive of the patron than are others. This support could translate into moderate overt support, non-discussion of the issue, or restrained opposition to the patron's specific initiative. In cases where clients' support involves issues outside the realm of their institutional responsibilities, such support is usually more straightforward. Even granting these qualifications, however, differences in attitude between the top decision maker's associates and others are to be found. They continue to be exhibited even when the top leader and his network are strong.

History has shown that protégés support their patron and his policy program. A flourishing patronage network constitutes the nucleus of a governing coalition. With an effective politician guiding it, a patronage network can influence policy making. It can play the critical role in seeing a patron's program brought to fruition. Such a network did so in the Brezhnev period. As we shall see, however, institutional reform can alter the structural bases upon which clientelistic networks rest. Institutional and procedural changes can transform the nature and behavior of network politics. They may be doing so in Gorbachev's USSR.

4 Patronage, Gorbachev, and the period of reform

The preceding chapters demonstrate that patronage networks have been central to Soviet political life. But contemporary dilemmas and political reforms are altering the fundamental conditions under which clientelistic politics operate. The late 1980s and 1990s are a period of transition, with Gorbachevian initiatives leading to a profound restructuring of Soviet power relations. Power and authority are being redistributed and shared among a widening set of actors. Reforms are changing the procedures by which policies are developed and implemented. These changes are transforming elite behavioral norms, including network politics.

Even in the Soviet polity of the Gorbachev period, however, patronage relations continue to help politicians to consolidate power, bridge interests, and forge coalitions. There is evidence that high-level officials still favor long-time associates, and aspiring politicians still use connections to ascend to the political hierarchy. Nevertheless, *perestroika* and the emergence of a Soviet *civil society* complicate politicians' efforts to transfer power to favored protégés.[1] The political opportunity structure is being fundamentally altered, as new interests influence elite recruitment and the policy process. Traditional patronage entourages that once so dominated Soviet political life are giving ground to short-term and multifaceted alliances that merge a variety of elite and societal interests. Contemporary powerful officials – system patrons – are still sponsoring allies and politicians into high-level positions, but these relationships are based less and less in long-term past associations and more in common interests and perspectives that conform with the needs of the present. Old-style networks are increasingly giving way to new interest-based coalitions.

Reform and a changing political opportunity structure

The institutional, procedural, and personnel changes of the latter 1980s and 1990s are altering the political environment in which Soviet politicians operate. A basic assumption of this study is that such institutional and procedural arrangements determine elite mobility and behavioral norms. Although the contemporary Soviet political scene is dynamic, the broad contours of an altered political opportunity structure are clearly evident in the early Gorbachev period.

A pressing issue agenda and a wideranging reform program have precipitated the changes. A decisive political elite, joined by the intelligentsia in advancing these reforms, is supported openly by many in the broader society. The radical nature of the reform program has necessitated some changes that have important implications for elite norms, in particular (a) the increased concentration of power among a limited number of top national actors, as set against (b) a system-wide decentralization of power and authority. A redistribution of power has provided the necessary political conditions for the advancement of the *perestroika* program. In order to achieve economic reform, the position of the top leader had to be strengthened and power decentralized to subnational actors. This power redistribution has enabled top reformers to consolidate their own power positions, and institutional changes below have helped to strengthen the positions of allied interests. The targets of these changes have been resistant anti-reform elements found in all quarters, especially in the party apparatus, state bureaucracy, and regional party leaderships. This resistance, rooted both in thought and institutional practices, has been evident at every level. The reforms necessary to counter this resistance have opened up the opportunity structure, presenting aspiring, upwardly mobile politicians with expanded career options. These reforms have also altered coalition-building and regime formation norms, leading the Gorbachev regime to look and act differently from its predecessors.[2]

The basic outline for political and institutional reform appeared in Gorbachev's report to the January 1987 CC Plenum, and the June 1988 XIX Party Conference and subsequent CC plenums acted upon his proposals. The result has been the emergence of alternative bases of power and authority. The revitalized Supreme Soviet, in its first sessions, took on a wideranging agenda and addressed matters of the highest policy priority.[3] Congress of People's Deputies (CPD) and

Supreme Soviet deputies were increasingly able to command public attention, influence the policy agenda, and effectuate responses from bureaucratic actors. Although still in a transition period, revitalized Supreme Soviet commissions and standing committees appear to be playing a heightened role in policy making. Governmental bodies have become more accountable to the Supreme Soviet and these committees. The Supreme Soviet's rejection of numerous ministerial nominees proposed by Premier Nikolai Ryzhkov attests to its enhanced power and authority.[4] Speaking to the July 1989 CC Plenum, Ryzhkov warned party leaders that the Supreme Soviet might not accept future CC recommendations as it had always done in the past.[5]

At the same time, the central party apparatus has been streamlined, its powers increasingly circumscribed. The twenty-four CC departments were consolidated into ten supra-departments, and their ability to influence policy and supervise lower-level agencies rendered increasingly suspect. The turmoil besieging these party bureaucracies has weakened the standing of central apparatchiki to the benefit of outside interests. Many apparatus officials are now being coopted from outside (e.g., from the influential, Moscow-based, think tanks), pushing long-established actors to the sidelines.

The creation of six top-level party commissions is of special relevance to our study of national policy makers. These commissions were made subordinate only to the Politburo and Gorbachev himself. They were given primary executive authority in developing policies and in overseeing the work of subordinate party actors. The sketchy information available to date suggests that their infrequent meetings and operations left the commissions less than dominating. But their emergence weakened the institutional position of the Secretariat and undermined that of the Politburo. It became clear that among Politburo members, those who chaired these commissions were especially favored in the evolving power hierarchy. And as we shall see, Gorbachev and the reformers consolidated their positions in most of these commissions.

All of these changes added to the already existing pressures on the government ministries and state committees. In the latter 1980s, the Council of Ministers was overhauled, with the total number of ministries and state committees reduced from nearly 100 in the late Brezhnev period, to 57 in early 1990. Government bureaucracies were consolidated and streamlined, the political structure disrupted. Comparable consolidations at lower levels led to cuts in republic and provincial staffs by 30 to 40 percent.

These party and state institutional changes enabled the leadership to redistribute assignments and shift responsibilities as initiatives were prepared and implemented. They helped to displace many incumbents and to open slots for new appointees, officials more committed to reform. These institutional reforms allowed Gorbachev and other reformers to shift power toward more pliable organizational actors.[6]

Ongoing procedural changes are also affecting elite recruitment and regime formation norms. In his concluding speech to the first session of the Supreme Soviet, Gorbachev spoke of a "socialist law-governed state," in which changes in rule would permit a wider spectrum of interests to influence the political process.[7] The Soviet system is evolving away from central command, as the regime develops more civil service type rules and applies more universalistic standard operating procedures in the functioning of bureaucracies. The regime is interested in depoliticizing party and state bureaucracies. Many diverse elements, including often-neglected CC members, are increasingly consulted and drawn into the policy process. Moreover, the growing reliance on multi-candidate, secret ballot elections in the selection of party and state officials is pressuring politicians to become more responsive to the reformist inclinations of both national leaders and constituents.[8] Yury Solov'yov's electoral defeat, subsequent forced retirement, and ultimate expulsion from the ranks of the CPSU illustrate the consequences for even the most powerful.[9]

Equally important, the nomenklatura system is under mounting pressure, as its utility in determining mobility is publicly called into question. The XIX Party Conference had recommended that cadres selections be made not through the use of the nomenklatura approach – which was characterized as "obsolete" – but through elections.[10] There has been subsequent public discussion about the misuse and obsolescence of this system.[11] The long-standing principle of democratic centralism is being reexamined and redefined by politicians and scholars.[12] In essence, democratic centralist norms are no longer being enforced in party and state organizations. This has visibly weakened party discipline and reinforced institutional decentralization, further opening elite mobility channels. No one preferred set of background characteristics now assures aspirants

Table 4.1 *Leadership turnover in leading party organs under Brezhnev, Andropov, Chernenko, and Gorbachev (initial months of power consolidation)*

	Brezhnev Oct. 14, '64 to Dec. 31, '65	Andropov Nov. 12, '82 to Feb. 13, '84	Chernenko Feb. 13, '84 to Mar. 10, '85	Gorbachev Mar. 10, '85 to June 30, '86
Politburo (N=12−14)	3 (3)	3 (2)	0 (0)	5 (6)
Secretariat (N=8−11)	3	3	0	8
CC department heads (N=23)	9	9	2	14
Republic party first secretaries (N=14)	2	3	1	4
Regional party first secretaries (N=115)	36	36	11	51

The numbers in parentheses refer to candidate members of the Politburo.

mobility success, as had been true in the past for the politically connected apparatchiki.

These institutional and procedural changes have permitted the massive turnover of personnel in top national and subnational political bodies, and this turnover is affecting the motivations and the behavior of ambitious politicians. Many political slots have opened up, with a new cohort of officials filling the openings. Although there are always cadre changes in the aftermath of a leadership succession, a comparison of the initial period of power consolidation for the most recent four regimes reveals considerably *higher* rates of turnover during the Gorbachev period for all top party actors, from the Politburo and Secretariat down to regional party first secretaries (Table 4.1). The high level of turnover has continued throughout the regime's first five years, signifying a genuine transformation of the ranks of the elite. Upon the fifth anniversary of Gorbachev's succession in March 1990, all but four of the twenty-five members of the Politburo and Secretariat had been elevated to their positions during his tenure. Likewise all but one CC department head, all republic party first secretaries, and 129 of 143 regional party first secretaries had been recruited since Gorbachev's rise.[13] These impressive turnover rates were the result both of the retirement of many Brezhnev regime incumbents and the elevation of politicians with more technocratic backgrounds who champion sweeping sys-

tem reform. They facilitated the emergence of post-Brezhnev networks and alliances.

As the political opportunity structure opens up, more interests and
actors are able to influence the mobility, regime formation, and
policy processes. Elite recruitment becomes more complex, as the
fundamental thinking and behavioral norms of the elite change. A
challenging issue agenda requires an elite that is capable of addressing society's problems. The development of such a cohort of new
officials is a task explicitly promoted by leading national reformers.[14]
As we shall see, officials with more impressive professional credentials and experience are being selected to head party and state
bureaucracies, and they are increasingly drawn from outside the
political establishment.[15] Mounting institutionalized pressures from
above (e.g., national reformers, beginning with the General Secretary) and below (e.g., constituents and CPD members) compel all
officials to alter their policy preferences and behavioral proclivities or
risk ouster. The growing number of party first secretaries who
simultaneously hold top elective positions reflects a new institutionalized mechanism requiring governing officials to secure broader
popular support.[16] Whether by elections or street demonstrations,
politicians have been pressured to conform with a mounting "radical
reform" agenda.[17] Anti-corruption trials have reinforced the notion
that officials should respect legal norms.[18] Notions that officials
should be held accountable before superiors, subordinates, and mass
interests have been growing stronger. Individual officials must
demonstrate that they possess the confidence of subordinates and
superiors that will allow them to effect desired policy ends. Accordingly, they assume greater responsibility in legitimating their own
right to hold positions of authority.

What is the impact of these changes on the elite mobility patterns
and regime formation efforts of the latter 1980s and early 1990s? How
have these structural and procedural changes affected incumbents
from past regimes? What opportunities have emerged for up and
coming politicians? And, of central importance to our study, where
do patron–client relations fit in this changing constellation of political actors?

The fate of Brezhnev-era network members

Incumbents from the pre-1985 period have not fared well in retaining
power in the unsettled Gorbachev period. In chapter 2 we saw that

the departure of patrons does not automatically result in the ousters of their associates. But what happens when the system patron – the party General Secretary – departs and a new national regime takes shape? Can protégés and clients survive? What conditions enhance the survival prospects of network members? The fate of Brezhnev and other network members is illustrative.

The impact and immediate consequences of a Soviet leadership succession are complex and have been subject to debate.[19] Nevertheless, there is general agreement that as a new regime consolidates power, it distances itself from its predecessor. This is done both for purposes of legitimation and for distinguishing a regime's innovations from the practices of the predecessor. The Andropov regime certainly lost little time in distancing itself from its predecessor. Although the first explicit attacks on Brezhnev came only after Gorbachev's succession, Andropov quickly moved ahead with policy changes in early 1983, with the intimation of more profound reforms later in the year.[20] Chernenko, while publicly committed to the reform effort begun under Andropov, was cautious in responding to the Brezhnev legacy.[21] As a close confidant of the departed leader and key member of the old team, Chernenko's very selection as party leader constituted an effort by established figures to maintain the status quo. But the pressing agenda of problems that helped bring Gorbachev to power only a year later necessitated a more open rejection of the Brezhnev legacy. Fundamental restructuring of the economy and polity required a radical reform program: a program that would be rationalized in large measure on the basis of failed Brezhnev policies.

These successions and policy changes had consequences for members of established patronage networks. Nearly all of those politicians closest to Brezhnev – the members of his own network – lost their positions (Table 4.2). The considerable institutional strength of the extended Brezhnev network meant the process of purges would proceed through stages, with nearly a decade needed to fully uproot it. Within weeks of Brezhnev's death the first set of trusted associates were removed.[22] Indeed, half of the identified Brezhnev network members were ousted during Andropov's brief fifteen-month tenure. In this initial stage of ousters, however, those retired were not the leading network members; they were second-rank officials who had been close to Brezhnev (e.g., Y.M. Churbanov, I.T. Novikov, S.P. Trapeznikov, and G.E. Tsukanov). The top Brezhnev period patrons, such as Chernenko and Ustinov, retained considerable

Table 4.2 *Turnover of Brezhnev era patronage network members,*
November 1982–January 1990[a]

	Fate of members		
	Retained N(%)	Ousted N(%)	Total N
Brezhnev network members	3 (8)	36 (92)	39
Brezhnev protégés' network members	21 (44)	27 (56)	48
All other networks' members	24 (44)	30 (56)	54

	When Removed			
	Andropov Nov. 12, '82 to Feb. 13, '84 N(%)	Chernenko Feb. 13, '84 to Mar. 10, '85 N(%)	Gorbachev Mar. 10, '85 to Jan. 1, '90 N(%)	Total N
Brezhnev network members	18 (50)	1 (3)	17 (47)	36
Brezhnev protégés' network members	5 (19)		22 (81)	27
All other networks' members	8 (27)	4 (13)	18 (60)	30

[a]Figures cover the period from Brezhnev's death, November 10, 1982, to
January 1, 1990, Gorbachev's fifth year in power. Figures do not include
those politicians who died during this period.

authority in the Andropov regime. Some high-level Brezhnev associates were already linked to Andropov (e.g., Aliev). Others cut deals
or were coopted by the new party leaders (e.g., Chebrikov).
Regionally well-ensconced Brezhnev associates such as Kunaev and
Shcherbitsky also maintained their high standing. But pressures
were being applied to ferret out weaker elements from the old
network and its allies. It was hardly surprising that the party
Secretary for cadres, Kapitonov, a key Brezhnev ally, was quickly
shifted out of his position after the November 1982 succession.

The practice of displacing Brezhnev associates and allies was
halted under Chernenko, though only temporarily. A.F. Vatchenko
was the only Brezhnev network member retired during this thirteen-
month period. The policy of turning out incumbents was also slowed
down. The only major patronage network to come under scrutiny
was that of the former Uzbek leader, Sharaf Rashidov, who had died

just months before Chernenko's succession, in October 1983.[23] From the perspective of cadres politics, perhaps the most significant development during this period was the death of Ustinov in December 1984, for an important pillar in the old extended Brezhnev network had departed the scene. Of greater long-term importance, however, were the growing power bases of Gorbachev, Ligachev, Vorotnikov, and others, all cultivated by Andropov and all associated with a growing opposition to Brezhnevism. Their power mounted until the 1985 succession outcome when a final assault on the Brezhnev network occurred.[24]

Under Gorbachev, senior Brezhnev associates were quickly vulnerable to retirement. The specific circumstances of these ousters varied, ranging from the discrediting of First Deputy Premier Aliev, who became the focal figure in an ongoing anti-corruption campaign, to the rapid easing out of the octogenarian Premier Tikhonov. The momentum from Andropov's drive to remove Brezhnev cronies was regained with zeal as remaining second-rank associates such as Arkhipov, Dymshits, Smirnov, and Yepishev were also unceremoniously retired. Concomitant with these high-level retirements were the ousters of junior officials who were part of the extended Brezhnev network. The public disgracing of selected members of the old regime (e.g., Grishin and Rashidov) was used to speed up the momentum for cadres renewal and reform in those politicians' former bailiwicks. Aliev's and Kunaev's clients fell as their patrons came under increasing pressure. Meanwhile, several of Ustinov's influential associates, primarily in the defense industries sector, became vulnerable in his absence and were retired.[25] The November 1989 retirement of Moldavian First Secretary Semen Grossu, the last surviving republic party leader from the Brezhnev era, constituted a final assault on a lingering Brezhnevist republic political machine.

By the end of the 1980s, only three of Brezhnev's associates – Konstantin Katushev, F.T. Morgun, and L.M. Zamiatin – still held CC/CAC membership. And these three were hardly the closest or the most important of the network's members. Katushev, who had been a CPSU Secretary in the later 1960s, had already been distanced from Brezhnev. He had experienced a career setback in the 1970s and in fact was in Cuba as Soviet Ambassador when Brezhnev died.

Brezhnev's closest associates had poor survival prospects, but those officials who were less directly tied to him – albeit members of his extended network through powerful intermediaries – had prospects of retaining their elite standing. Politically well-ensconced extended network members could survive the constant political disruptions of the 1980s. While 56 percent of extended Brezhnev network members were removed, 44 percent survived into the 1990s. Those who survived had been linked with intermediary actors whose standing was not compromised during the 1980s. A number of them were members of the Kirilenko Sverdlovsk network with which Andropov had fashioned an alliance in the latter days of the Brezhnev regime. In fact, many who rose in Sverdlovsk during Kirilenko's tenure as a senior secretary and Politburo member came to assume critical roles in the Andropov–Gorbachev regimes.[26] Other "survivors" were tied to holdovers such as Katushev, who carved out particular domains of specialty (in his case, foreign trade).

A good number of "survivors" were part of Shcherbitsky's Ukrainian entourage.[27] The increasingly isolated national political position of the conservative Brezhnevist Shcherbitsky did not preclude him from maintaining a firm network of more hardline supporters in his Ukrainian bailiwick. Shcherbitsky was retired at the September 1989 CC Plenum (he died of a long-term illness less than six months later), but an associate who had advanced under him in Ukraine, Andrei Girenko, was elevated to a CPSU secretaryship at that same plenum.[28]

Members of other networks dominant during the Brezhnev period also had reasonable prospects of surviving politically. As of early 1990, 44 percent had retained their elite standing. Members of institutionally secure networks that had been led by honorably retired politicians fared better in the turbulent latter 1980s than those of other networks. Some members of the Moscow group remained – especially those with ties to Demichev, whose career spanned several central party and governmental agencies.[29] Identified associates of Dolgikh, Gromyko, Kisilev, Solomentsev, and Zimyanin – none of whom had been publicly disgraced in retirement – also remained.[30] But as the 1990s began, almost none of the associates of the most prominent members of the Brezhnev regime remained. Indeed, the April 1989 *en masse* "retirement" of 110 "dead souls" meant the departure of nearly all remaining Brezhnev, Kosygin, Podgorny, and Suslov associates, with the number of retired associates of all Brezhnev period leaders totaling forty-two.[31]

Evidently, those officials well-connected to honorably departed leaders and to leaders who had distanced themselves from Brezhnev have been able to withstand the pressures of the 1980s. But do other career and background factors help to explain the survival prospects for incumbent network members? A systematic analysis of career characteristics does not reveal any combination of factors that determines individuals' prospects of political survival beyond their proximity to the discredited past leadership. The role and tenure considerations that helped explain clients' prospects of survival *during* a given regime (see Table 2.9) do not help to explain cross-regime survival patterns. Employing the same associational measures used in chapter 2 results in very weak or nonexistent relationships between these factors and prospects of survival.[32] Neither long-serving administrators (*qua* specialists) nor longer-serving apparatchiki had better prospects for surviving the regime change. Those who survived appear to have had technical or career expertise that made them useful to successor regimes, though no statistically significant associations are evident.[33] Generally, these officials had carved relatively narrow power bases that were not threatening to newly emerging powers – at least not in the short run. Some were able to hook up with powerful actors or rising stars of the post-Brezhnev period. A prominent example is N.E. Kruchina, who worked with Shelepin in the Komsomol, was elevated by Andropov in 1983 to be CC Administrator of Affairs, and now works with Gorbachev in that same capacity.

The apparent vulnerability of former network members should be put in perspective by noting that given the massive personnel changes of the interregnum and early Gorbachev periods, most incumbent officials were vulnerable to retirement regardless of whether they were tied to patronage networks. Numerous long-serving party and governmental officials not tainted by network connections were retired.[34] Many identified "nonclients" also did not survive the political vicissitudes of the later 1980s. No single set of background or experiential conditions provided incumbents with guarantees of political security.

Thus, regime changes do affect the standing of networks and network members as the constellation of political actors is reset. Some survive the period of power transition, but most do not. The turnover of personnel – especially powerful officials of the predecessor regime – makes room for new appointees, but more importantly it constitutes a critical precondition for the formation of a new governing regime. The vulnerable close associates of the departed leader could be removed rather quickly; powerful protégés only succumbed to longer-term pressures that transcended network politics and that generally included mounting policy reforms. These incumbent politicians, albeit with considerable experience in the practicalities of politics, represented potential – and often real – obstacles to the emergence of a new regime that was attempting to advance a radical reform program. Although some incumbents came to terms with the rising tide of reform, by the 1990s few of them were left in top decision-making positions.

The political landscape of the Gorbachev period

The Soviet national leadership exhibited a diverse range of political interests during the consolidation of the Gorbachev regime. Political changes opened up the opportunity structure allowing new elements on the fringes of the political establishment to be coopted into the national leadership. In background and function, the types of politicians recruited corresponded to those we identified for the eighteen-year Brezhnev regime, though the representation of groups had changed (Table 4.3). Through the mobility channels of the political hierarchy, however, growing numbers of recently recruited leaders were rising to high national office outside of entrenched patronage networks. In the Gorbachev era, traditional patron–client entourages were giving way to new network associations, increasingly grounded in common policy interests and perspectives.

Associates of Gorbachev period Politburo and Secretariat patrons have continued to constitute a significant – although diminished – element of the overall leadership. Among *all* CC/CAC members for the period running from Gorbachev's first party congress in February 1986 through his fifth year as leader in early 1990, 27.1 percent had patronage ties to top national figures. This was a heterogeneous client group, including politicians who rose with Gorbachev and other contemporary leaders, and numerous politicians who first came to national prominence under Khrushchev and Brezhnev period officials.[35] Some of these officials – in particular the holdovers from previous regimes – were already under mounting pressures during the first years of the Gorbachev leadership, and most were retired by the end of the decade. But during this five-year period, officials connected to rising post-Brezhnev politicians assumed a growing number of key party and government responsibilities as the broad outline of the new regime became clearer. As of January 1990, nearly one-quarter of all CC/CAC members still exhibited identifiable patronage connections to senior officials.

These overall client totals become more impressive when we recall

Table 4.3 *Identified clients and nonclients in the CC and CAC, and their political longevity, January 1990 (average number of CC/CAC elections)*

	N	%	Average number of elections
Clients	**96**	**23.9**	**2.4**
Gorbachev network	15	3.7	1.7
Other networks	40	10.0	1.8
Former leaders' networks	41	10.2	3.1
"Nonclients"	**305**	**76.1**	**1.8**
Party apparatchiki	87	21.7	1.9
Administrators	83	20.7	1.9
National functionaries	34	8.5	1.5
Scientists	9	2.2	2.6
Military	24	6.0	1.9
Tokens (including heroes)	68	17.0	1.7
Total N	**401**	**100**	**2.0**
Other deceased, retired and ousted[a]	**128**	**100**	
Clients	48	37.5	
"Nonclients"	80	62.5	

[a]These include the 110 so-called "dead souls" who were retired in April 1989, and all other officials who left CC/CAC membership between the XXVII Party Congress in February–March 1986 and January 1990.

that only approximately half of all identified "nonclients" were genuinely serious politicians with clout in the highest national circles. Those non-clients who were party apparatchiki and government administrators constituted a formidable group of officials, holding many senior posts in the command structure.[36] But as we saw in the earlier Brezhnev study, other nonclient CC/CAC members assumed more representative roles and lacked national power. Taking this into account, we find that roughly one-third of the more influential national-level politicians exhibited career ties to recently departed or still powerful Politburo/Secretariat patrons. The considerable diversity in the career paths of these clients makes it difficult to generalize about all network members. What is important is that during a period of political upheaval and mounting reform, many officials were still climbing to the pinnacle of power as members of patronage networks.

Not all politicians rose to power in this way. The institutional changes and political confusion of the 1980s facilitated the emergence of a governing cohort with a less cohesive and more varied political background than its immediate predecessors. Analysis of the aggregate population of Gorbachev-period politicians reveals that no single element, identifed on the basis of functional and patronage considerations, dominated the national leadership. No single network assumed a commanding position within the national hierarchy. It is striking that after Gorbachev had been formally in power for five years, his identified network of protégés and immediate clients numbered only fifteen.[37] Gorbachev's institutional powers as General Secretary and President have been vast; arguably, they have been greater than those of any Soviet leader since Stalin. He also has accumulated considerable authority among the elite and the masses in promoting his policy interests, including new cadres policies. But this power and authority did not translate into a large traditional patronage network.

In early 1990, the combined membership of other top-level networks represented only 10 percent of the total population of CC/CAC members. This number is not insignificant, but it was divided among diverse and potentially rival interests. Among these were groups of politicians who had risen from different institutional and regional settings. Prominent contemporary officials such as Ligachev, Ryzhkov, and Sliun'kov were at the center of these networks. In addition, the combined membership of departed patrons' networks also equaled 10 percent, and as we have seen, certain of these officials from previous regimes did hold positions of some authority. No one sector, institution, or entourage was especially well-favored in this evolving constellation, and, on the basis of institutional power, no one group made any advances in power comparable to those of the earlier Brezhnev network.

There were important differences in interest and perspective among the emerging networks. We need only contrast reform-oriented Gorbachev network members, the more reluctant reformers tied to Ligachev, and the remnants of the Shcherbitsky Ukrainian group to sense this diversity. There have continued to be important checks and balances among these contending networks and interests. Their diversity clearly underscores the importance of coalition-building efforts by senior politicians. Gorbachev may be the most authoritative contemporary actor, and the Gorbachev group may be the single most important, but he and they have had to work with others who themselves command considerable resources. The need to effectively build bridges has been reinforced by the arrival of so many relative newcomers to the contemporary national political scene. Using CC/CAC membership as a basic indicator of an individual's national political standing, length of membership in these bodies is useful in determining a politician's national tenure. We find that the average CC/CAC tenure of Gorbachev and other contemporary network members has been less than ten years (Table 4.3).[38] Most of these network members attained national elite standing only after Brezhnev's death in 1982, while two-thirds entered the CC/CAC only after Gorbachev's succession to power in 1985. Their length of tenure thus has been comparable to that of the often less influential "nonclients." In stark contrast is the predictably higher tenure of former leaders' network members (approximately fifteen years, on average). The associates of former leaders are politically experienced and institutionally well-grounded. Some of these officials have developed independent bases for maneuvering (e.g., A.N. Aksionov and A.I. Vol'sky), while others have been coopted by post-Brezhnev groups and officials (e.g., Anatoly Dobrynin and V.V. Zagladin). By 1990, none held senior national posts, but many were powers to contend with in the decision-making labyrinth.

In the first five years of the Gorbachev regime, the institutional strength of contemporary patronage networks clearly lay not in their membership numbers but in their strong profile in top national political bodies. As of January 1990, the cohort of network members – including both patrons and clients – still constituted an imposing political element within the overall leadership (Table 4.4). The select positions held by the associates of Gorbachev, Ligachev, Ryzhkov, Sliun'kov, and others generally have been in the top strata of the party and government hierarchies. Most networks' institutional powers have emerged out of the traditionally dominant central party organs. In early 1990, identified network members represented over half of the combined Politburo and Secretariat membership, and over half of CC department heads. Important network patrons – Ligachev, Sliun'kov, and Razumovsky – chaired three of the six CC commissions, while senior Secretary and Politburo member Aleksandr Yakovlev and his confidant Vadim Medvedev chaired two others. We have already commented on the relatively limited size of the Gorbachev network, yet it merits noting that he

Table 4.4 *Network members in leading party and state bodies, January 1990*[a]

	Gorbachev and allied networks	Other networks	Former leaders' networks
Politburo (12)	3 (4)	5	
Secretariat (13)	1	3	1
CC department heads (10)	4		2
Council of ministries (74)	1	6	2
Republic leaders (44)	1	1	1
Obkom first secretaries (143)	7	7	6

[a]The membership sizes of the given bodies are noted after each institutional actor. For the Politburo row, numbers in parentheses represent candidate members who were network members; there were 7 candidate members in early 1990. The heading "republic leaders" refers to the first secretaries, chairmen of the councils of ministers, and chairmen of the supreme soviets of the 15 union republics.

and his associates have collectively become a dominant element in the Politburo, Secretariat, and CC apparatus. They thus have been in a decisive position to structure the issue agenda and mold policies. Premier Ryzhkov likewise has been able to advance several trusted associates to top government posts directly under his purview (e.g., several deputy premiers). Other senior politicians have done likewise.

These nation-level networks also had a presence in several influential subnational party organizations, as three republic and twenty provincial first secretaries exhibited patronage ties to them. Regions that were traditional network bastions have continued to be linked to senior politicians (e.g., Belorussia with Sliun'kov, Sverdlovsk with Ryzhkov). But in the early Gorbachev period the tails of these national patronage networks have not been long. Relatively few of the total number of critical republic and oblast positions have been held by the clients of senior national politicians. This pattern in part reflects the fact that contemporary national leaders have had more narrowly defined subnational careers, not moving across regions in the manner of earlier generations of officials. These leaders have also been in high national office for shorter time periods. Generally, they moved rapidly from the periphery to top posts under Andropov (e.g., Ligachev, Sliun'kov), and thus have not been as able to cultivate expansive networks of trusted lieutenants.

But this seeming inability to develop more geographically expan-

sive networks also reflects the new structural and procedural conditions now sweeping the Soviet system. Politicians – both high and
low – have been under mounting pressures that weaken their ability
to transfer power and authority directly to their clients. Two basic
subnational recruitment patterns have emerged in the post-Brezhnev
period: local officials with central apparatus experience who were
politically distant from besieged local political machines have returned to their old stomping ground; and officials from outside the
local establishment have been coopted to assume top prefectural
roles. The opportunities for placing associates have become more
limited, leaving national networks with fewer links to subnational
units.

In formal organizational terms, the political position of contemporary networks is moderately weaker than that of Brezhnev period
networks, even at the end of the Brezhnev regime's first five years of
consolidation. In spite of the unprecedented number of turnovers in
the later 1980s, the extended Gorbachev network – including his
protégés and clients – is smaller than Brezhnev's network was at the
same point in the development of his regime (see Tables 2.4 and 2.6).
The same is true for other networks: Brezhnev's rival networks were
larger and institutionally better grounded than those of Gorbachev's
contemporaries. There are no contemporary networks comparable in
size and position of power to those of Kosygin, Podgorny, and
Suslov (see Tables 2.6 and 2.8). Recalling that the expansion of
networks gained momentum after the Brezhnev regime's first years
of consolidation, we find no evidence of a comparable tendency in
the early 1990s. To the contrary, beyond the strategic placement of a
limited number of trusted associates, we find an open political arena
in which many politicians' career interests are merged by other – and
not past career – considerations.

These observations do not signify that contemporary national
leaders are politically weaker than their predecessors, though their
formal political bases appear to be less firm. Rather, they suggest that
we must look elsewhere to understand the roots of contemporary
politicians' power and authority. Their political standing is increasingly tied to their ability to effectively address the pressing policy
problems they have identified. Politicians' performance is all the
more critical to their political standing because they themselves had
championed the institutional and procedural reforms that now
underlie the reinvigoration of the Soviet sytem.

It is beyond the scope of this study to trace the evolution of the reform program and the efforts of national officials to revitalize Soviet society. But a look at selected aggregate demographic and career characteristics of contemporary network members suggests these politicians often have the ability to meet their increased performance expectations. This is an educated cohort of politicians whose backgrounds have been diverse and multifaceted. Compared with other CC/CAC members, they have comparably high levels of education; one-quarter of them have advanced educational training. They have worked in many institutional settings, though as already noted, they have generally not served in as many different sub-national settings as their predecessors. In fact, their career pasts tend to have bridged a wider range of organizational and sectoral contexts than those of their peers. This is very much a post-Stalinist group: three-quarters of the identified network members joined the CPSU after 1952. These politicians were socialized in the heady days of Khrushchevism and reform. Rational-technical and corporatist con-tentions raised in regard to Brezhnev period officials appear to be more applicable to these contemporary politicians. Among three major cohorts comprising the Gorbachev national leadership – con-temporary network members, past network members, and "non-clients" – the former look to possess that syndrome of background and experiential characteristics most conducive to addressing the challenges of reform.[39]

Nevertheless, these protégés and clients have advanced with particular senior politicians, through varied institutional settings, and on the basis of different types of clientelistic relations. An examination of the dominant contemporary networks enables us to better understand the diverse interests comprising the leadership and influencing the *perestroika* program. Gorbachev and his asso-ciates have become the core for an extended network, encompassing both senior officials allied with the General Secretary, and their associates. Beyond these are rival senior politicians who have culti-vated their own networks: networks that constitute an important political constraint on a powerful party leader and his supporters. As in the past, the absence of formally institutionalized checks and balances leaves patronage networks the formidable actors. Individu-ally, these networks help bind politicians' career interests: collect-ively, they help balance the power interests of rival groups.

Contemporary patronage networks

The Gorbachev network

The Gorbachev network was varied in composition, encompassing (a) politicians with traditional patron–client ties to Gorbachev extending over a considerable time period; (b) politicians who linked up with Gorbachev only after he became a senior Moscow official in 1978; and (c) others who were cultivated clients who advanced under Gorbachev's institutional prerogatives as General Secretary. A review of Gorbachev's network in the first five years of his regime reveals several conclusions about his patronage proclivities. Nearly all of his trusted subordinates were of the post-Stalin generation, having had their formative career experiences in the 1950s. Most were party professionals, highly educated, with experience in both national and provincial positions. Many rose in his area of specialty, agriculture. Some were from Stavropol, but many linked up with him when he supervised national agricultural policies. These associates proved their worth in an area their patron knew well, and were subsequently posted to important positions outside of the agricultural domain. In order to hold their positions and continue to advance, protégés and clients had to perform well. Gorbachev's sponsorship did not shield them from pressures that could halt their advance. During the first five years of the Gorbachev leadership, a number of sponsored protégés and clients suffered career setbacks – including early retirement. In such cases the General Secretary was willing to cut his losses, moving on without compromising his own standing.

The Stavropol politicians have assumed influential – often troubleshooting – roles in the Gorbachev regime. V.G. Afonin, who had worked under Gorbachev in Stavropol and was responsible for the province's industrial sector, was brought to Moscow to head the CC Chemical Industry Department (1983) and oversee the restructuring of that sector. When the central party apparatus was reorganized a few years later, Afonin was chosen to guide the important Kuibyshev oblast that at the time was racked by worker demonstrations (1988). His selection was not an accident: with no previous experience in Kuibyshev, Afonin was better able to oversee the transformation of the local party machine while simultaneously helping Gorbachev to counter the considerable influence of Politburo member and RSFSR Premier Vitaly Vorotnikov, who was from the province.

Other Stavropol colleagues of Gorbachev had similar backgrounds and abilities. A.D. Budyka was appointed to several important national posts in administering Soviet agriculture.[40] B.M. Volodin was selected in 1984 as the Rostov Ispolkom Chairman, helping the new Rostov First Secretary – and Gorbachev associate – Aleksandr Vlasov to wage what would be a model anti-corruption campaign in this important region. Two years later, when Vlasov was selected as USSR Minister of Internal Affairs, Volodin took over the first secretaryship, continuing Vlasov's initiatives. The long-time Stavropol official, S.I. Maniakin, who had been the Krai's Ispolkom Chairman (and a full CC member) when Gorbachev's career was in its early stages, was elevated under Gorbachev to chair the USSR People's Control Committee (1987). This was also an important assignment in the democratization drive, for Maniakin was empowered to streamline the inspection process and reformulate the process of citizen investigations.[41]

Among long-term Gorbachev associates, some were more able than others to adjust to the new reform environment. Gorbachev could not safeguard the elite standing of those who alienated important elements within their domains of responsibility. V.I. Kalashnikov, for example, had worked under Gorbachev in Stavropol and his career had taken off with Gorbachev's. Kalashnikov moved to head the RSFSR Ministry of Land Reclamation and Water Resources (1982), and two years later was elevated to the important Volgograd province as first secretary. He shared many common views with Gorbachev, at one time earning a reputation as a new-style reformer.[42] But, in fact, Kalashnikov alienated his Volgograd constituency and lost the confidence of establishment reformers, suffering political embarrassment in confirmation hearings (for a vice premiership) before the Supreme Soviet in June 1989, and falling from his Volgograd first secretaryship in January 1990. Another close client, V.S. Murakhovsky, assumed an important troubleshooting role under Gorbachev, first replacing him as Stavropol party leader in 1978, then advancing in 1985 to head the newly-formed Gosagroprom, the supra-ministry overseeing the reform of Soviet agriculture. With agricultural reform a priority, and with the new Gosagroprom a highly visible symbol of ongoing reform, Murakhovsky was entrusted with a set of responsibilities that was critical to the fledgling regime's initial policy success. The lackluster performances of both Gosagroprom and Murakhovsky, however, led to its abolition and his early retirement in 1989.

Beyond Stavropol associates, Gorbachev's network included officials cultivated since his arrival in Moscow in 1978. Most of these
officials worked with Gorbachev in the agriculture sector. He had
secured a reputation as a thinker and experimenter and Gorbachev
attracted reform-oriented agricultural specialists.[43] He relied heavily
on bright and thoughtful specialists, who often enjoyed meteoric
advances under his patronage in the 1980s. V.I. Boldin, Gorbachev's
major advisor on agricultural issues since 1981, advanced to head the
important CC General Department, where he essentially oversaw the
flow of information among top party organs. A.P. Lushchikov, who
had worked with Gorbachev's mentor Kulakov, came to head Gorbachev's personal staff and was a senior assistant to him for over a
decade. I.I. Skiba was advanced three times in five years under
Gorbachev's sponsorship, eventually heading the newly consolidated CC Agrarian Department in 1988. Finally, N.E. Kruchina, who
had worked with the then Agriculture Secretary Gorbachev, became
a key supporter in the central party apparatus by the latter 1980s. His
background in agricultural management and party organizational
matters helped him to become CC Administrator of Affairs in 1983,
and he maintained his high standing amidst the reorganizations of
the latter 1980s.

Similar to Stavropol associates, these clients were politically vulnerable if they did not perform adequately. An especially prominent
case involved Viktor Nikonov, whose past party organizational
experience, knowledge of agriculture, and shared views with Gorbachev had all helped him to rise to Politburo and Secretariat membership in the second half of the 1980s. Nikonov was a reputed
innovator. He had pressed for agricultural reform and had experienced rapid mobility in the Gorbachev regime's early years. But like
Kalashnikov and Murakhovsky, he did not adapt to the political
developments of the latter 1980s. He was increasingly associated
with the tired approaches of the past and he became a scapegoat for
failed reform measures. As a result, when the agricultural sector was
once again reorganized in Fall 1989, Nikonov was retired.[44]

Not all of Gorbachev's patron–client connections at the national
level emerged out of the agricultural sector. A.S. Cherniayev, who
was a central apparatus specialist on international affairs, became the
General Secretary's top foreign policy assistant in 1986. He probably
first met Gorbachev in the early 1950s, when he was a lecturer at
Moscow State University. He had risen through the party apparatus,
working with Yakovlev in the CC Science Department in the 1950s

and with Ponomarev in the CC International Department in the 1960s and 1970s. He shared the reformist inclinations of Gorbachev and ally Yakovlev, and by the late 1980s it was clear Cherniayev was one of the chief architects of the foreign policy "new thinking." Another one-time associate, Anatoly Luk'yanov, had been a government and party official for several decades before experiencing a series of rapid advances under Gorbachev. Luk'yanov, who had been in Moscow State University's law program with Gorbachev, and who had worked under Chernenko on upgrading the system of soviets, assumed quite prominent responsibilities in the late 1980s. From heading the CC General Department – the chancery of the central apparatus – to serving as party Secretary overseeing legal institutions, security and intelligence, Luk'yanov was arguably the top lieutenant in Gorbachev's expanding entourage. With the upgrading of the Supreme Soviet, Luk'yanov's role as First Deputy Chairman (1988) identified him as the trusted protégé stewarding the ever more important institutional base of Gorbachev's authority.[45]

This core group of entourage members came to hold an impressive array of positions under their patron, although only one was a member of the Politburo as of early 1990. Yet Gorbachev's power and authority were not grounded in this traditional patronage network. He had inherited a number of Kulakov's associates, and he had forged some important connections when he was a party Secretary, but five years into his tenure as General Secretary his immediate network was concentrated in select institutions and posts. Most protégés and clients were to be found within the central party apparatus, in positions dealing with priority policy matters such as agriculture and foreign policy. Certain trusted associates assumed *troubleshooting* roles, either at the national level or in the locales. But we must look beyond this immediate network to understand Gorbachev's organizational might. He forged important connections with other upwardly mobile officials who shared common policy perspectives and career interests. Several politicians, not members of Gorbachev's immediate network, but allied with him or sponsored by him, became pillars in an extended Gorbachev network. The logic of the radical reform period was that *political sponsorship* and *alliance building* undergirded the development of a powerful, institutionally well-grounded, coalition of interests. Politicians with minimal or no previous career ties to Gorbachev rapidly became key figures in that emergent coalition. The General Secretary's ability to rally considerable political forces to his side was of utmost significance in the formation of a governing national regime.

An extended Gorbachev network

In the first five years of the regime, the extended Gorbachev network encompassed both senior politicians in the Politburo and Secretariat and others whose careers had advanced since the 1985 succession. These politicians had much in common with Gorbachev's own network members. They were a highly educated group, primarily of the post-Stalin generation; in many cases their career pasts were multidimensional, transcending several bureaucracies. But their connections to Gorbachev were apparent in their career advances under him or under his senior lieutenants, especially Razumovsky, Shevardnadze, and Yakovlev. These politicians developed their own networks and, when combined, all of their network members constituted a formidable element within the national political elite.

I have already commented that Gorbachev's reputation as a reformer drew reformist elements to him, and these elements were rewarded with growing authority in the latter 1980s. Among these were officials with considerable experience on the Moscow political scene who had reputations as establishment reformers. Often these officials became members of Gorbachev's "brain trust," first serving as advisors before occupying weighty positions. Some were initially cultivated by Andropov (e.g., the defense industry specialist Oleg Baklanov). These reformers were critical in developing new policies and helping the reforming regime consolidate power. Ivan Frolov and Yevgeny Primakov were especially noteworthy among those officials cultivated by Gorbachev who became important parts of his extended network.[46]

Ivan Frolov became a prime ideological innovator of the emergent regime. He had supported the Khrushchev liberalization policies of the 1950s, but had experienced a rather uneven career under Brezhnev. Gorbachev gave him several successive influential positions. Selected as chief editor of *Kommunist* in 1986, he transformed it – the most authoritative theoretical organ – into a mouthpiece for reform. Three years later he became chief editor of *Pravda*, turning it around after several years of sliding subscriptions and growing disinterest among readers. By the end of 1989, he was not only a party Secretary, but a leading figure in the attempt to reconcile Marxism–Leninism with the logic of more radical reform.[47] Yevgeny

Primakov was also an important member of the Gorbachev team, assuming a leading role in the development of Soviet foreign policy "new thinking." No newcomer to the Moscow policy-making scene, he experienced three major career advances between 1985 and 1990, advancing into the Politburo as a candidate member in 1989. Frolov, Primakov, and other elevated advisors have helped Gorbachev stay near the cutting edge of establishment reform thinking, better enabling him to anticipate developments and outmaneuver rivals.[48]

Beyond these advisors turned politicians, numerous officials who publicly supported Gorbachev reform thinking saw their careers flourish during his tenure. These politicians are better thought of as shorter-term clients of the party leader. Aleksandra Biriukova, who advanced to be a USSR Deputy Premier and Politburo candidate member, emphasized the heightened priority accorded the light industry area. V.I. Mironenko, selected from outside the national apparatus to head the All-Union Komsomol, reorganized the Komsomol's leadership and helped reset its policies. The two officials selected to serve as USSR Minister of Internal Affairs also enjoyed career advances while articulating reformist lines. Aleksandr Vlasov had met Gorbachev when he was posted to the northern Caucasus in Chechen-Ingush Obkom in the latter 1970s; they shared common economic management, reform, and anti-corruption interests. Since Gorbachev became a senior Secretary and then General Secretary, Vlasov was appointed as Rostov First Secretary (1984), USSR Minister of Internal Affairs (1986), a candidate member of the Politburo (1988), and RSFSR Premier (1988): all in the span of four years. His successor, V.V. Bakatin, experienced comparable mobility, enjoying three promotions in Gorbachev's first five years as party leader. As a provincial party leader he had revealed himself as a reformer among his peers, championing the Gorbachev reform line.[49] He continued to do so as the top national police official.

In selected institutional settings and policy areas, cultivation of such short-term clients strengthened the organizational position of the governing coalition of reformers that made up the extended Gorbachev network. I use the term *coalition*, rather than faction, because this group of officials was grounded in a wide range of career and policy factors. They shared common reformist inclinations, even if particular issue stances varied. Their careers were often linked. But all had enjoyed enhanced mobility and authority under a guiding coalition patron. Within this coalition were the entourages of several politicians who became senior members of the contemporary regime. These senior politicians aligned themselves with Gorbachev for various reasons, and their power and authority rose as a result. They must be distinguished from clients because they brought considerable resources to the alliance. Although not long-term protégés, they became leading members of the Gorbachev team.

Georgy Razumovsky had a past association with Gorbachev and took public positions on important issues – especially the cadres questions for which he was responsible – entirely consonant with Gorbachev's expressed thinking.[50] He enjoyed a meteoric rise under Gorbachev, moving from the Krasnodar first secretaryship to become the OPWD Head (1985), a Party Secretary (1987), a candidate member of the Politburo (1987), and a CC Commission Chair (1988). He espoused the reform line throughout the latter 1980s, supervising cadres matters and distancing Gorbachev rival Yegor Ligachev from influencing recruitment questions. Several of his protégés became highly visible in the Gorbachev era. I.K. Polozkov had worked with Razumovsky in Krasnodar, and he became a regional leader championing Gorbachev's domestic reforms. Krasnodar's more open selection of cadres was cited as an example for others as the party democratization initiative progressed.[51] A.A. Khomiakov was a political troubleshooter dispatched to one problem-ridden province, elevated to head another important province, and then designated to chair the RSFSR Gosplan (1989). Gorbachev and the national reform coalition had rather tenuous links to provincial party organizations, but through Razumovsky and his network, several important connections were forged.

Another pillar of this extended network, Eduard Shevardnadze, did not bring many colleagues from his native Georgia to the highest levels, though T.N. Menteshashvili (Secretary of the USSR Supreme Soviet) and D.I. Patiashvili (Shevardnadze's successor as Georgian party First Secretary) did advance under him in the 1970s.[52] But Shevardnadze has, since his arrival in mid-1985, transformed the Foreign Ministry, displacing dozens of Gromyko associates and bringing in an entire cohort of new generation policy makers and analysts.[53] His past association with Gorbachev and his reformist inclinations made him a likely candidate for a senior position within the emergent regime.[54] As such, he helped to design a new foreign policy line and provided national reformers with additional clout in the highest reaches of the decision-making establishment.

Aleksandr Yakovlev was arguably the most powerful member of the national regime after Gorbachev. Politically resurrected by

Andropov and Gorbachev in 1983, he was a full member of the Politburo and a senior Secretary within two years of Gorbachev's succession. As a leading architect of the reform program, he was influential on every major domestic and foreign policy issue. But the strengths he brought to the regime and extended network were experience and competence, not a vast entourage of clients. Yakovlev's network was small, its members found primarily in his own area of expertise, propaganda and culture.[55]

Before his demotion to Ambassador to Canada in 1973, Yakovlev worked with Y.A. Skliarov in the CC apparatus (Propaganda Department). Like Yakovlev, Skliarov did not fare well during the latter Brezhnev years, with both men falling foul of Mikhail Suslov. But with Yakovlev's return in 1986 he quickly became head of the CC Propaganda Department.[56] Vadim Medvedev, who also worked with Yakovlev in the central party apparatus in the early 1970s, also suffered Suslov's disfavor, and was "rehabilitated" only after Suslov's death. Medvedev was already well-versed in ideological and propaganda matters when he became a party Secretary in 1986. Elevated to a full membership in the Politburo two years later, he emerged as a leading member of the Gorbachev team, first helping to develop a new policy toward Eastern Europe, and subsequently helping Yakovlev in the restructuring of Soviet ideology.[57]

By 1990, the extended Gorbachev network had become large and diverse. Although there were cross-cutting connections in the careers of certain members, there was no one sector, region, or interest that bound these politicians together. Most came together on the basis of common reform inclinations and career interests that stemmed from their promotion of Gorbachev's reform program. But the high stakes of the reform program they were collectively promoting caused their career fortunes to become increasingly interconnected.

These reformist politicians had to deal with other interests that stood outside of this allied set of networks – interests that were often threatened by the reform program. For example, several important networks led by powerful national politicians emerged. Their organizational and geographical bases generally varied from those of the extended Gorbachev network, and they championed alternative policy perspectives. These networks and their leaders arose as potential rivals, representing important political constraints on the evolution of the national political elite in the Gorbachev period.

Rival politicians and networks

In addition to Gorbachev, Yury Andropov elevated or resurrected a number of officials who played critical political roles in the succeeding decade. A number of them developed networks of some influence. Similar to Gorbachev's network, their entourages tended to be narrowly defined in regional or sectoral terms. Like the Gorbachev group, these networks grew as their patrons advanced to senior national posts, and by the end of the 1980s they had become formidable.

The most important of these rival networks was that of Yegor Ligachev, the putative political counter-weight to Gorbachev. As a rallying symbol within the establishment of contemporary orthodoxy and resistance to reform, Ligachev developed a following that descended into many national bureaucracies and regional party organizations. Brought to Moscow by Andropov to help purge the leadership, Ligachev already had earned a reputation for fighting corruption, emphasizing discipline, and fostering limited economic reform. In building a network of associates, he drew primarily on two sources: his old stomping ground, the Tomsk province; and the OPWD which he led for three years (1983–85). Several politicians who worked closely with Ligachev had advanced to prominent positions with his support. A.G. Mel'nikov, his top lieutenant and successor in Tomsk, rather quickly advanced to head the CC Construction Department (1986), overseeing a major turnover of personnel in that sector. After his department was abolished as part of the streamlining of the central party apparatus, Mel'nikov was dispatched to the important Kemerovo prefecture as First Secretary (1988). Throughout the latter 1980s he assumed a high profile in challenging many aspects of the reform program while advancing conservative views very compatible with Ligachev's stated positions.[58] Another client from Tomsk, Y.I. Litvintsev, was appointed First Secretary of the important industrial province of Tula, where he subsequently garnered national attention for his Novomoskovsk experiments in agro-industrial management.[59] Yet another Tomsk client, P.Y. Slezko, who had served under Ligachev in the OPWD, became Ligachev's assistant, and subsequently assumed a deputy chairmanship of the Party Control Committee (1988).

As a senior national leader, Ligachev was in the position to help many officials with compatible interests and views. F.I. Loshchenko, once Ligachev's superior in Novosibirsk, was a victim of the reform movement. Public pressure forced him out of his Yaroslavl first secretaryship in 1986, yet he was still able to secure high-level support to land a national nomenklatura position as USSR Goskomrezerv Chairman. Many who served in the OPWD during Ligachev's three-year tenure were able to advance to important regional leadership positions.[60]

Ligachev's career path crossed that of many officials who were likely allies in the struggle over reform.[61] This study likely undercounts his clients, as his supervision of the OPWD enabled him to sponsor numerous officials who are not captured by our decision rules. But as the darling of establishment conservatives, Ligachev clearly forged ties with politicians who shared common views and whose future standing was affected by his evolving position within the national hierarchy. He informally led a broader coalition of interests that, while smaller than the extended Gorbachev network, was similar to it in transcending many institutional and sectoral interests. As was true for Gorbachev, Ligachev's power and authority were based far less in a patronage network and far more in his political standing as the advocate of a particular programmatic vision.

The Sverdlovsk province, which gave rise to Andrei Kirilenko and his influential network in the Brezhnev period, continued to provide a cohort of officials in the succeeding decade. Some politicians tangentially tied to Kirilenko (e.g., Kolbin and Riabov), survived his November 1982 retirement, and their careers continued to thrive in the Gorbachev period.[62] Not surprisingly, all of these Sverdlovsk politicians had extensive experience with industry, and many fitted our definition of a Soviet technocrat: educated, grounded in an area of expertise outside of the party machine, and often possessing significant managerial experience. The members of this Sverdlovsk cohort made careers that were tightly interconnected: many studied together, served directly with one another, and ascended the political hierarchy together. A number assumed important high-profile roles, some allied with the Gorbachev reformers and others allied with more conservative forces. The heterogeneity of the group was evident in the divergent public positions of iconoclastic reformer Boris Yeltsin and Ligachev supporter L.F. Bobykin, two politicians with Sverdlovsk connections.

The key figure emerging out of the Sverdlovsk network during the Andropov and Gorbachev periods was Soviet Premier Nikolai Ryzhkov. Brought to Moscow by Kirilenko, he rose to senior standing under Gorbachev. Ryzhkov was an advocate of economic and managerial reform throughout the 1980s and early 1990s. His reputation for administrative efficiency and political acumen emerged over the past few years.[63] Ryzhkov elevated a number of protégés to high government positions during his tenure as Premier. Both First Deputy Premier Yury Masliukov and Deputy Premier L.A. Voronin advanced into senior Council of Ministers posts within months of Ryzhkov's appointment as Premier. Both were members of the Sverdlovsk network, both had extensive experience in the military–industrial complex in which Ryzhkov himself had risen, and both became top members of the national economic administration. Y.P. Batalin, another Sverdlovsk official and protégé of Ryzhkov, also advanced to a deputy premiership in 1985, and was selected to chair the supra-ministry dealing with construction (Gosstroi) in 1988.

As was true of former Premier Kosygin, Ryzhkov constructed a high-level team of officials who collectively dominated the upper echelon of the governmental bureaucracy. His power base was clearly the Council of Ministers Presidium, since in the wake of the 1989 reform of the legislature and government, few of the ministers and state committee chairpersons were tied to him. His national-level bailiwick was the top governmental planning agencies where he served before, and his network did not reach far beyond this. Ryzhkov had connections through a broader Sverdlovsk network, but he was no Kirilenko, and in the absence of such a powerful patron, this regional cohort was too varied in postings and perspectives to constitute a single political force. Again, as we found true of Gorbachev and Ligachev, the Soviet Premier derived his primary authority from past achievements and contemporary reputation, rather than from a traditional patronage machine. By the end of the 1980s, his public posture, as revealed in his outspoken July 1989 CC Plenum comments, cast him in a centrist position between the reformist extended Gorbachev network and conservative elements including the Ligachev network.[64]

Finally, the Gorbachev period also witnessed the emergence of another nationally prominent Belorussian network, led by Nikolai Sliun'kov. Encompassing ten CC/CAC members, this network's members were once rivals of the Mazurov network of the Brezhnev period. Belorussian network politics of the Brezhnev period had favored the Mazurov and Brezhnev groups.[65] Most members of the Sliun'kov network only emerged in the latter Brezhnev period, having made their early careers in Minsk. They moved to republic and national prominence after the 1982 national succession, when the rival networks' patrons had departed the political scene.[66]

Sliun'kov rose to be the republic's First Secretary in 1983. He had made his early career in Minsk, moving up in industrial management and later party work. A technocrat with experience in Gosplan, he was especially active in political networking activities (e.g., with both Gorbachev and Ryzhkov) in the late 1970s and early 1980s. As the Belorussian party leader, Sliun'kov purged the republic's leadership, elevating many with past Minsk connections. Among his Minsk protégés elevated were G.S. Tarazevich, who became the Belorussian Supreme Soviet Chairman, and M.V. Kovalev, selected as the republic's Premier.[67] During this period other politicians, not from Minsk, but apparently able to cut deals with Sliun'kov, also advanced as Sliun'kov's own career progressed.[68] As a senior Secretary and Politburo member with a past reputation for economic reform, Sliun'kov was given considerable responsibility in the administration of the country's economic life. His ties to his home republic remained strong, though his immediate successor as First Secretary was not a close protégé.[69] Like other contemporary networks, Sliun'kov's network was narrowly focused, with his national authority primarily derived from his good working relations with other senior politicians.

Other national leaders of the Gorbachev period cultivated associates, though none built comparable networks. Both Vitaly Vorotnikov and Lev Zaikov, for instance, assumed influential roles in the national leadership, but neither has developed a large entourage.[70] Other politicians – transitional figures in the Gorbachev regime – also elevated selected associates, though their entourages were not large.[71] The turbulent early years of the Gorbachev regime brought many personnel changes; the composition of leading party and state bodies constantly changed. But few patronage networks emerged as formidable actors in the Soviet policy process.

Networks, coalition building, and the Soviet *new politics*

The Gorbachev regime emerged rapidly after the March 1985 succession. As we have seen, its networks were more limited in size and more narrow in scope than their predecessors. Elite recruitment and coalition-building norms reflected an altered political environment. Short-term sponsorships of upwardly mobile officials were favored, and transitory alliances involving senior officials and their networks became common. Top leaders relied upon selected long-term protégés for key posts, but they cultivated many more upwardly mobile officials lacking those associations but sharing common issue and career interests. We have also seen how leaders, especially Gorbachev, relied upon experienced officials who were already institutionally well-situated. Relationships between current leaders and these incumbent officials are better defined as alliances rather than sponsorships, for these officials had past records of accomplishment and already developed institutional bases rather than past associations. Their loyalties to new senior politicians – like the loyalties of sponsored, short-term clients – were grounded in current policy and career interests and not in long-term past associations. The resultant alliances were fragile, but they were not to be underestimated. The case of Defense Minister Dmitry Yazov and his group is illustrative.

Yazov enjoyed almost meteoric advance under Gorbachev, moving from the Far Eastern Military District to head the Defense Ministry and to become a Politburo candidate member in less than two years. He must be viewed as an important member of Gorbachev's governing coalition. Members of a "Far Eastern military cohort" were not closely connected with the military establishment of past regimes, and their ranks included generally younger, post-Stalin, professionals. Within the professional military establishment, Yazov was relatively more supportive of the reform program during its initial phases – a fact that helps explain why he leap-frogged past several senior military leaders to become Defense Minister.[72] Although in the overall national discussion Yazov was critical of certain "excesses" of reforms (e.g., *glasnost* and the "negative" reporting of military issues), he championed the central initiatives of the reform program: democratization, fighting corruption and bureaucratic inertia, cutting defense spending, and developing a more defensive military strategy.[73] It is hardly coincidental that Gorbachev publicly defended Yazov during the Defense Minister's July 1989 Supreme Soviet confirmation hearings, emphasizing his role in promoting restructuring in the armed forces. It is also not a coincidence that a number of Yazov's protégés have assumed important posts since his move to Moscow and that, like him, their policy positions relative to professional peers leaned toward the reform program.[74]

It is difficult to assess the power and authority of the Gorbachev-led extended network and allied interests. It has never been easy to assess any coalition's strength, and this is even more true when the

Soviet system is in transition. There are methodological constraints hindering our ability to systematically account for these sponsorship and alliance relationships. The evidence adduced in the preceding pages reveals that Gorbachev has been at least as active as any recent predecessor in cultivating all types of like-minded subordinates, but we often lack the firm evidence that would leave us confident in our judgments regarding systematic identifications. Thus, in these analyses, only those officials who enjoyed *two* separate career advances under Gorbachev or other top leaders were identified as sponsored clients and members of their networks. Given the stakes involved in such advances, these measures best capture those officials most directly linked to national leaders' career and power interests. But national leaders' sponsorship of subordinates certainly transcended these more evident cases to encompass other, more subtle, political relationships. As a result, we have undoubtedly undercounted the number of individuals linked with senior politicians through sponsorship and alliance arrangements. We may be underestimating the influence of expansive – albeit diverse – Gorbachev period coalitions. But given available information, we can focus on two basic considerations for some reliable indication of a coalition's strength. First, we can assess the institutional positions of extended network and alliance members within the policy process (something we have already partially done). Second, we can consider the expressed positions of these actors on the most pressing issues of the day, particularly on the development and implementation of the *perestroika* program. Although a thorough survey of both would be a massive undertaking in and of itself, a few observations may be offered.

We have already seen the dominance of Gorbachev network and allied interests in the traditionally important party and government organs, especially in the Politburo and Secretariat. We have also noted that extended network and allied officials directed at least three of the more recently formed CC commissions. But of growing importance in the transitional early 1990s, the memberships of party and state bodies have included a significant number of associates of Gorbachev and his senior lieutenants (Table 4.5). Unlike any other network or potential coalition of networks, extended Gorbachev network members were to be found in all six CC commissions, with some of these politicians among the most influential members.[75] These politicians and other extended network members never constituted a majority in any commission, but their presence signified that

Table 4.5 *Network members in CC Commissions, RSFSR Buro, the Presidium of the Supreme Soviet, and the Presidential Council, 1990*

	Total number of members	Gorbachev and allied networks	Other networks	Former leaders' networks
CC Commissions				
Agrarian	22	5	2	3
Ideology	25	4		4
International affairs	23	4		2
Legal affairs	20	2	2	3
Party organization and cadres policy	25	5	3	1
Socio-economic	21	2	6	3
RSFSR Buro	16	3		
Presidium, Supreme Soviet	41	3	2	
Presidential Council	15	4	1	

the Gorbachev national network had a considerable ability to influence the deliberations of all these planning bodies.[76] The Socio-Economic Commission was the only one that contained a good number of members from rival networks (in this case, associates of Ryzhkov and Sliun'kov); arguably it was in that broad area that rivals were most effective in blocking the rapid emergence of reforms. The membership of the RSFSR Buro – a body first championed by conservatives as a forum from which to challenge reformist inclinations in the Russian Republic – also included several extended Gorbachev network members, while no associates of rival Politburo members were to be found in its ranks. Even the newly formed Presidential Council (March 1990), representing a wide spectrum of interests and views, included a significant number of members either tied to or allied with Gorbachev.

More important, however, is the fact that network and extended network members holding these and other positions had important policy-making prerogatives in areas of key importance to Gorbachev and the reform program. For at least the last half of the 1980s, Razumovsky was a key figure in the supervision and renewal of cadres, as Yakovlev and Medvedev were in the areas of ideology, propaganda, and culture. The momentum for reform was clearly sustained by key media figures who became important elements within the extended network. Shifts in national newspaper and journal editorships brought to the fore reformers who were critical parts of the governing team. The politically influential roles of Frolov and Burlatsky cannot be overemphasized. In the area of legal reform and the transformation of the soviets, the critical roles of associates and extended network members such as Luk'yanov and the political scientist G.K. Shakhnazarov cannot be denied. The foreign policy changes that became a hallmark of the Gorbachev period and that were essential to his reform drive were the result of the efforts of Shevardnadze, Yakovlev, Primakov, Dobrynin, and other network members and allies.

If there were areas where this extended network was less pervasive, they entailed the economy and subnational leaderships. There had been some allied reformist officials in high government posts dealing with the economy (e.g., Deputy Premier Abalkin), but their overall presence was modest. In the administration of the economy, other interests had more pronounced direct roles. Among networks identified here, those of Ryzhkov and Sliun'kov – especially if combined into a broader coalition of officials – were more influential. And in subnational administrative units, relatively few of the over a hundred party first secretaries were directly tied to the extended Gorbachev network. It is hardly coincidental that it was these areas, less subject to the political will of the dominant national reform coalition, that were among the primary sources of resistance to reform efforts.

The governing team of Gorbachev associates, extended network members, and allies operated in a broader context in which both conservative and radical reform elements applied pressures. The 1985–90 Gorbachev regime had a history of changing alliances among numerous parties in forming and maintaining a governing coalition. In the period 1983–86, alliances with Ligachev, Ryzhkov, Sliun'kov, and Vorotnikov – among others – were key in successfully challenging incumbent politicians and past policies. As the regime became consolidated and its program became more radical, these rival politicians increasingly distinguished themselves from the policy preferences of establishment Gorbachev reformers. As subordinates were sponsored and networks grew, Ligachev became a rallying point for post-Brezhnev conservatives; Ryzhkov and Sliun'kov became mouthpieces for more hesitant technocratic elements especially within the government establishment; and Vorotnikov became a champion of a new conservative RSFSR elite cohort. By the late

Table 4.6 *Policy positions of selected top leaders, 1989 Congress of People's Deputies election speeches*

	Components of political reform	Support for *radical* economic reform	Characterization of ideological change	Identified achievements of reform program
Gorbachev	Accountability, socialist pluralism[a]	Specific	Advances	Economic, ideological, political, social
Luk'yanov	Accountability, socialist pluralism	General	Advances	Economic, ideological, political, social
Medvedev	Accountability, socialist pluralism[a]	Specific	Advances	Economic, ideological, political, social
Razumovsky	Accountability, socialist pluralism[a]	General	Advances	Economic, ideological, political, social
Yakovlev	Accountability, socialist pluralism	General	Advances	Economic, ideological, political, social
Ligachev	Diverse one-party system		Dangers	
Ryzhkov		General		Economic
Sliun'kov	Diverse one-party system	General		Economic, political
Vorotnikov	Diverse one-party system	General	Dangers	Economic, political
Zaikov	Diverse one-party system	General	Dangers	Economic, political

[a]Explicit use of term *pluralism*.

1980s, the public pronouncements of these politicians and their associates revealed mutually compatible and overlapping perspectives, suggesting a potential coalition of conservative opponents to the Gorbachev reform line.[77]

A full analysis of the evolving policy debate among top officials for the 1985–90 period goes beyond the limits of this study. But drawing on my approach in analyzing the Brezhnev era debate, we can briefly overview one set of election speeches – delivered during the 1989 Congress of People's Deputies election campaign – to gauge the broad policy proclivities of top politicians. We have the statements of more and less reformist members of the national leadership. As we will find, an examination of their treatments of selected issues reveals that leaders' articulated policy positions are related to network politics (Table 4.6).

By early 1989 the broad contours of the Gorbachevian reform program were clear. Compared to past elections, 1989 candidates provided quite wideranging discussions of that program and the dilemmas before Soviet society. While touching upon many different themes, election candidates remarked upon four broad policy considerations that we may systematically examine to measure attitudes. First, they spoke about the components of political reform, which might include notions of officials' accountability, pluralism, and the one-party system. In their discussions of political changes, they accentuated what might be understood as either more reformist or more cautious stances on the pace and direction of democratization. Second, they addressed *perestroika*, with their commentaries ranging from general to specific in supporting what some of them called *radical* economic reform. Third, they discussed ideological reforms, dwelling either on the advances already witnessed or the dangers implicit in ideological changes. Finally, the speakers enumerated the achievements of the reform program, their discussions spanning various domains. National leaders provided contrasting treatments of these complex issues, with their relative emphases reflecting their areas of expertise and responsibility. But their broad orientations can be grouped into more and less reformist perspectives, with Gorbachev team members assuming a more supportive reformist posture and other top leaders being more restrained and less supportive.

Extended Gorbachev network members provided more detailed and positive assessments of the reform program and its results. They developed the notion of the accountability of officials and the party to mass interests; they spoke of a new socialist pluralism; and they accentuated positive developments stemming from democratization. In citing economic and ideological gains and other achievements of the reform program, these leading Gorbachev associates exhibited firm support for the rapid changes sweeping the CPSU and the country. Thus, Medvedev spoke of the market as "a flexible tool" for the coordination of Soviet economic life; Razumovsky stressed the gains from a "socialist pluralism of opinions and attitudes"; and Luk'yanov detailed the democratic strides resulting from the revitalization of the system of soviets.

In sharp contrast, the five leading politicians outside the extended Gorbachev network assumed more cautious – and sometimes critical – stances on these same policy considerations. None of them emphasized notions of accountability or pluralism; rather, they stressed the threat posed by greater diversity within the one-party system. Perhaps given that all five politicians were involved in the country's economic life, it is no surprise that they offered more balanced discussions of the problems and payoffs of *perestroika*. But where they were detailed in illuminating problems, they were general and vague in commending the radical reform program. As for ideological changes, all of these politicians were skeptical, focusing their attention on implicit dangers. Except for Ligachev, whose analysis and prognosis were especially gloomy, these rival officials identified selected economic or political achievements; but they exhibited none of the zeal displayed by top Gorbachev loyalists.

There was a need for a *quality debate* addressing the profound problems afflicting Soviet society; at last, it began. That debate significantly widened the spectrum of expressed views, as is evident in Table 4.6, but it also brought all politicians – junior and senior – under new and visible pressures. High-level alliances shifted, as politicians who once were major supporters of Gorbachev increasingly distanced themselves from him (e.g., Ligachev) or were even ousted (e.g., Chebrikov). That debate directly affected the functioning of the networks themselves. By 1990 there was evidence of policy disagreement among members of the extended Gorbachev coalition that we did not find in the extended Brezhnev network.[78]

There is a conceptual and methodological overlap among traditional patronage associations, sponsorships, and alliance building in extended networks such as that of Gorbachev. For example, the ties linking Gorbachev, Luk'yanov, Razumovsky, Shevardnadze, Yakovlev, and their associates have encompassed divergent considerations. Given the breadth of career, institutional, and policy interests among members, I prefer to conceive of the extended Gorbachev network as a broad-ranging coalition or unified set of sponsorships and alliances rather than as a faction. All of the extended network's senior members had significant career advances while promoting reformist thinking. They supported the Gorbachev program, both in its broad outlines, and in the more specific policies involving their own areas of responsibility. Their career futures became increasingly inter-related as their own achievements increasingly depended on the achievements of their fellow members. The extended network they headed was further augmented by other officials and interests that, at least in the short run, were part of informal alliance arrangements.

Patronage networks bridge career and policy interests, but the increasingly formalized checks and balances system that is emerging with the reform program is altering their centrality to Soviet political life. The political prerogatives that permit politicians to cultivate selected officials are increasingly circumscribed. Even the most powerful can no longer automatically place trusted associates as well – as Gorbachev was reminded in May 1989, during his protégé Luk'yanov's tribulations in being confirmed as First Deputy Chair-man of the Supreme Soviet.[79] All national leaders – including reformers – are now compelled to deal with the very forces they labored to create. The politics of the early 1990s entail ongoing institutional changes that as of this writing are not harnessed by any actor or group. We thus find that officials who are not accountable to any higher party authority – for instance Congress and Supreme Soviet deputies – have increasing influence on those above them. An analysis of the memberships of Congress and Supreme Soviet commissions and committees revealed almost no national network members within their ranks. Top politicians did sponsor selected network members into the governing Supreme Soviet Presidium (Table 4.5), but network influence did not directly extend below. The logic of the *new politics* and the public debate runs counter to that of traditional patronage networks. The *new politics* and ongoing debate have shown patronage relations to be dysfunctional to the country's political life. Reformers have contended they are building a civil society on the bones of putatively corrupt, rejected networks of officials. And when self-described reformers resort to old style patronage politics, they risk media exposure and condemnation. The fates of numerous contemporary "reformers" illustrate these severe consequences.[80]

It may be that the reforms of the latter 1980s and early 1990s are altering the motivations that guide the behavior of Soviet politicians. The politically ambitious still desire to gain and hold onto power, but the qualities once necessary to accomplish these ends are changing. The Brezhnev regime, whose core system goals were control and stability, rewarded loyalty and reliability. The Gorbachev program, which stresses system transformation, seems to consider competence and commitment to reform goals as the hallmarks of a superior candidate for advancement. The national regime appears to be promoting a new type of official in this period of rapid change. Are aspiring politicians *rational* in relying less on traditional network means and more on their competence and reformist leanings?

The dynamism of the times and the open disputes among both elite and mass elements make the stakes of the political game for all officials very high. The acceleration of policy change and mounting crisis environment only reinforce the centrality of authority building. Authority increasingly stems from an individual's ability to identify and address the serious problems facing Soviet society. The relative power and authority of both Gorbachev and Ligachev, for instance, are the direct result of their ability to deal with pressing issues. The networks and alliances I have analyzed also rely more on common understandings of current problems and appropriate responses than on the fortuitousness of long-term past associations. But these are fragile bases of power. Contemporary politicians will have to contend with a more fickle political temper than did immediate past generations of Soviet officials.

The 1990s are no doubt a transition period. The mechanisms binding politicians' interests are clearly changing. Informal groups, emerging as nascent political parties, are helping to bring interests together by openly articulating divergent policy preferences. They are paving the way for legalized associations of competing interests that will no longer be bound to an outwardly monolithic governing coalition. In the aftermath of Gorbachevian reforms, we will again need to consider the utility and relevance of patronage networks to Soviet elite politics and political life.

5 Patronage and regime formation in Lithuania

The Soviet political structures and norms that we examined at the national level also functioned in the diversity of cultural and developmental settings that constitute the USSR. Our exploration of Soviet national politics naturally concentrated on an elite population that was overwhelmingly Slavic and drawn primarily from the Russian Republic. More than any single cohort, that elite developed the system and its norms. But these same norms – especially those involving patronage politics – have been central to the politics of non-Slavic and subnational settings. An examination of two very different republics, Lithuania and Azerbaidzhan, reveals the critical role of networks in the political life of the locales. Networks have been central to subnational regime formation and governance, helping national authorities to influence an expansive and diverse periphery.

Though culturally and developmentally divergent, Lithuania and Azerbaidzhan were long dominated by powerful networks. In the traditional Soviet systems, the structure and logic of political power in a European Baltic republic and a Muslim Central Asian republic were comparable. The attendant norms of regional political machines were likewise comparable. Even Moscow's relations with the Vilnius and Baku regimes were similar.

Before the tumultuous events of the late 1980s, Lithuania was among the most stable of the Soviet republics, even though it had been incorporated into the USSR against its will. The Lithuanian Communist Party (LCP) leadership proved to be especially reliable: its guiding figure, Antanas Snechkus, and his successors dominated the republic's political scene for fifty years. Petras Grishkiavichus, who succeeded Snechkus in 1974 and ruled Lithuania until his death in 1987, developed a formidable network, with key members of his governing team guiding the republic until the Lithuanian National

Reconstruction Movement, Sajudis, came to power in March 1990. In this chapter the broad contours of this regional political machine are explored, and the considerable prerogatives vested with reliable subnational leaders examined. We also consider the impact of the Soviet *new politics* on subnational governance: in particular, the rapid undoing of a dominant network and the transformation of the traditionally strong tie of a regional leadership to national authorities. Lithuanian politics of the late 1980s and early 1990s suggest the effects profound institutional reform could have on the political norms of a society and its elite. The experience of the Grishkiavichus regime revealed the strengths of an institutionally well-entrenched political machine, but the rapid emergence of an independent popular front revealed that machine's fragility. As a powerful and long-dominant coalition of officials surrendered the reins of power to a group of intellectuals and political novices, traditional network politics gave way to the politics of open debate and democratic reform.

Continuity and change in Lithuania

On January 22, 1974, Antanas Snechkus, the LCP First Secretary, unexpectedly died after leading Lithuania for nearly forty years. Snechkus had been the republic's dominant figure and his passing represented a critical juncture in Soviet Lithuania's history as it underwent its first leadership succession. His death was also a milestone of sorts for the Soviet Union, marking the first time a republic leader died in office, resulting in an unanticipated succession. This leadership change provided an opportunity for a transformation of the political elite that had guided Lithuanian politics since the 1944 establishment of Soviet power. With the selection of a new republic boss came the likelihood of a new governing coalition of politicians and the emergence of a new dominant patronage network.

The size and complexity of the interlocking set of organizations in the Soviet system made the political tasks before the top decision maker enormous. In Lithuania, the top leader oversaw an apparatus of fourteen CC departments and forty-nine regional and major city party organizations. He also assumed ultimate responsibility for the operation of forty-eight ministries and state committees and their subordinate bodies. The first secretary had to effectively coordinate the various party-state bodies. This meant, above all, effectively

Bracauskas

guiding the all important party apparatus. As one party document put it, the first secretary had to "ensure that all departments and workers act purposefully, directing their efforts at organizing the masses. The proper organization of the work of the apparatus presupposes the efficient allocation of assignments and the exercise of personal responsibility in executing them."[1] Perhaps of even greater importance, the republic party first secretary represented the republic and its leadership before the national authorities.

Although the magnitude of the tasks before a new party first secretary was immense, the resources available to him in his own bailiwick were considerable. What personnel recruitment strategies were used as a regime formed? To what extent did a new leader rely upon patronage connections as a governing coalition emerged? Were there particular organizational and political prerequisites that underlay the republic leader's authority building efforts?

The 1974 Lithuanian succession did not transform the republic's politics. It did, however, facilitate the reformulation of the governing elite and provide a second generation leader with an opportunity to mold his own political machine.

This succession occurred against the backdrop of a stable leadership that Moscow had only recently pressured to make certain domestic political and economic adjustments. The LCP had long pursued the broad goals set out by the national leadership. Snechkus had headed the LCP since June 25, 1940, and had worked in the party since the 1920s.[2] He served closely with many LCP members who assumed critical roles in the postwar regime. After the disbanding of the Lithuanian Bureau of the All-Union Communist Party Central Committee (AUCP CC) in March 1947, Snechkus and other former underground partisans oversaw the sovietization of the republic.[3] Snechkus guided the expansion of the LCP from the creation of primary party organizations in all districts, to the establishment of a higher party school in Vilnius. By 1947, the first collective farms were being established. The Lithuanian political and economic scene was normalized by the mid-1950s, proving to be more stable and predictable than those in the neighboring Baltic republics. Investment decisions and political priorities determined in the 1944–53 period held firm, as the traditionally prominent light and food industries continued to receive priority. There was less emphasis on the rapid and extensive industrialization of Lithuania, especially in comparison with Estonia and Latvia. Under Snechkus, the fuel and power, machine-building, agricultural machinery, and building materials industries were developed. But by and large, efforts at transforming the republic's economy were not as extreme as in the Baltic and other republics.[4] At the same time, the Snechkus regime proved relatively effective in subduing Lithuanian nationalism and in controlling the Catholic Church, although the republic did have a dissident movement and one of the higher incidences of samizdat.

A major reason for political stability in Lithuania, and for Snechkus's own longevity, was that the republic's leadership remained loyal to Moscow while nativizing the party and state apparatuses. The June 1953 LCP CC Plenum had sanctioned the nativization of party cadres. Many non-natives (especially Russians) were removed from positions of responsibility. In 1949 only 50 percent of CC members were Lithuanian; in 1964 over 60 percent were Lithuanian; and, by the 1970s well over 70 percent were Lithuanian.[5] The Lithuanian experience of leadership nativization contrasted markedly with that of neighboring Baltic republics where levels of representation of the indigenous population were considerably lower. Turnover of top-level personnel and frequent purges of selected sectors and institutions were more common in those republics. Even by the mid-1960s, Lithuania's representation of natives within the top leadership was more substantial than most Soviet republics.[6] The Snechkus policy of local cadres recruitment continued into the 1970s. It helped moderate ever-present nationalist sentiments. It also helped insulate Lithuania from outside influences considered undesirable by Moscow.

Political stability in Lithuania also derived from a stability in the ranks of cadres that stemmed in large measure from Snechkus's own durable political machine. His network was fairly large, encompassing the top *Buro* and Secretariat, and extending down into the party apparatus and Council of Ministers. This is hardly surprising, since Snechkus had been in the Secretariat since 1926 and had been First Secretary since 1936. His machine survived not only the postwar Stalin era of societal and political transformation, but the turbulence of the Khrushchev years. Thus, when the neighboring Latvian party leadership underwent a massive purge in 1959, the LCP leadership remained quite stable. It was only in the mid-to-late 1960s that prominent members of Snechkus's machine began leaving the scene, and their departures were generally due to death and retirement, not ouster. At the time of Snechkus's death, most of the top leadership had been in power for a considerable period of time. As of early 1974, *Buro* members had been serving for an average of thirteen years.

Secretariat members had been in their slots for an average of at least fourteen years, while members of the Council of Ministers' Presidium had served for nearly ten years. There was comparable continuity in personnel at lower levels. The network's demise and the regime's reformulation came only with the death of the patron.

Three and a half weeks lapsed from the time of Snechkus's death to the selection of his successor. The length of time the LCP leadership took to deliberate over a successor revealed the stability of the republic and its elite: it indicated that Moscow did not impose an automatic choice upon the republic. This is clear in contrast to the time period accorded other republic party organizations in the midst of a succession: during the Brezhnev and immediate post-Brezhnev period a delay of over three weeks in the replacement of a republic party boss was unprecedented. When a first secretary was ousted, announcements of both the ouster and the selection of a new first secretary were usually made together or were separated by only a few days at most. When a first secretary died, presumably unexpectedly, the time period was slightly extended. But even for such long-serving first secretaries as Masherov (Belorussia) and Rashidov (Uzbekistan), replacements were found within a week.

The February 1974 succession brought a power struggle for Snechkus's mantle between the First Secretary of Vilnius, Petras Grishkiavichus, and the republic Party Secretary for Industry, Al'girdas Ferensas.[7] The LCP leadership's decision to appoint Grishkiavichus required Moscow's approval, but the evidence suggests the decision was made in Vilnius and not imposed from above. Grishkiavichus was not the automatic designee of either the Vilnius or Moscow elite. In fact, his selection came as something of a surprise. Yet the leadership that selected him had earned the confidence of the national authorities.[8]

Cadres turnover and the Grishkiavichus team

The selection of a new party leader was the first step in the emergence of the new regime. Months before the Lithuanian succession there had already been public acknowledgment of the need to rejuvenate the republic's leadership. Analysis of aggregate career data demonstrates two crucial developments during the five-year period of Grishkiavichus's consolidation of power: first, the significant turnover of personnel, at both the republic and regional levels; and second, the elevation of trusted associates of the new party

Table 5.1 *Number of changes in top Lithuanian party and state positions,*
1974–1981

Positions (N)	1974–76	1977–79	1980–81	Totals
Buro members (11)	2	2	1	5
Secretaries, CC (4)	1	2	1	4
Heads, CC departments (14)	10	7	3	20
Ministers and chairmen of state committees (48)	7	1	2	10
First secretaries, raikoms (46)[a]	15	14	1	30

[a]This category includes the first secretaries of the two leading gorkoms,
Vilnius and Kaunas.

leader. As Table 5.1 indicates, these changes characterized both party
and state policy-making and policy-implementing institutions.

We can identify a pattern of power consolidation similar to that we
saw at the national level, i.e. a pattern that reflects both the
institutional prerogatives of the republic first secretary and the
structure of power relations among party and state bodies. Because a
republic leader's power is directly connected to the party apparatus,
he is able to initiate immediate and sweeping changes there.
Predictably, a high proportion of CC department heads – the
command posts of the republic party apparatus – were replaced
during the power consolidation period. Simultaneously, the ranks of
top state officials – especially the ministers and state committee
chairmen – were also altered. Although the level of personnel
rotation among state officials was less dramatic, it was the key posts
that were affected. More than one-third of all Council of Ministers
members were replaced during the 1974–79 period. After 1979, the
pace of change slowed down. Even organizations outside of Vilnius
were affected by the succession. At the regional level, twenty-nine of
forty-six regional first secretaries were replaced between 1974 and
1979; many of these changes occurred soon after Grishkiavichus's
own elevation.

Many of those elevated in the wake of the 1974 succession were
new to the institutions and levels of authority to which they were
appointed (especially CC department heads). Others were lateral
transfers, in some cases having been shifted from CC departments to
head ministries. The infusion of new blood enabled Grishkiavichus
to enhance his influence over strategically important organizational

Table 5.2 *Placement of Grishkiavichus associates in top party and state positions, 1974–1981*

Positions (N)	Associates			
	1974–76	1977–79	1980–81	Totals
Buro members (11)	2	2	0	4
Secretaries, CC (4)	1	1	1	3
Heads, CC departments (14)	5	1	1	7
Ministers and chairmen of state committees (48)	6	1	1	8
First secretaries, raikoms (46)[a]	4	4	0	8

[a]This category includes the first secretaries of the two leading gorkoms, Vilnius and Kaunas.

slots, while preserving the political acumen of experienced incumbents.

The configuration of political actors was significantly altered during the post-succession power consolidation period. The extent of the changes that took place is all the more striking when we examine the five-year period before the succession. Between 1969 and 1974, there were no personnel changes in the influential *Buro* and Secretariat. In fact, the few changes that occurred during the 1960s generally involved routine retirements of elderly or ailing incumbents. Within the government, only ten of forty-six Council of Ministers members were replaced. There were more personnel changes in the CC apparatus as ten of sixteen department heads were either transferred or removed; many of these changes came during the year and a half before Snechkus's death and were the result of pressures from Moscow to invigorate the Lithuanian economy. However, in general, the last five years of the Snechkus regime – and even the decade of the 1960s – were a time of genuine cadres stability. Indeed, many of those retired had been long-serving party and state officials who had held positions since the 1950s and early 1960s.

The personnel turnover that followed the 1974 succession was especially important because a significant number of Grishkiavichus protégés and clients assumed important party and state positions. Within just a few years, Grishkiavichus had recruited numerous past associates and sponsored fast-rising newcomers into responsible positions (Table 5.2). The significance of these personnel changes cannot be over-emphasized; the positions of incumbents were weakened, as the power and profile of the new leader's trusted lieutenants and allies expanded. Many institutionally well-ensconced elements were put on the defensive. These changes provided a political and organizational momentum that helped the new leader more rapidly form a governing coalition.

The new party leader's political base began within his own realm of responsibility, the OPWD, now headed by his former assistant, V.S. Astrauskus. The OPWD was an important institution because it monitored cadres recruitment and mobility for both the party and state apparats (including regional, district, and city party commit-tees). Astrauskas, who had a multifaceted career that had taken him to numerous organizational and regional settings, was a trusted protégé who would become a senior member of the regime. Assoc-iates from the OPWD were transferred to head a number of impor-tant CC departments including the Administrative Organs Department (1974) and the General Department (1975). Influence over these supervisory and policy-making departments ensured the Grishkiavichus network's influence over key state bodies, including the apparatus of the Council of Ministers. As a result, within the first year of his own appointment, the new First Secretary was in an organizationally strong position within the LCP apparatus. Although overseen by national level bodies. Grishkiavichus and his team quickly became responsible for all cadres matters within the LCP, and thus institutionally able to monitor all subordinate party and government organs.

The expansion of the Grishkiavichus network involved the pro-motion of associates to head other departments critical both to the Lithuanian economy and to cultural and educational issues dominat-ing the policy discussion in Vilnius. Grishkiavichus quickly pro-moted an associate, L.K. Maksimovas, to head the Industry and Transport Department – a department that assumed a special impor-tance in light of previous criticisms from both Moscow and the republic second secretary.[9] Of comparable importance was the 1975 elevation of a protégé, A.A. Kiriushchenko, as chief of the LCP's Light and Food Industry Department. Historically, Lithuania's light and food industries constituted a critical part of the republic's economy. Because the republic was annually near or at the top in per capita production of milk, meat, and other dairy products, Moscow always gave special attention to the performance of its food industry. Other areas of special concern for Moscow included the republic's high tech industries, manifestations of nationalism, and the effective socialization of Baltic youth. It was no coincidence that several Grishkiavichus associates successively headed the CC Science and Higher Education Department from the mid-1970s into the mid-1980s.

The political position of the first secretary within the central republic party apparatus was significantly boosted by concomitant changes in the membership of the LCP *Buro* and Secretariat. These two bodies represented the zenith of political power in a Soviet republic. The party *Buro* was the republic's chief deliberative body. It was composed of the top dozen politicians whose institutional affiliations spanned the range of party and state hierarchies. Subject to the constraints set by Moscow, the republic party first secretary, as the presiding official within the *Buro*, set the agenda and directed the *Buro's* actions. As the leading member of the Secretariat, he supervised the activities of the other republic secretaries who, themselves, coordinated and oversaw all of the subordinate republic, regional, and local party organizations. Given the policy-making and supervisory functions of the *Buro* and Secretariat, changes in their composition could aid the first secretary in further consolidating his position. The number of members of these two bodies was necessarily limited, since the number of slots was small. In the Lithuanian case of the mid-1970s, however, the new party boss gradually augmented his position through the retirement of several incumbents and the elevation of protégés and clients.

In 1971, only one of the eleven full members of the LCP *Buro* was a protégé or client of the then First Secretary of Vilnius, Grishkiavichus. By 1976, just two years after his succession to the top party post, three of his associates were full members of the *Buro* (out of eleven total), and three associates were candidate members (out of four total). By early 1981, nearly half of the *Buro* members had career connections to the First Secretary. Among these were Astrauskas, A.Y. Chesnavichus, V.V. Sakalauskas, and L.K. Shepetis – associates who were now the key figures running the party organization and the republic.

Retirements, transfers, and promotions within the party Secretariat also bolstered Grishkiavichus's standing. The long-serving Secretary for Agriculture (R.-B.I. Songaila) already had ties with Grishkiavichus. But Ferensas, the Secretary for Industry, had been Grishkiavichus's main rival in the 1974 leadership struggle. By mid-1977, a fast-rising client, A.-M.K. Brazauskas, had replaced Ferensas, who was shunted off into a trade union slot that had some public visibility but limited influence.[10] Just a year earlier, another client (L.K. Shepetis) became the LCP Secretary for Propaganda and Agitation: a move helpful to a first secretary who was publicly prodding the Lithuanian leadership in its struggle against nationalist tendencies and foreign cultural influences.[11]

Meanwhile, in the top governmental bodies, Grishkiavichus associates were also advancing. Several found their way into the Presidium of the Council of Ministers as vice-chairmen. Over one-third of all ministers and state committee chairmen were elevated during the regime's first five years, and a number of them were Grishkiavichus associates. Analysis of these elevations reveals them as a crucial means by which the new party leader strengthened his grip on the policy process: experienced protégés from the CC apparatus were routinely transferred into government positions that entailed duties in the same area of responsibility. Thus, a protégé who had headed the CC Science and Higher Education department was appointed Minister of Culture; another who was in charge of the Trade and Services Department became Minister of Social Welfare; and a third protégé from the Science and Higher Education Department became Minister of Education. In addition, the head of the Light Industry Department became Minister of Light Industry. Through these transfers Grishkiavichus consolidated his own position and allowed experienced incumbents to retain their political elite status, albeit in less influential posts. Trusted protégés now supervised these experienced – but perhaps politically less reliable – officials who lacked connections to the republic leader.

This pattern of personnel transfer enabled Grishkiavichus to cope with a major challenge facing any decision maker in the Soviet context: the need to secure bureaucratic leverage in translating initiatives into policy. There were limits to the number of loyal associates upon whom the top leader could rely as he expanded his power base into various organizations. Moreover, the ouster of less reliable incumbents was often a waste of needed competence and experience. Soviet leaders at all levels have long complained of the dearth of qualified and competent personnel to fill positions. Reassignment of such incumbents to less powerful administrative positions – supervised by reliable associates – enabled the leader and his network to strengthen their position within the overall set of interlocking bureaucracies in the face of a limited pool of loyal associates. Many Snechkus-era incumbents experienced this fate (Table 5.3).

Table 5.3 *Direction of mobility of incumbents*

Positions	Transferred promoted	Demoted ousted	Retired died	Unknown
Secretaries, CC	2	0	0	0
Heads, CC departments	3	6	1	0
Ministers, chairmen of state committees	3	5	8	2
First secretaries, raikoms[a]	7[b]	11[b]	0	3

[a]This category includes the first secretaries of the two leading gorkoms, Vilnius and Kaunas.
[b]In those cases where information on the subsequent position was unavailable, reelection to the CC/AC was considered to reflect transfer/ promotion, and non-reelection was considered to reflect demotion/ouster.

This strategy of selective personnel transfer from party to state positions directly related to the policy dilemmas of that time. Several of the cited cases of personnel transfer involved issue areas that were problematic for the republic. The Lithuanian leadership was concerned about increasing manifestations of nationalism and dissent in the republic. The cultural thaw and expanded foreign contacts of the latter 1960s and early 1970s had strengthened the underground dissident movement. That nationalism and dissent had culminated in the appearance of the underground *Chronicle of the Lithuanian Catholic Church* and in riots stemming from the self-immolation of a nineteen-year-old student in spring, 1972.[12] In the economic realm, ongoing problems included the need to expand consumer goods production and provide incentives to enhance worker productivity. Transfers of experienced – but supervised – incumbents were conducive to the coordination of activities across the responsible party–state bureaucracies. Although some of the politicians transferred had, in fact, been demoted, their continuing status as members of the governing elite now rested upon their performance within the state administration. They were now supervised by Grishkiavichus associates who held their former party positions. A total of six top incumbents within the party apparatus were shifted to important governmental policy implementation posts during the period of power consolidation.

Patronage and other political considerations were clearly critical to post-succession recruitment and mobility patterns. Other factors – including expertise and background – also influenced the personnel

Table 5.4 *Political fate of Snechkus protégés, by level of education*[a]

Level of education	Retained N(%)	Removed N(%)	Total N(%)
Higher education	10 (91)	1 (9)	11 (100)
Secondary education	3 (25)	9 (75)	12 (100)

[a]Where: Chi Square = 7.64; D.F. = 1; Significance Level = 0.006; Fisher's Exact Probability = 0.002.

norms of the Grishkiavichus regime. Rational-technical criteria affected the career-building efforts of incumbents and aspirants. However, the patterns were complex. Using level of education and range of previous posts as indicators of professional expertise, the backgrounds of newly recruited officials did not reveal higher levels of education or significantly stronger career backgrounds. These rational-technical factors, however, were relevant to the survival prospects of incumbents, including close associates of the departed Snechkus. Some Snechkus protégés retained positions in the Lithuanian hierarchy, at least through the first five years of the Grishkiavichus regime. Those with expertise, as measured by level of education, were more likely to survive the power consolidation period: among the twenty-three identified Snechkus protégés, nearly all with higher education kept their positions, while most of those with lower levels of education were removed (Table 5.4). Meanwhile, Grishkiavichus protégés and clients who were elevated were better educated than the incumbent Snechkus elite (Table 5.5). Indeed, the Grishkiavichus cohort exhibited a higher level of education when compared with other Lithuanian politicians of the 1970s. Grishkiavichus's recruitment of trusted lieutenants did not entail the advance of a less competent group of politicians.

As for professional background, the Grishkiavichus cohort did not incorporate a wider range of institutional or sectoral interests than its predecessor, yet if the Grishkiavichus team was not a more varied group, it did tap a somewhat different set of interests. The new regime was disproportionately composed of politicans whose careers had been made in institutional settings important to the career past of the new party First Secretary. Among the hundreds of politicians who comprised the LCP's top ranks there were certainly representatives of all major sectoral and regional interests, but representatives of the LCP OPWD and the Vilnius party organization assumed

Table 5.5 *Levels of education of Grishkiavichus protégés and clients, Snechkus protégés, and all other politicians*[a]

Level of education	Grishkiavichus protégés and clients N(%)	Snechkus protégés N(%)	All other politicians N(%)
Higher education [of which are	30 (79)	11 (48)	95 (70)
candidate or doctor]	[7 (18)	4 (17)	17 (13)]
Secondary and lower	8 (21)	12 (52)	41 (30)
Total N's	38 (100)	23 (100)	136 (100)

[a]Where comparing Grishkiavichus and Snechkus associates with all other politicians the Chi Square = 0.04; D.F. = 1; Significance Level = 0.839.

decisive party and state positions within the new regime. These institutions were certainly powerful, but their preeminence in supplying upwardly mobile personnel was no coincidence: past career connections with the new party leader were critical in explaining the changing composition of the top leadership.

Geriatric and generational factors were not important in the post-1974 transformation of the Lithuanian leadership. In the final years of the Snechkus regime these considerations had explained personnel turnover. A close look at the demographic attributes of both the ousted incumbents and the new recruits of the post-1974 period reveals only marginal age differences between these two groups. Incumbent party secretaries and CC department heads, for instance, were only slightly older than their successors; the average age of incumbent senior secretaries was less than 55.[13] Only one of the incumbent secretaries or department heads was over 60 years old and he retired. Transferred incumbents were hardly at an age requiring retirement. Most were of the same generational cohort as the new party boss.

Among top government officials, the picture was somewhat different. The age difference between incumbents and newcomers was more pronounced: incumbents were on average 58 years of age compared to an average of 46 years for their replacements. Of those replaced for whom career information on subsequent activities was available, half retired or died. In comparison with party personnel, retirement or transfer of government officials sometimes reflected nonpolitical considerations. But in these cases the average age of incumbents removed from office was still under 60.

As with age, generational considerations were also irrelevant to turnover. Examination of the backgrounds of both incumbents and their replacements reveals both groups were of the same generation: born in the 1920s and socialized into the LCP and republic politics in the late 1940s and 1950s. Most officials were products of the late Stalin and Khrushchev periods, having made their careers during Snechkus's lengthy stewardship.

No systematic differences in demographic factors emerge between those ousted and those elevated. The political importance of incumbents' positions, however, did influence their prospects of career survival after Snechkus. There was a positive relationship linking the probability of ouster, the importance of an incumbent's position, and the strength of that incumbent's political connections to the former top leader. Incumbent protégés in politically prominent positions (e.g. Chairmen of the Council of Ministers and of the Supreme Soviet, head of the People's Control Commission, heads of CC departments) were almost sure to be removed. Those in less visible posts or in posts requiring technical expertise (e.g., the heads of the Lithuanian Znaniye Society and the Archive Administration of the Council of Ministers) were retained. The experience of Snechkus holdovers indicates that certain *golden parachute* options were open to politicians desiring to maintain an elite status, i.e., they could move into positions that were politically less important but that carried some prestige and required specialized expertise or experience.

There were other incumbents within the political hierarchy who survived the leadership succession and who apparently maintained positions of authority in the new regime. A number of these politicians, for instance G.O. Zimanas, the "Lithuanian Suslov" (then the editor of the Lithuanian party theoretical organ, *Kommunist*), and Y.A. Bernatavichius, the former top agricultural specialist and aide to the First Secretary, had been close to Snechkus. Both were critical figures in the pre-1974 hierarchy. Neither remained as politically influential, but both maintained their elite status well into the new regime.

There was one important institution outside of the emerging Grishkiavichus coalition that continued to be headed by individuals who rose during the Snechkus regime: the Lithuanian security forces. Security force officials were a potential check on the party leadership, assuming watchdog functions for Moscow. During the 1970s, both top security forces' leaders were native Lithuanians, but neither was a protégé or client of Grishkiavichus. Y.U. Mikalauskas, the Minister of Internal Affairs, was a party apparatchik who had worked in that ministry since 1963, when he became deputy minister. Y.Y. Petkiavichius transferred into the Lithuanian KGB in 1960, and became its chairman in 1967. Both men had been involved in republic-level affairs since the mid–1950s.[14] They maintained their positions in the period after Grishkiavichus's selection, and Petkiavichius was even promoted back into the party *Buro* as a candidate member in 1976.[15]

Established elements in the Lithuanian political hierarchy thus could accommodate themselves to the new governing coalition, but mostly in less crucial posts or in settings outside of the new party leader's direct purview. Influential politicians in the party apparatus not linked to Grishkiavichus and his network were more expeditiously purged. There were certain relatively "independent" actors who represented potential constraints on the governing coalition. Operating behind the scenes was the Moscow-approved and non-Lithuanian second secretary. There was also an apparently more independent security forces sector, not penetrated by the local party machine, and at least partially responsible to national ministerial authorities. Although the governing network was institutionally strong, it was still subject to Moscow's scrutiny.

By the end of Grishkiavichus's first five years in power, he and his team had carved out a formidable niche within the top party and state organs. Few senior figures from the previous regime retained their positions. Some influential figures had been rotated, but they were to be found primarily in government posts. A growing number of Grishkiavichus associates had settled into the key political positions in the republic. The public posturing of the republic second secretary, and the close ties of national party functionaries monitoring the LCP, signified Moscow's awareness – and at least tacit approval – of these developments in Vilnius. The new party leader was firmly in control of his bailiwick.

Political change and the Lithuanian periphery

A patronage model of traditional Soviet politics predicts that lower-level political changes will directly result from higher-level personnel turnover. Assuming Moscow supports a new republic leadership, there should be minimal obstacles to the transformation of lower-level bodies. In the Lithuanian case, the turnover and rotation of republic-level officials did prove important to the politics of many subordinate regional party committees and major city organizations.

There was an almost immediate change in the Vilnius city and regional leaderships, with some protégés of the new Lithuanian leader moving up to republic-level posts with him and others advancing to key city organizational slots. Among these slots were the city's new First Secretary, V.V. Sakalauskas, and city executive committee chairman, A.-A.P. Vileikis. Meanwhile, Grishkiavichus selected a protégé and a client respectively as Vilnius regional first secretary and city second secretary.

Personnel changes in Vilnius were predictable, not only because of the prominence of the capital city, but because it was the immediate past domain of Grishkiavichus; yet comparable organizational changes also occurred in other major cities including Kaunas, Lithuania's second most important city. After a lengthy period of leadership stability during the Snechkus era, Kaunas underwent a major shift in the composition of its leadership. The "revitalization" of the Kaunas political elite began in 1975, when both the city party first secretary and executive committee chairman were removed. The Kaunas leadership had not had ties to Grishkiavichus. It represented a set of interests that traditionally competed with those of the capital city of Vilnius. There was a discernible past rivalry between the officials of these two major party organizations: a rivalry in which Kaunas politicians, by and large, had fared poorly. Was the shift in the Kaunas party leadership an attempt by the new republic leader to further consolidate his position in an area with fewer personal loyalties? Given that his major political rival, Ferensas, had made his early career in Kaunas and its Komsomol and party organizations, was this an effort to purge a hostile elite?[16] Or were these changes the result of pressures associated wth events such as the Spring 1972 student riots? Open manifestations of anti-Soviet nationalism had made the city's leadership vulnerable for some time; but it does not seem coincidental that its leadership was transformed only as the new regime was consolidating power. At the very least, the Kaunas establishment felt the pressure of that new regime.

The political links between the new First Secretary and his regime and other incumbent regional leaders were generally weak or nonexistent. The basic strategy was to reorganize regional party leaderships. Often leaders were rotated or demoted; only a minority of

regional first secretaries were permanently retired. These arrangements served to weaken what might have been Snechkus-era local
machines. Over one-third of the regional party committee first
secretaries were replaced during just the first two years of Grishkiavichus's tenure. Another third were replaced by the end of the power
consolidation period. The limited career data for the newly
appointed regional party leaders makes it difficult to identify these
politicians' career connections, if any, to past republic incumbents.
Relatively detailed biographical and career data were available for
only thirty of the new secretaries; even less information was available for their predecessors. Nevertheless, eight of the thirty newcomers could be identified as associates of Grishkiavichus. And in
tracing their placements among the forty-six regions, a recruitment
pattern emerges: these eight clients ended up in charge of some of
the most politically and economically important regions of the
republic.

Available Soviet data permit a rank ordering of the Lithuanian
regions and major cities according to their economic and political
importance. Relative economic importance was based on two
measures reflecting the agricultural and industrial productivity of
regions.[17] The relative political importance of regions was calculated
by determining the percentage of LCP members found in each
region.[18] Thus, we can consider the relationship between economic
and political importance of regions, likelihood of leadership change,
and likelihood of placement of Grishkiavichus associates.

Analyses of variance for the entire population of regions did not
yield statistically significant differences (at a 0.05 level of confidence)
in overall economic importance between Lithuanian regions where
leadership changes did and did not occur. But the relative industrial
importance – and the relative political importance – of regions did
differentiate between these regions at nearly a 0.05 level of confidence; and in examining the ten most politically important regions –
including the five largest cities in the republic – it was found that
leadership changes occurred in nine. The same results obtained for
the top ten economic regions. As the Lithuanian leadership was
being transformed in the wake of a succession, pressures for sub-
republic personnel changes were especially keen in the major cities
and priority regions.

These sub-republic leadership changes took an even greater significance because they often involved the selection of trusted associates of Grishkiavichus. The inclusion of the patronage element into

Table 5.6 *Analyses of variance among three populations of Lithuanian regions (no leadership change/change/change with recruitment of client), by economic and political importance*

Significance	N	Coefficient	Means	F-Statistic
Industrial Importance				
No change	23	0.0339		
Change	17	0.0065		
Change-client	9	0.0373		
Grand total	49	0.0107	7.83	0.001
Agricultural Importance				
No change	23	0.0106		
Change	17	0.0091		
Change-client	9	0.0093		
Grand total	49	0.0099	0.268	0.766
Economic Importance				
No change	23	0.0140		
Change	17	0.0156		
Change-client	9	0.0467		
Grand total	49	0.0206	9.07	0.001
Political Importance				
No change	22	0.0126		
Change	15	0.0149		
Change-client	9	0.0550		
Grand total	46	0.0217	6.45	0.004

an analysis of variance across three groups of regions (no leadership change, change, change-client) resulted in a statistically significant relationship between the importance of regions and leadership recruitment (Table 5.6). Associates of Grishkiavichus tended to be transferred into the most important regions. Of the nine politically significant regions that underwent leadership changes four involved the selection of a Grishkiavichus client. Similarly for the industrially and economically most significant regions, eight of the top ten underwent changes, and five of these involved the selection of clients.

It is difficult to assess the impact of these recruitment and regime formation patterns on the politics and life of the various regions. Soviet authorities did not publish the relevant regional-level industrial and agricultural productivity figures after 1974, so we cannot consider the policy implications of the Grishkiavichus network's penetration of regional party organizations. It should be noted, however, that after the consolidation of the new regime the ranks of the regional leaders stabilized. Personnel turnover was regularized and proceeded at a much slower pace. The republic party leader was not inclined toward the constant rotation and turnover of personnel – whether in the locales or in Vilnius. The Lithuanian cadres policy mirrored the "stability of cadres" tendency of the Brezhnev national regime.

In Lithuania, republic-level leadership change did affect lower-level officials, especially in the important regions. The emergence of a governing coalition, formed around the new party leader and his network, encompassed critical actors in the periphery, strengthening institutional connections to Vilnius. That governing coalition remained firmly in charge throughout Grishkiavichus's tenure.

Policy making in subnational settings

Assessing the policy implications of traditional regional-level patronage networks is challenging due to a paucity of information on the policy process at the subnational level. It is difficult to judge the relative power and influence of politicians beyond drawing inferences from their organizational affiliations and public profiles. Donna Bahry has demonstrated systematically the real resource constraints operating on subnational officials. Her work has revealed the limited latitude permitted these officials as they attempt to influence the policy process.[19] Moreover, republic newspapers and theoretical organs have not provided a sufficient number of speeches and articles by the various decision makers to permit a comprehensive analysis of issue debates; and, until recently, politicians were very reluctant to diverge from the CPSU line. They tended to pick up themes and positions already articulated elsewhere especially by the national leadership. Since the policy agenda was set in Moscow, at best we can examine the roles of top-level republic officials in presenting that agenda in their administrative domains.

Several propositions based on our knowledge of the Soviet system and past events, however, can help us consider the political implications of a patronage network *qua* governing coalition in a Soviet republic. First, forging a coalition based in part on patronage connections has helped to link key institutions and interests within an administrative unit. This was evident in the Lithuanian case, as strengthening the sluggish economy required the coordination of activities of various institutions, ranging from the transportation and

construction ministries, to the party organs overseeing those organizations, including the CC departments and the CC itself.[20] The thrust
of many public remarks made by responsible officials was that
greater coordination among these organizations was essential to
assure plan fulfillment. Criticisms from Moscow pointed to problems
in integrating the activities of republic, regional, and lower-level
institutions. The governing coalition developed by Grishkiavichus
embraced those institutional actors who could enhance the coordination of activities. The regime's recruitment strategy itself was
conducive to such coordination for it enabled the leadership to
bridge party and state organs in key areas through the selective
movement of officials.

Second, assuming Moscow's dominance of the political process, a
unified regional team was in a better position to implement the
broad policy program hammered out elsewhere. The parochial
interests of divergent institutions had to be merged even if positive
incentives to do so did not exist. A major role of republic leaders was
to guarantee such constraint across interests. Their positions were
strengthened if they stood atop large networks, and even larger
coalitions, that already encompassed the primary institutional actors.

Third, by forming a unified coalition, the republic or provincial
leader was better able to guarantee some political stability in that
region – a critical objective from Moscow's standpoint. The hierarchical, centralized decision-making structure of the Soviet system
limited the maneuverability of regional bosses, no matter how strong
their local positions. The system of both positive and negative
incentives further dissuaded regional leaders from veering out on
their own paths. During the Brezhnev period, the 1972 ouster of
Ukrainian party boss Piotr Shelest was an important reminder to any
republic leader of the consequences of deviating too much from
Moscow's line. Moscow attempted to deal with the pronounced
centrifugal tendencies in the periphery by appointing reliable representatives to positions of power and authority.

Did Moscow's confidence in these regions and their stability imply
that the local elite enjoyed limited discretion regarding policy
implementation? Was a region such as Lithuania susceptible to a
type of "feudal arrangement" in which the local "baron" and his
coterie had a certain degree of leverage vis-à-vis the center? If so,
what kind of discretion did they have?

The consolidation of power by a republic or provincial secretary
had limited relevance to the content of the policy agenda of the

region. The constraints set by Moscow were too great to allow more than limited discretion; yet, considering the tasks associated with the implementation of that policy agenda, there is evidence that the republic leader does have some discretionary political power. Bunce's work on investment allocations in the Soviet system demonstrated that there were marginal changes in expenditures when a republic leadership changed, just as occurred at the national level with successions.[21] Although certain expenditure patterns remained constant (e.g., allocations to heavy industry), others were subject to change (e.g., allocations to consumer goods). Bunce's investigation of nearly a dozen republics in the 1970s indicated that agricultural investments were also affected by leadership successions. There was some room for leverage across varied regional settings. The national leadership's evaluation of the political reliability of a regional party organization determined whether such leverage would be granted. Our assessment of the impact of a region's stable governing elite on its policy agenda depends in great measure upon our understanding of the decision-making process at this intermediate level of authority. It is clear that regional leaders were constrained by Moscow, but it is uncertain to what extent they were inhibited by their own peers and subordinates. The Shelest case in Ukraine also demonstrated that regional leaders were constrained by events and forces operating within their own republic. Building the political might and authority to master potential forces of change was extremely important in maintaining Moscow's favor and one's own power.

Republic leaders' authority stemmed not only from their organizational strengths but from assuming a public profile that would allow them to guide the public policy discussion. It also stemmed from the performance record of their regime. One way to assess the position of such leaders is to examine their role in the ongoing public discussion of the party's program. Were the republic party leaders presenting the agenda, raising the primary issues and articulating the appropriate approaches? As they consolidated their own base of power, to what extent did they become preeminent in any such discussion? Were there contrasting views and did they cover anything beyond the means of policy implementation?

In considering the party leader's role in the policy discussion we must distinguish between what I understand as "high" and "low" politics at the subnational level. My focus is on the general policy program offered by the CPSU and the way it was restated by the republic or regional party apparatus, i.e., "high politics" at the subnational level. This is to be distinguished from technical matters, or issues simply involving means of implementation of those policy thrusts, i.e., "low politics." As Idzelis notes in his study of the branch principle in Soviet and Lithuanian planning and management, matters of organization and implementation can have important implications not only for the economy but for political stability within a province. Debates among specialists over territorial planning or branch planning could be important because advocacy of the former could represent an attempt to advance the interests of the region and its native population. But while policy-relevant, these matters do not structure the actual debate among politicians; they more likely reflect the concerns of specialists responsible for administering the "high politics" directives of the politicians.[22] I am therefore more interested in assessing the party, network, and governing coalition leader's role in presenting Moscow's agenda to his republic constituency.

Grishkiavichus and the Lithuanian policy agenda

The Lithuanian policy discussion of the mid-1970s was structured by two important considerations. First, the republic generally evinced a stability not characteristic of most other republics; but, second were the concerns that had arisen in Moscow over the republic's economy and the LCP's ability to cope with Lithuanian nationalism and religious observance. These concerns were publicly expressed in a major speech delivered by the Second Secretary, Valery Kharazov, to an LCP CC Plenum in November 1973. They were followed up by comments made by the national party ideologist Mikhail Suslov, who criticized "shortcomings" in Lithuania said to encompass economic failures and problems of anti-Soviet nationalism.[23] Two months later the republic was in the throes of a succession.

The context for the policy agenda during the early phase of Grishkiavichus's tenure was determined by Moscow and identified by both Suslov and Kharazov. They proclaimed that an era of political lethargy had set in, and they portrayed the LCP leadership as less energetic in coping with an ever-complicated agenda of political, social, and economic issues. The national leadership's critique of the republic centered on three broad sets of concerns: (1) growth problems in the Lithuanian economy; (2) challenges to the ideology and culture posed by new manifestations of anti-Soviet nationalism; and (3) shortcomings in the work of the LCP that extended to the primary party organization level. The public remarks made by Suslov and Kharazov laid out the broad contours of these problems but did not detail specific solutions. In fact, Kharazov's comments to the November 1973 CC Plenum restated in the Lithuanian context many points made by General Secretary Brezhnev on recent trips to Ukraine and Kazakhstan.[24]

What was Kharazov's role in the Lithuanian setting? Second secretaries, usually Slavs drawn from outside of the republic to which they are posted, traditionally assumed an overseeing role for the Moscow leadership in the periphery. Because second secretaries were directly accountable to the CPSU apparatus and CC, some scholars have viewed them as the main political actors responsible for cadres selection in the republic, and thus consider them the republic's prime political movers.[25] They have even been viewed as the top decision makers within the republic.[26] Most observers have stressed their role as a watchdog and mouthpiece of Moscow in the periphery. Second secretaries' power, however, has been constrained by the relative brevity of their service in the republics. The five politicians who served as Lithuania's second secretary from 1955 through 1980, for instance, only remained there an average of five years – a figure only slightly above the average for all republic second secretaries.[27] Generally, second secretaries had not previously served in the republics for which they assumed short-term responsibility, and when they left these positions, they usually moved into other territorial units with different types of responsibility.[28] As a consequence, second secretaries were in a better position to *monitor* republic politics and officials than they were to direct them. Kharazov's length of service, relatively low profile, and subsequent transfer out of Lithuania, were typical. He trumpeted Moscow's concerns before the succession, but afterwards the new party boss dominated the discussion, setting out the broad tasks before the republic and its leadership.

During the first years of the new regime Grishkiavichus assumed an immediate high profile in addressing the range of issues on the political agenda. His speeches and published articles treated those issues in detail and suggested concrete solutions. In an April 1974 speech before the LCP *aktiv*, Grishkiavichus offered his first comprehensive discussion of the republic's issue agenda. He highlighted the accomplishments and dilemmas of priority sectors (e.g., Lithuania's dairy and meat industry). Referring to Brezhnev's recent speech in Alma-Ata on agricultural issues, he offered a similar set of

comments and solutions,[29] Grishkiavichus picked up other Brezhnev
themes as he provided a *tour d'horizon* of Lithuanian economic
difficulties. Problems with capital construction, transportation and
distribution of produce were discussed in detail. He identified
problem-ridden regions and organizations.[30] Grishkiavichus made
these public criticisms while instituting leadership changes in those
sectors and recruiting his associates into influential positions.

Public appearances provided the republic party boss with the
opportunity to congratulate and chide regional and local party and
state organs for economic successes and failures.[31] While he spoke,
his network performed: members attended lower-level organizational meetings and effected personnel changes stemming from
Grishkiavichus's criticisms. During the first year and a half of the
new regime, organizational meetings occurred in such important
cities and regions as Vilnius, Kaunas, and Shvenchensky.[32] Officials
from the First Secretary's old domain within the CC apparatus –
some of them protégés or clients – were the senior officials in
attendance as lower-level leadership questions were entertained.[33]
They often oversaw the recomposition of lower-level leaderships
through the recruitment of Grishkiavichus loyalists.

During his first year as party leader Grishkiavichus focused on
reviving the republic's economy, but as his regime was consolidated
he devoted more attention to a broader range of concerns, including
ideology and culture.[34] The Supreme Soviet election campaign of
1975 provided him and other leaders with an opportunity to survey
the accomplishments (largely economic) of the past year. Meanwhile,
he pointed out specific shortcomings that merited the personnel
changes that would continue during the next few years.[35]

In the public discussions of his early years of rule Grishkiavichus
coopted themes raised by Moscow – including those articulated by
Kharazov in late 1973 – to link a broad program of directives with the
Lithuanian leadership. For example, his September 1975 CC Plenum
speech again stressed the Brezhnev themes of specialization and
concentration of agricultural production on the basis of "inter-
enterprise cooperation" and "agro-industrial integration". He
described these as providing the "main direction for the future
growth of agriculture". By the end of this power consolidation
period, he had addressed the major concerns of his superiors and
suggested solutions fully compatible with their line. In the mean-
time, through appointments, he had consolidated his own position
within the Lithuanian hierarchy.

Where Grishkiavichus dealt with the broad agenda, the details were left to be developed by others. Other top politicians assumed supporting roles in the public discussion of the regime's early years. Grishkiavichus's main rival, Ferensas, assumed a high public profile, making a number of speeches and attending several major party meetings.[36] By virtue of his senior secretarial position, his comments were focused almost exclusively upon the major economic issues of the day: matters of capital construction, methods of improving plan fulfillment and trade across economic sectors, and solutions to structural problems undercutting Lithuania's productivity; but, as Grishkiavichus's position strengthened Ferensas's profile lessened. His demotion in late Spring 1977 left him outside of the major policy-making bodies, though he retained his CC membership throughout the entire Grishkiavichus era.[37]

Other leading politicians, such as the Premier Jozas Maniushis, Supreme Soviet Chairman Antanas Barkauskus, and Grishkiavichus client (and soon to be LCP Secretary for Culture) Lenginas Shepetis, also assumed public profiles, but their roles were to provide specific information on their areas of special responsibility.[38] Their role was to support, and not to initiate, as they reacted to themes set out by Grishkiavichus.

As the regime consolidated power, Second Secretary Kharazov assumed a lower public profile. While addressing himself to the broader political issues raised in his November 1973 address, he focused on more limited party organizational concerns. His criticisms of party practices within specific regional and local organizations were fully compatible with Grishkiavichus's political interests. For instance, in his address to the March 1975 CC Plenum, he directed special attention to shortcomings in the Kaunas gorkom.[39] Indeed, he chided K.K. Lengvinas, its first secretary, for not following up on criticisms of the Kaunas gorkom's ideological-cultural work that had been raised in a 1971 LCP *Buro* meeting. Kharazov had had a higher public profile before the 1974 succession.[40] Now he merely trumpeted the specific concerns of Moscow, instead of providing a comprehensive treatment of the state of the economy or of other issues of republic-wide importance.[41] His public suggestions to *Buro* members (and the LCP generally) that they be more self-critical and develop "the moral and political qualities" required of "the modern leader" were delivered while the *Buro* and LCP apparatus were already undergoing personnel changes initiated by Grishkiavichus.

The guiding position Grishkiavichus assumed in the republic's public political discussion by late 1975 remained throughout his tenure. It was reinforced by his network's expanding base of power. He had primary responsibility for laying out the party's program as it applied to Lithuania, adopting the critical themes and concerns articulated by the national leadership. He was the primary figure who publicly acknowledged the shortcomings of party and state organs and leaders; other top network and coalition members only supplemented his pronouncements and discussions.

Grishkiavichus's authority was reflected in his high public profile and his leading role in the policy discussion. It was enhanced by the republic's strong economic performance. Lithuanian industrial productivity rates, for instance, were growing well above the national average.[42] The negative trends of the latter Snechkus years were reversed and the republic experienced economic growth rates placing it among the leaders of the fifteen republics. While there were continued incidents of Lithuanian nationalism, the LCP leadership's containment efforts were more successful than the efforts of neighboring republics.[43]

The position of the republic first secretary in his own region and *vis-à-vis* Moscow suggested a feudal power arrangement. This arrangement strengthened the position of national authorities within the country's extensive and diverse periphery. Moscow's broad objectives were realized as the regional patron articulated the CPSU line, maintained social and political stability, and supervised sustained economic growth. In return, the patron first secretary enjoyed significant organizational and political discretion in consolidating his position and that of his group. In this system the continued goodwill of the political center assured the authoritative position of the favored regional patron. This remained true until the late 1980s, when democratization and power decentralization began to transform the rules of the political game, and Lithuanian politicians struggled to adapt.

Democratic reform and the transformation of network politics

We have seen that the overriding policy goals of the early Gorbachev regime departed considerably from those of preceding regimes. In their desire to restructure the economy and society, national reformers were intent on opening up subnational politics. This meant dismantling conservative regional and local leaderships and recruiting new officials who shared those reformist visions. In Lithuania, and eventually in all republics, national reformist pressures not only undermined subnational party organizations but gave rise to the emergence of unexpectedly strong popular fronts which weakened the hold of traditional patronage networks.

Pressures on the Lithuanian leadership emerged even before the death of Grishkiavichus on November 14, 1987. The *glasnost* campaign enunciated by senior national officials found immediate resonance in the republic. LCP politicians found themselves under immediate pressure to initiate political and economic reforms. Grishkiavichus and his colleagues, as products of the Brezhnev era, were wary of the openness initiative, and their network was quite strong. By Grishkiavichus's last LCP Congress in January 1986, the majority of all *Buro* and Secretariat members were his associates. His network and regime were hesitant to respond to mounting pressures; they won few friends in Moscow or Vilnius.

Grishkiavichus's successor, Ringaudas-Bronislovas Songaila, the long-serving Agriculture Secretary (1962–85) and Supreme Soviet Presidium Chairman (since 1985), was a protégé who continued the cautious policy toward openness and democratization.[44] While there was some personnel rotation, during Songaila's short eleven-month tenure the Grishkiavichus network remained strong. Among the top political bodies, only two *Buro* members, one LCP secretary, six CC department heads, nine ministers, and three regional party leaders were replaced. Appointments suggested the routine movement of personnel and many of those recruited were already part of the established network. The most noteworthy of these changes was the appointment of Grishkiavichus associate Astrauskas to the Supreme Soviet Presidium chairmanship.[45]

Songaila's rise and power consolidation coincided with the accelerated growth of pro-democracy forces in the republic and a growing pressure for subnational reform from Moscow. During 1988 many official groups (e.g., the Lithuanian Writers' Union) gained heightened independence, and iconoclastic informal groups such as Sajudis emerged.[46] Meanwhile, Moscow officials pressured the Vilnius leadership to be more responsive to the reform interests of these groups. Aleksandr Yakovlev's well-publicized visit to Lithuania on August 11–13, 1988 made the intentions of national reformers clear: the LCP leadership was explicitly advised to be more active in promoting *perestroika* and democratization.[47] Yakovlev conveyed the central regime's desire that the LCP work with the popular front and other societal interests; he suggested a cooptive rather than confrontational strategy.

Songaila did not prove adept in responding to the mounting challenges. In his first major speech as party leader, delivered to the January 1988 LCP CC Plenum, Songaila criticized nearly all top officials and departments for past performances and emphasized their need to implement reforms.[48] He adopted a cautious public position on developments in the republic that lent nothing to the momentum for political change. In fact his regime paid lip-service to reform efforts while emphasizing greater party and society-wide "discipline": a euphemism for repression of the growing informal groups. Songaila and other leaders emphasized the dangers of extremists who were said to manipulate nationalist themes and to advocate Lithuanian independence. His regime's attitude toward Sajudis was clearly hostile.

The Songaila regime attempted to balance its conservative, status quo, political preferences with some concessions on selected issues that were important to the broader society. LCP delegates to the XIX CPSU Conference supported greater Lithuanian autonomy and an opening up of the political process. But Songaila did not cede any significant powers to Sajudis or other societal representatives; and in his address to the XIX CPSU Conference, he commented on the party's need to enhance its influence over popular movements and informal groups.[49] The October 1988 Lithuanian Supreme Soviet's approval of the old national flag, anthem, and holiday was the regime's final action to appease Lithuanian nationalists without sacrificing real political power.[50] But the use of force by police against Vilnius demonstrators only a week earlier had revealed the regime's real intentions *and* abilities in dealing with the mounting democratization challenge. The governing network was clearly on the defensive.

Within weeks of the late September violence senior members of the regime were publicly distancing themselves from the policy actions and Songaila was forced from office.[51] The new LCP First Secretary, Al'girdas Brazauskas, immediately tried to separate his regime from that of his predecessor: in his first press conference, he expressed serious reservations about Songaila's ability to cope with the challenges of reform noting that mistakes had been made.[52] He even wished Sajudis well and called for mutual understanding with the LCP. Brazauskas quickly proved to be a different kind of politician – one who was more flexible and conciliatory in confronting the now considerable political forces operating outside the party establishment.

Brazauskas had risen under the sponsorship of Grishkiavichus to occupy a senior position in the regime. He was experienced and technically adept, having served for over twenty years in the industrial and construction sectors; but he differed from his predecessors in temperament and style: he was independent minded and innovative in tackling policy problems.[53] As LCP leader, he proved to be an able competitor in the more open and democratic Lithuanian political arena; but his ability to draw popular support and to work with Sajudis and other challengers not only necessitated major policy changes; it depended upon the dislodgement of traditional network politics.

Brazauskas initiated major leadership changes almost immediately. In early Fall 1988 there had been public calls for the ouster of various senior officials, including the unpopular Ideology Secretary Shepetis and the Moscow-selected Russian Second Secretary Nikolai Mit'kin. There was strong public pressure to appoint officials who articulated pro-reform lines. Yet Brazauskas appeared to desire distance from the increasingly discredited ruling political machine. Although part of that machine, he increasingly distinguished himself from it in his expressed views. It is not clear to what extent he actively worked against his senior colleagues, but his personnel and organizational decisions resulted in the removal of many top officials. Mit'kin was replaced by the more popular, though ethnically Russian, Vladimir Berezov, who had been more responsive to Lithuanian interests; Shepetis was unceremoniously removed from the *Buro*; and Supreme Soviet Presidium Chairman Astrauskas and Premier Sakalauskas were "retired" in the wake of electoral defeats. Beyond these high-level changes, an impressive number of other republic and regional officials were ousted: from Brazauskas's selection as republic leader October 20, 1988 to V. Landsbergis's election as Lithuanian President March 11, 1990, all *Buro* and Secretariat members (excluding Brazauskas himself), eleven CC department heads, sixteen ministers, and thirty-two regional first secretaries were replaced! In fewer than eighteen months Brazauskas accomplished what Grishkiavichus had needed over a decade to do. Beyond the sheer numbers, the turnover also entailed the recruitment of officials from outside of the Vilnius establishment. Most of those recruited were younger, post-Stalin generation officials, from middle-rank or regional settings, and *not* part of the Grishkiavichus network. New senior officials such as K.V. Glaviatskas and I.-V.I. Paletskis were recruited from outside the mainstream party apparatus; their reputations had not been tarnished by the Snechkus–Grishkiavichus record.

These personnel changes were important in helping Brazauskas consolidate his position and build authority with the Lithuanian populace, but in the increasingly open and decentralized Lithuanian political arena his stated political views were more important. Brazauskas exhibited a willingness to work with Sajudis. In a speech to its founding congress within days of becoming Lithuanian First Secretary, Brazauskas said the LCP leadership was now making "a new, more objective political assessment" and that it was "capable of adjusting its activity in a self-critical way."[54] Regarding Sajudis, he commented that "on fundamental questions we [the LCP and Sajudis] are of one mind and can cooperate fruitfully." Yet from the beginning, his policy approach was multifaceted: he demonstrated a commitment to promoting Lithuanian aspirations while maintaining working relations with national authorities. He was a champion of reform, but reform within the system. Among Lithuanian reformers, he was a moderate, attempting to bridge the LCP establishment, more mainstream elements within Sajudis, and national reformers. Thus, in November 1988, under his influence, the Lithuanian Supreme Soviet chose not to follow Estonia's lead and failed to pass a Sajudis-backed declaration on Lithuanian national sovereignty, but it did declare Lithuanian the official language of the republic. A few months later, at the February 1989 LCP CC Plenum, the party leadership condemned what it described as the growing radicalism and extremism of Sajudis. But the same Plenum also ousted Shepetis, replacing him with the more moderate Valerionas Baltrunas.

Brazauskas took an approach to power consolidation that diverged from that of his predecessors and his counterparts at the national level. His power and authority came to rest upon his own popular standing and his image of being a new style politician equipped to help Lithuania make the transition toward greater sovereignty and pluralism. The backing of the LCP organization became less important to his immediate political needs; in fact, to became a liability as he approached popular elections.

Structural changes in the system and new political conditions necessitated this different power-consolidating strategy. A multiparty system was emerging, as was a more decentralized political process. Power was increasingly shared among competing political interests. Leaders were more openly accountable to the broader society, as the now less regulated media applied growing pressure on all political actors. Dozens of Sajudis publications were issued; for the first time, a rival organization had effectively challenged the LCP.[55]

As the 1980s came to an end, Sajudis – and not the LCP – was driving the republic's issue agenda.[56] The LCP and regime were exposed to more direct outside scrutiny, subject to newly legitimate notions of public accountability, and left vulnerable to competitive secret-ballot elections. It was these elections – first to the national Congress of People's Deputies (CPD) and then to the republic Supreme Soviet – that altered the regime and displaced the remnants of the old network. They revealed that the network and the LCP no longer had a lock on political power.

Sajudis was formally legalized on March 16, 1989 – just days before the CPD elections. Its strength was so great that it could afford to withdraw its candidates running against both Brazauskas and Second Secretary Berezov to help ensure that these party reformers would be elected. This self-confidence was vindicated by the election results: only one candidate officially backed by Sajudis lost in the elections. Moreover, the results constituted a dramatic political setback for the LCP, as highly visible candidates such as Astrauskas and Sakalauskas, among other *Buro* members, were overwhelmingly defeated. Even younger and more recently appointed LCP officials fared poorly (e.g., S.A. Gedraitis and B.A. Zaikauskas).

The turbulence of Lithuanian domestic politics stemmed from the political calculus of national reformers. Both political instability and reform were intended to help reinvigorate the country's economy; but the situation was dynamic and developments went beyond what was anticipated. Moscow's reading of the situation in Vilnius changed as the LCP became unable – or unwilling – to channel developments. In Fall 1988 the reform program of the LCP and Sajudis was characterized as reasonable, but by February 1989 Moscow emphasized LCP timidity in responding to challenges coming from an ever more extremist Sajudis.[57] The May 18, 1989 Lithuanian Supreme Soviet approval of an amendment granting the republic sovereignty was a critical first step taken by the Lithuanian leadership in its march toward full republic independence. Less than a year later, the republic formally broke away.

An important consequence of Gorbachevian reforms was the

fracturing of the LCP into more and less reformist factions. Brazauskas and the "moderates" worked with Sajudis, attempting to coopt national independence efforts. More orthodox officials adopted conciliatory reformist stances.[58] But mounting pressures led to the late 1989 convocation of the XX LCP Congress to approve more radical policy change.[59] The result was a further transformation of the leadership ranks, an even more explicit acknowledgment of past policy mistakes, an acceptance of a more limited role for the LCP in the republic's political life, and the enunciation of the LCP's independence. The LCP took the first formal steps in restructuring its relationship with the CPSU; but in the process the established political machine left by Grishkiavichus was ruptured.

What drove the LCP leadership to adopt this radical platform? Most importantly, party officials were reacting to the dilemmas posed by a more open and democratic political arena; they understood that the party would not survive another overwhelming electoral defeat that was anticipated if their public positions were not further altered.[60] Perhaps ironically – but to save the LCP – most remaining senior members of the old network and their supporters joined together at the Congress to overwhelmingly approve (855 of 1,033 delegates) the LCP declaration of independence. Brazauskas and Berezov, together with J.-V.J. Paleckas (Ideology Secretary) and K.V. Glavechas (Economic Affairs Secretary) assumed leadership of the now explicitly pro-independence LCP. Unpopular officials such as Astrauskas and Sakalauskas were completely dropped – even from CC membership. Within weeks it was apparent that this new reformist group had pulled nearly two-thirds of the overall LCP membership to its ranks.

But the LCP leadership was no longer united. Approximately 160 Congress delegates split and formed an LCP based on the CPSU's nationality platform. Led by the conservative historian, M.M. Burokevichius, its leadership included mostly minor figures from past regimes. Although the CPSU broke formal ties with the reformist LCP and recognized this LCP-CPSU Platform faction, it still understood the considerable clout of the former. Thus, in his remarks to the February 1990 CPSU CC Plenum, Gorbachev concluded that "separatist sentiments" prevailed in Lithuania, but he recommended that the CPSU "show maximum restraint, respect, and attentiveness" in its attitude toward the LCP.[61]

Beyond the LCP split, the structural political reforms of 1988–89 resulted in a more profound outcome: the transfer of power to

Sajudis in March 1990. Sajudis officials had begun to assume formal positions nearly a year earlier (e.g., the July 1989 selection of Kazimera Prunskene as Deputy Premier), but the 1990 elections enabled Sajudis to form the first non-Communist republic government in modern Soviet history. Brazauskas, who had assumed the Lithuanian presidency in early 1990, was forced to turn it over to Sajudis leader Vytatus Landsbergis just two months later. With that transfer of power, a new democratic phase was ushered in.

The transformation of Lithuanian political life clearly affected the conduct of Soviet center–periphery relations. Developments not only in Vilnius but throughout the Baltic permitted the forging of intra-Baltic linkages. In little more than a year, the establishment of various formal and informal political, economic, and societal links (e.g., the May 1989 Baltic Council and the September 1989 Baltic Parliamentary Council) constituted a new collective Baltic posturing vis-à-vis Moscow.[62] In addition to the profound changes in Vilnius, the breakdown of a once reliable political machine and the demo-cratization of a republic's political process contributed to the reali-zation of a long-held Moscow fear: the emergence of a common anti-Soviet front both within one republic and across several others.

The demise of Lithuanian patronage politics?

Did the developments of 1988–90 constitute the demise of patronage politics in Lithuania? At the very least, the political reforms signifi-cantly weakened the dominant machine and made it very difficult for officials to transfer power and authority to favored subordinates. The means used by politicians to achieve power and authority had changed. Brazauskas relied upon his own popular standing – instead of a dominating network – to maintain his authority. This strategy proved effective, as his popularity rating throughout 1989 and early 1990 remained higher than that of any other politician or organi-zation, including Sajudis.[63] But Brazauskas could not transfer these fluid resources – popularity and authority – to other politicians or the LCP; and their defeat left him unable to retain the top leadership position.

As the 1990s began, the CPSU no longer controlled the levers of power that had once assured its decisive control of Lithuania. The most fundamental lever, i.e. the ability to direct personnel decisions, was gone.[64] And the basic thinking of most Lithuanian politicians was transformed, as their actions were increasingly motivated by democratic norms. Deputy Premier Prunskene succinctly captured that changed thinking in comments made during Gorbachev's January 1990 visit to Vilnius:

> The members of the former republic party organization chose independence for the LCP, having their own reasons for doing so. For me it was, among other things, a means of getting out of an internal contradiction involving the incompatibility of participating in a democratic movement and, simultaneously, in a party with deeply rooted traditions of iron rule – a party that has even subordinated the Constitution to that rule – of being in the same party with people, some people of dubious reputation, fervent opponents of democracy and of restructuring itself . . . . (*Pravda*, January 15, 1990)

Moscow's democratization drive had transformed Lithuanian politics. The March 11, 1990 Lithuanian decision to void the USSR and Soviet Lithuanian constitutions opened a new page in Soviet history. But when we turn to another republic rocked by political changes, Azerbaidzhan, we find a very different situation. Here domestic pressures and pressures from Moscow severely taxed a long-dominant network and led to several leadership changes. But unlike Lithuania, the reform program could not alter the basic norms and fundamental importance of patronage politics.

6   Azerbaidzhan and the Aliev network

Both the national and Lithuanian studies revealed how the structural conditions of the traditional Soviet system encouraged patronage networks to flourish. We have also seen, however, how changes in those underlying conditions have altered the norms by which officials are recruited and regimes are formed. Looking beyond the Slavic and Baltic settings, cultural and institutional structures have given patronage networks a special buoyancy in the Transcaucasian and Central Asian republics.[1] Azerbaidzhan has had an especially strong reputation for pervasive mafia-type networks. Azerbaidzhani patron–client relationships have been rooted in geographical and clan ties that transcended the political rivalries of the Soviet period. Local mafias flourished in Azerbaidzhan, seemingly removed from the direct influences of outside actors even though events in Baku were closely monitored by Moscow[2]. Azerbaidzhan is an especially appropriate setting to consider the conduct and consequences of patronage politics. We can put our earlier findings in perspective by identifying elite recruitment and regime formation norms in Azerbaidzhan and by examining the complex evolution of Soviet center–periphery relations in another regional setting. We can also consider the constraints on national regimes that attempt to root out subnational patronage networks.[3]

The structure of the Azerbaidzhani policy process and the manner of power distribution within the republic are similar to those of Lithuania, but the dilemmas of Azerbaidzhani elite politics must be considered against a background of general domestic stability. Azerbaidzhan and its party organization were traditionally among the most stable and politically reliable of the non-Russian and Muslim republics. Its geopolitical significance made it a priority for national authorities from the earliest days of Soviet power. Azerbaidzhan's reliability was a function, in part, of its pre-Soviet past.

Unlike its regional neighbors, it did not have one national, historical, and cultural tradition that marked it as a distinct geopolitical unit.[4] Historically, the nationalism that was an ongoing concern in many non-Russian republics was not especially salient in Azerbaidzhani politics. Unlike Lithuania, Azerbaidzhan had little anti-Soviet nationalistic activity. Before the developments of the *perestroika* period, there were no significant alienated Azerbaidzhani intellectual groups and no viable samizdat. Although Moscow had been compelled to reassert its will on a number of occasions in different Transcaucasian and Central Asian republics, this had not been necessary in Azerbaidzhan. Economically, it was a key non-Slavic unit within the USSR, especially because of its wealth in energy resources. Its political reliability and economic productivity served as a model for other Transcaucasian republics as well as for neighboring non-Soviet states.

As we have seen, traditional Soviet center–periphery relations have had a feudal nature. In the Azerbaidzhani case, the presence or absence of Moscow's support has been critical to the functioning and fate of its regimes. Beyond this, however, the Azerbaidzhani case provides graphic evidence of the functional and dysfunctional dimensions of political patronage in the Soviet system. A regime could emerge and a patronage network consolidate power and govern the republic for a considerable time period. A regime's fate ultimately rested on Moscow's evaluation of the economic and political consequences of the network's governance, but even where those consequences were disastrous, it would be replaced by another regime that rapidly evolved into a new governing network. The emergence of a dominant network could allow a political and economic reinvigoration of the republic, as occurred in the 1970s. It could also result in policy inertia. A review of Azerbaidzhani politics in the 1970s and 1980s, however, reveals compelling evidence of a regional network's staying power, even in the face of considerable pressures from above and below. Indeed, Azerbaidzhani elite politics of the 1970–90 period demonstrate the *resilience* of patron–client relationships, even in the face of a national regime that was actively opposing them.

Azerbaidzhan of the Brezhnev period

A plenum of the Azerbaidzhani party CC was unexpectedly convened on 14 July, 1969 to consider the serious political and economic problems that had arisen over the previous decade. A day later *Bakinsky Rabochy* announced the transfer of the First Secretary Veli U. Akhundov to a position in the Azerbaidzhani Academy of Sciences and his replacement by the republic's KGB Chairman Geidar Aliev. Akhundov, just months earlier elected a member of the Azerbaidzhani Academy of Sciences, had been the republic's party leader for a decade of relative political tranquility. He had moved quickly into the top republic party position, having been a party secretary and the Chairman of the republic Council of Ministers only a year before his ascent as party boss of Azerbaidzhan. His ten-year rule, however, proved unexceptional. His rise to power had been linked with an effort to revive the moribund Azerbaidzhani economy. His strong ties to Nikita Khrushchev could have helped him reinvigorate the republic; but, by the end of the 1960s the republic's economy had failed to recover; its growth rate was still low in comparison with other Soviet republics. In addition, the republic party organization's corruption and political incompetence contributed to the republic's economic woes. These problems were hardly new, but their presence confirmed that Akhundov had done little better than his discredited predecessors.

The 1969 leadership change and the subsequent evolution of Azerbaidzhani politics was a direct result of the deteriorating state of the republic's economy and party organizational problems. The Azerbaidzhani economy had been stagnating, in comparison not only with most other Soviet republics, but with its regional neighbors as well. The deterioration that began during the 1960s was indicated by various measures of the republic's economic strength, including industrial labor productivity, overall industrial productivity, and growth of national income. Compared with other Soviet republics, Azerbaidzhan's overall performance during Akhundov's ten years in power was ranked twelfth, fourteenth, and fifteenth respectively for these productivity indicators.[5] These results did little to commend Akhundov and his regime to the national authorities.

The economic troubles of Azerbaidzhan in the 1960s could not be dissociated from longer-term developmental trends. The oil reserves, which long had been the basis for the expansion of the Azerbaidzhani economy, were greatly depleted. Although the republic's economy expanded in the 1950s and 1960s with the development of machine building and other industries, the low level of technology and the need for highly trained personnel constrained more rapid expansion. From the end of World War II to the July 1969 Plenum, the republic had the lowest rate of industrial growth of any Soviet republic. Natural gas exploitation, mining, and the production of cement (a major export to over thirty countries by the mid-1970s) also provided some potential for economic growth. But the limited amount of arable land made economic expansion in the agricultural domain highly unlikely. National expenditures for agriculture were more likely to be targeted to Georgia, Kazakhstan, and Uzbekistan where agricultural industries were much stronger and had more pull in Moscow than in Azerbaidzhan.[6]

As the Azerbaidzhani economy suffered these slowdown problems, the party apparatus came under mounting attack for serious organizational problems. Criticisms were directed at performance failures associated with corruption, matters of party discipline, and what were termed problems of "localism" in the recruitment, placement, and functioning of cadres. The public discussion of cronyism and local networks continued throughout the 1960s. By the May 1966 CPSU CC Plenum, even General Secretary Brezhnev was publicly criticizing the Azerbaidzhani leadership for neglect in monitoring the republic's economic growth. He cited organizational corruption as a major problem requiring prompt attention. A July 7, 1966 *Pravda* article explicitly criticized the Azerbaidzhani leadership for such shortcomings.[7] Although these problems were hardly new to the republic, its party leadership was held responsible for not adequately addressing them.

Akhundov's regime proved rather complacent: there were few policy changes in Baku's efforts to resolve the republic's economic woes and party organizational problems. The culpability of the Akhundov group was made known after the July 1969 CC Plenum, when most top republic leaders were publicly criticized as either participating in or condoning corrupt mafia networks. As a result, Akhundov was "retired" to an academic position.[8] Yet this routine leadership change, with the comfortable retirement of a party boss into privileged obscurity, proved to be but the first step in a major transformation of Azerbaidzhan's leadership. Within five years of Akhundov's ouster and Aliev's succession, the republic's political elite was almost entirely reconstituted. This transformation of the Azerbaidzhani political elite was an ongoing process that continued throughout the First Secretary's thirteen-year tenure. A large number of incumbents were ousted and many new cadres – often tied to the new party leader and from outside the republic party apparatus – were moved into positions of responsibility. This leadership turnover involved most party and state organizations, and it extended into nearly all of the regional and major city party organizations. An Aliev patronage network would rapidly come to dominate Azerbaidzhani politics for the next decade.

Aliev's policy of extensive and regularized personnel transfer proved to be an important component of his strategy to combat resistant regional officials. Such resistance generally resulted when subordinates – especially those in the periphery – became institutionally ensconced, developing comfortable political arrangements that enabled them to hold on to power. The rotation of cadres helped Aliev and his regime weaken these arrangements by keeping the political scene fluid. During the initial power consolidation period (1969–74) this cadres turnover involved ousters of Akhundov and other influential incumbents and affected the mobility of new personnel. It later increasingly entailed the periodic shifting of individuals across regions and organizations. The political consequences for Aliev were positive, as Azerbaidzhani productivity data revealed considerable growth and a much better national standing during his tenure. This economic turnaround more than caught the national leadership's attention and by the early 1980s Aliev was a full member of the CPSU Politburo and had been coopted into a senior government position in Moscow. The extent of the free hand given Aliev after the July 1969 Plenum reflected not only the high degree of Moscow's concern over the domestic deterioration that had set in over the previous decade. It reflected the importance of Azerbaidzhan to Moscow's broader regional calculations.

Aliev and the transformation of the party elite

The selection of KGB Chairman Aliev to head the Azerbaidzhani party organization represented a different succession strategy that had important consequences for the governing political elite.[9] In essence, one clientelistic network was replaced with another. The new network was made up of politicians who had moved up a hierarchical ladder other than that of the central republic party apparatus in Baku. This group of officials rose in the republic KGB and security forces apparats; many had served in the Nakhichevan ASSR. By the early 1970s, these "non-party" officials, most of whom were native Azerbaidzhanis, had assumed the central position in a new constellation of political actors.

Aliev had been in charge of the Azerbaidzhani KGB since 1966.

His roots were in the Nakhichevan ASSR, and his career was almost exclusively in the security forces apparatus. He had worked in the organs of internal affairs since 1941, serving in both Nakhichevan and Baku. His growing prominence within Azerbaidzhan became evident only in 1964, when he was appointed deputy chairman of the Azerbaidzhani KGB. At the time of his 1969 selection as party First Secretary he was not even a member of the republic party *Buro*, let alone a party secretary. He became a full Azerbaidzhani CC member – a necessary prerequisite for republic-level political elite status – only at that July 1969 Plenum.

The organizational and policy expectations associated with this new party boss diverged from those associated with a party apparatchik whose political base rested squarely in the CC apparatus. Aliev's important political contacts fell outside that apparatus. The skills he brought to the party leadership involved cadres discipline and organizational control. He did not have evident skills in economic management and innovation. Aliev's selection signaled the application of a particular set of solutions to the stagnating republic: a set of solutions grounded in the reestablishment of discipline within the hierarchy of party and state bodies.

The promotion of a sectoral representative to head the Azerbaidzhani Communist Party (AzCP) represented a genuine challenge to the incumbent governing group. His selection was regarded with suspicion and suggested more than a routine turnover of the top party official. General Stalinist period norms notwithstanding, the former republic party boss Mir D. Bagirov, who had risen through the security forces, had terrorized Azerbaidzhan for two decades while working out of his security police domain. When he was finally removed in 1953, it was not expected that the police forces would ever again be given such wide-ranging political authority.[10] The advancement of Aliev thus underscored the likelihood of more profound change in the republic.

Unlike the 1974 Lithuanian leadership change, when Moscow assumed a low profile in the resolution of the succession question, the quick and smooth replacement of Akhundov by Aliev revealed a more decisive Moscow role. The decision to replace Akhundov with Aliev was formalized and publicized on July 14, with Ivan Kapitonov, the CPSU Secretary responsible for cadres affairs, attending the Baku meeting. The arrangements for Akhundov's move into the republic's Academy of Sciences had already been made.[11] Aliev's selection apparently had the strong support of General Semyen

Tsvigun, the First Deputy Chairman of the USSR KGB, who had worked with Aliev earlier in his career. Tsvigun, Brezhnev's brother-in-law, had nominated Aliev for the Azerbaidzhani KGB position and had secured the support of the then KGB boss Yury Andropov. Thus Tsvigun, who headed the Azerbaidzhani KGB from October 1963 to June 1967 before being transferred to Moscow, was in a strong position to sponsor Aliev. The new Azerbaidzhani leader was quickly coopted into the CPSU CC, addressing its December 1969 Plenum.[12]

A central contention of this study is that in the traditional Soviet system, the succession of a new party first secretary has been a critical stimulus for cadres renewal in subordinate party organizations. The Azerbaidzhani and Lithuanian case studies reveal an identifiable, almost routine, process whereby a new regime is created and a new policy program – or a new variant on Moscow's program – is presented. As is true at the national level, there have been no procedural rules enabling a new leader to automatically replace incumbents of the previous regime. The republic first secretary, however, has directly influenced personnel matters within the CC apparatus beneath him. Particular departments of that apparatus (e.g., the organizational–party work department) have been especially important to the power consolidation needs of a new leader and regime. Personnel changes within the central party apparatus enhanced the party leader's prospects of influencing the policy agenda, as well as the recruitment and mobility patterns within both the state apparatus and subordinate regional party organizations. A new republic leader has enjoyed a mandate of sorts from Moscow to initiate those changes vital to his reconstituting of the governing coalition. The Aliev experience of the early 1970s is illustrative.

Table 6.1 summarizes the rate of cadres turnover in leading Azerbaidzhani party and state organizations in the period immediately following Aliev's succession. Extensive personnel turnover occurred within all leading party and state bodies, and at both the republic and regional levels. The speed and extent of personnel turnover and regime formation in Azerbaidzhan were noteworthy, exceeding those found in the Lithuanian case. Within just two and a half years of Aliev's succession, the AzCP CC *Buro* included only one Azerbaidzhani member *not* recruited by the new party boss.

Among the republic party secretaries, three of four were rather quickly replaced. These changes signified that the top party apparatchiki overseeing the republic's agricultural and industrial sectors

Table 6.1 *Leadership turnover in Azerbaidzhani party and state organizations, July 1969–December 1974*

Positions	Total N	July–Dec. 1969	1970	1971	1972	1973	1974	Total changes[a]	Turnover %
Buro	10[b]	2	1	5[c]				8	80
Secretaries, CC	4		1	2				3	75
Heads, CC departments	14	4	4	3	2		2	13	93
Ministers and chairmen of state committees[d]	5	6	16	8	3	2	9	38[e]	68
First secretaries, raikoms	57	5	19	11	2	5	11	45[f]	79

[a] As based upon available biographical data. In some cases, changes are known to have taken place, but the dates of the changes are unknown. These cases necessarily could not be included here.

[b] The membership of the CC Buro varies by year. The figure used is for the Buro membership as of the July 1969 CC plenum.

[c] Two candidate members of the Buro were selected at this time, too.

[d] Of the 7 members of the Council of Ministers Presidium, 6 were replaced between 1969 and 1972.

[e] While there were 35 changes between 1969 and 1973, there were 5 cases where a ministry or state committee experienced 2 changes during this time period. For purposes of calculating the percentage turnover of ministers and state committee chairmen, there was a total of 30 ministerial and state committee chairmen changes. These figures do not include those cases where ministries and state committees were created or abolished. Such institutional changes likely transcend the career fates of specific politicians. Were such abolished or newly created organs included, then a total of 6 slots entailed 47 personnel changes during the July 1969–74 period.

[f] The "Total changes" figure of 45 reflects the total number of regions which had leadership changes. A number of regional party leaderships experienced several changes during this 5½-year period.

were Aliev appointees, as was the secretary responsible for propaganda. Only Sergei V. Kozlov, the Russian Second Secretary appointed by and ultimately accountable to Moscow, retained his position throughout this period. Having become Second Secretary in May 1968, Kozlov remained in Baku until he was transferred back to Moscow in 1977.[13]

Within the CC apparatus – the command staff of the republic party organization – eight of thirteen department heads were replaced. Two of the most important departments, the OPWD and the Administrative Department, had been headed by two close associates of Aliev's predecessor, who were quickly ousted. The Agriculture, Culture, Science and Higher Education Departments, which had been subject to serious criticisms in the period before the July 1969 succession, also experienced rapid leadership turnover. By the beginning of 1975, only five Akhundov-period incumbents still headed CC departments, but they were all responsible to recently promoted republic party secretaries who were closely linked to Aliev.[14] All these personnel changes guaranteed that apparatus slots would be available to favored Aliev loyalists.

The high level of personnel turnover within the AzCP organization was matched by a comparable replacement of state officials. The republic's Council of Ministers was reconstituted, as two-thirds of all members were replaced in less than five years. Six of seven members of the Council's ruling Presidium were removed. These changes in the state bureaucracy were almost as immediate and extensive as those in the party apparatus directly headed by Aliev. Those officials slated for removal generally headed agencies that were critical to the political and economic life of the republic (e.g., Gosplan, Trade, Finances, Communications, Internal Affairs, and the KGB). But it was also important to *cleanse* the influence of the previous republic leader. The health area had been Akhundov's area of specialty and it was targeted for special criticism by his successor. Speaking at his first AzCP Congress as republic leader, Aliev pointed to the corruption in the Narimanov Medical Institute, where Akhundov had worked earlier and had close connections. The Minister of Health F.M. Vekilov, a protégé of Akhundov, was ousted in early 1970 – signifying the beginning of a mass purge of the Health Ministry. Some incumbent government officials retained their positions, but they generally headed the more visible but politically less important ministries and state committees (e.g., Foreign Affairs, Nature Conservation, Vocational and Technical Education, and Cinema).

Table 6.2 *Percent turnover in membership of leading party and state organs in the 5-year period following the succession of a new republic party first secretary, Brezhnev period*

Republic	Buro (F) %	(N)	Secretariat %	(N)	CC depts. %	(N)	Ministers %	(N)
Armenia (1966–71)	43	(7)	25	(4)	58	(12)	41	(37)
Belorussia (1965–70)	38	(8)	100	(4)	67	(9)	58	(24)
Georgia (1972–77)	64	(11)	100	(4)	100	(13)	73	(52)
Kazakhstan (1964–69)	56	(9)	50	(4)	56	(9)	68	(34)
Latvia (1966–71)	11	(9)	50	(4)	55	(11)	36	(33)
Lithuania (1974–79)	30	(10)	75	(4)	57	(14)	35	(48)
Turkmenistan (Dec. 1969–75)	57	(7)	50	(4)	73	(15)	56	(43)
Ukraine (1972–77)	43	(7)	40	(5)	68	(19)	34	(56)
Azerbaidzhan (1969–74)	67	(9)	75	(4)	62	(13)	66	(56)

Sources: Author's biographical files for the political elite of Azerbaidzhan, Kazakhstan, Lithuania, and Ukraine; Grey Hodnett and Val Ogareff, *Leaders of the Soviet Republics, 1955–1972*, Canberra: The Australian National University, 1973; and Val Ogareff, *Leaders of the Soviet Republics, 1971–1980*, Canberra: The Australian National University, 1980.

The impetus for personnel renewal extended beyond the republic leadership to include most regional party organizations. Nearly 80 percent of all regional first secretaries were replaced as the new regime consolidated power. Some were simply transferred to comparable posts in different regions. Many, however, were ousted. Biographical information available for demoted regional first secretaries does not reveal their new postings, but the absence of later institutional references to them suggests that their political careers were terminated with Aliev's rise.

The political needs of a new leader with a mandate for change require the opening up of organizational slots. The magnitude of the opportunities made available to Aliev and his growing network is underscored by the low rate of personnel change before the July 1969 succession. From 1964–69, only 36 percent of the Azerbaidzhani *Buro* (N = 14) and 38 percent of the CC department heads (N = 13) were changed. Within the governmental apparatus, only 21 percent of the forty-eight Council of Ministers members were changed. These personnel changes, involving less than half the number for the post-succession period, generally entailed the routine rotation or retirement of cadres. A review of the biographical précis for the officials affected also reveals that these changes usually involved secondary administrative positions, and not the top party and government positions.[15]

The expectation of a post-succession transformation of the governing elite, confirmed in both the Azerbaidzhani and Lithuanian cases, is fully substantiated by comparable levels of personnel turnover in all Soviet republics after leadership changes (Table 6.2). In all republics where a new party first secretary came to power during the eighteen-year Brezhnev period, extensive personnel turnover occurred in both party and state apparats, with those changes extending from the republic level down to the regions and major cities. Incumbent regimes were disbanded as new governing coalitions emerged. Turnover rates were especially high in cases where Moscow publicly signaled its loss of confidence in the republic leadership (e.g., the crackdown on the Georgian CP and allegations of major corruption by top officials). In such cases there was a felt need to fully reconstitute the party hierarchy. The new party leader was given full authority to do so. This certainly proved true in both Lithuania and Azerbaidzhan.

Table 6.3 *Mobility of Aliev protégés and clients into leading party and state organizations, July 1969–December 1974*

Positions	Total N	Total changes	Number of Aliev associates	Aliev associates as % of total change
Buro	10	8	6	75
Secretaries CC[a]	4	3	3	100
Heads, CC departments	14	8	6	75
Ministers and chairmen of state committees	56	37	7	19
First secretaries, raikoms	57	45	13	29

[a]Does not include the party first secretary.

The Aliev patronage network

The ouster of incumbents from the past regime was the critical first step in the transformation of the republic's political leadership. Patronage ties were critical in the promotion of aspiring politicians who comprised the new ruling coalition. A significant number of Aliev protégés and clients were provided with the opportunity to move into important positions in Baku and the various regions (Table 6.3).

Thirty-five politicians who assumed political positions within the republic and regional apparats – and who at some point were AzCP CC/AC members – can be identified as protégés or clients of Aliev. Though Aliev drew loyalists from many settings, a good number were long-term associates who had served with him in the KGB. Within the emerging leadership there were also many from the Nakhichevan ASSR, where Aliev had begun his career. Five of his identified associates had been stationed there with him in the 1950s and early 1960s. Under the new party boss, second-level officials in Nakhichevan now ascended to the top ranks of the republic's leadership. All three new republic party secretaries, recruited between 1970 and 1971, were closely tied to Aliev.[16] A number of the other new party *Buro* members were his associates, including the new Chairman of the Supreme Soviet, K.A. Khalilov, the new Chairman of the Council of Ministers, A.I. Ibragimov, and Khalilov's First Deputy Chairman, I.A. Ibragimov.[17] These highly placed, rapidly recruited protégés bolstered Aliev's political muscle. Through their elevations, Aliev quickly secured a dominant position atop all political hierarchies; but his organizational strength stemmed first from the rapid alteration of the CC department leaderships. Through the immediate consolidation of his position in several key departments, especially the OPWD responsible for personnel recruitment and mobility, he was able to expand his own base and that of his coterie.

Three-quarters of the new CC department heads were Aliev associates. In the OPWD a protégé, R.G.K. Mamed-zade, was the initial appointee, succeeded a few years later by another protégé, I.N. Askerov. These officials not only oversaw personnel recruitment, but were responsible for the evaluation of party work. Other associates of the First Secretary came to head the Culture, Ideology, Propaganda and Agitation, Science and Higher Education, and Transport Departments immediately after the 1969 succession. The pattern revealed in the national and Lithuanian studies was repeated: a new political leader consolidated his power within the traditionally authoritative core party apparatus. His dominance of that apparatus, combined with the selective elevation of associates and allied officials into the top decision-making bodies, enabled him to expand his influence outward into the government and the public arena.

There were fewer Aliev associates among the new officials leading government bodies; combined they only constituted 19 percent of all new appointments. But those associates who were promoted assumed some of the more influential slots available. Several new members of the Council of Ministers' Presidium were tied to Aliev, including its chair. Unlike the experience in Lithuania, Aliev associates dominated the agencies responsible for security matters (e.g., KGB, Ministry of Internal Affairs, and Ministry of Justice).

Most members of the Aliev network assumed positions within republic-level organizations, in institutions directly subordinate to the First Secretary and his top lieutenants. But there was a discernible dispatching of protégés and clients to leadership positions within selected regional party organizations. Thirteen of the forty-five regional party leadership changes that occurred during the 1969–74 power consolidation period entailed the posting of Aliev associates. The placement of so many associates in important prefectural posts is striking when considering the practical limits on the size of a politician's patronage entourage – especially that of a politician at mid-career. No politician cultivates a limitless number

Table 6.4 *Analyses of variance among three populations of Azerbaidzhani regions (no leadership change/change/change with recruitment of associate), by political importance of region*

	N	Mean	F-Statistic	Significance
No change	12	0.007		
Change	32	0.009		
Change-associate	13	0.047		
Grand total	57	0.018	3.11	0.05

of reliable associates. Loyal associates are a *scarce* resource that must be carefully utilized. But the challenges for an Azerbaidzhani leader attempting to cope with the political machines in the republic's locales required not simply personnel turnover, but the careful placement of trusted loyalists as prefects. Aliev's strategy for expanding his influence into the Azerbaidzhani periphery was twofold: he would oversee leadership changes in most regional party organizations, and place his trusted associates in the most important of them.

Using regional-level political and economic measures similar to those applied in the Lithuanian study, I can assess the relative importance of different regions. Employing data on party membership by region permits a rough rank ordering of the regions according to total number of Communists, used here to measure the relative political importance of the regions.[18] An analysis of variance reveals a discernible difference in the relative importance of those regions where there was no leadership change and those regions where there was. Nearly all of the politically important regions experienced leadership change though the relationship is not statistically significant given that only twelve of fifty-seven regional party organizations did not experience a leadership change. However, if we differentiate among those regions that had a leadership change, those that had no change, and those that had a change involving the promotion of an Aliev associate, we find a positive correlation that is statistically significant (Table 6.4). Aliev associates assumed leadership positions in the salient regional and city party organizations. All ten of the most important regional party organizations experienced leadership changes between 1969 and 1974.[19] Six of these changes involved the promotion of Aliev clients or the transfer of Aliev protégés.

Table 6.5 *Analyses of variance among three populations of Azerbaidzhani regions (no leadership change/change/change with recruitment of associate), by economic importance of region*

	N	Mean	F-Statistic	Significance
No change	12	0.006		
Change	32	0.008		
Change-associate	13	0.051		
Grand total	57	0.018	3.20	0.05

Most of the regional leaders who were Aliev associates were shorter-term clients and not protégés. By and large, they did not have career ties with Aliev before his selection as First Secretary. Rather, they moved up quickly under Aliev after July 1969, assuming "trouble-shooting" roles in the periphery. There were a few protégés among these regional party officials, but most protégés occupied responsible positions in Baku. Those protégés posted to the locales served in the most important regional party leaderships, for instance in Baku City and the Nakhichevan ASSR.

Analysis of the economic importance of regions, leadership change, and recruitment of Aliev associates during the 1970s reveals a similar pattern.[20] Using a single measure of the relative economic importance of the fifty-seven regions within Azerbaidzhan, the likelihood of leadership change and client placement can be considered in economically important areas. There is a statistically weak relationship between a region's economic significance and the likelihood of leadership change. Again this is a function of the high number of cases where leadership changes occurred. But when the clientelism element is factored in, the relationship proves to be statistically significant (Table 6.5). The economically important regions experienced leadership changes in which associates of the new republic leader moved into those critical top positions. By the end of the power consolidation period, few regions had escaped leadership purges, and those that did were the least politically and economically influential.

The high profile of important regional party organizations such as those in Baku, Kirovabad, and Nagorno-Karabakh made the presence there of Aliev loyalists all the more significant. Public discussions of economic and other issues often concentrated on the experience of these regions and cities, setting expectations for other settings. In addition, these regions were the primary source of the cadres reserve for future elevations to republic posts.

The few pre-1969 incumbents who survived the leadership succession were not necessarily opposed to the new regime. The lack of career connections to Aliev, and the absence of any behavioral data revealing support (or lack of support) for Aliev's policy changes, do not allow us to draw hard conclusions. In fact, many of those regional leaders who survived the early period of extensive turnover maintained power throughout much of Aliev's thirteen-year tenure. There is no evidence that they possessed a base of power somehow independent of the republic party boss. The effective placement of associates in key regional party slots suggests that there must be a threshold number of placements necessary for a leader to reorient the expectations and behavior of subordinates within the broader cohort. Since most regional leaders under Aliev were new, had not served previously in their new domains, and were politically dependent upon the republic leadership for their appointment, the cohort of regional officials appeared all the more reliable to the new Baku authorities.

The identified pattern of protégé and client placement throughout the republic had real implications for Aliev's efforts to deal with the Azerbaidzhani economy, indicating an organizational rather than economic reform approach. As the primary overseers within the administrative apparatus, the new AzCP secretaries were critical to policy formulation and supervision in their respective areas. Working with loyalists heading CC departments this group of top officials was in a commanding position to promote republic-wide policy initiatives. Any serious effort to address the issues of economic lethargy and corruption required such a network of politicians. Established leaders in the politically and economically important regions were replaced with politicians linked with the new administration in Baku. The "family circles" from the past regime that often operated in intermediate and lower-level territorial jurisdictions were beheaded.[21] As a consequence, Baku was in a better position to contend with the problems posed by resistant regional and local politicians and their organizational networks, i.e., problems of information distortion and improper interpretation and execution of policy. At the same time, as other scholars of Soviet local politics have observed, the loyalty of such lower-level appointees was directed upwards, to the leadership that dispatched them, rather than to their constituents below.[22] The transformation of the leadership of regional party organizations enhanced the likelihood that Baku policy changes would have direct relevance to local policy implementation.

The massive purging of the Azerbaidzhani political elite resulted in the quick and almost complete removal of Akhundov loyalists. The strength of incumbents' political connections to the deposed leader were critical in determining whether they were survivors or casualties of the 1969 leadership change. We have already seen that connections with the new boss significantly enhanced mobility opportunities. By the same token, career connections with the ousted party boss severely limited the survival chances of incumbents. Among the fifteen state ministers removed, five were Akhundov associates. This is a significant figure considering there is less career data for the pre-1969 period, making it more difficult both to identify Akhundov protégés and to tap the full dimensions of his patronage network. Although incumbents generally did not survive the leadership succession, three of the five incumbents who did were associates of Aliev. Among the regional first secretaries, three of four identified incumbent Akhundov clients were ousted by 1974, while all four linked with Aliev were retained and promoted.

Overall, of the twenty-two politicians identified as Akhundov protégés, all but one were demoted or ousted after the July 1969 Plenum. Six of these protégés were republic party secretaries or heads of CC departments, and *all* had been removed by 1972.[23] Of the Akhundov associates in the Council of Ministers, all were retired by 1971, and all of the seven associates serving in the regions and major cities had gone by 1973.[24] Some incumbents from the Akhundov period survived the leadership change; some even experienced promotions (Table 6.6). But very few retained responsible positions in the regime by the end of the 1970s.

The political legacy of the Akhundov regime made it difficult for incumbents to survive. Akhundov's political disgrace, combined with the presumed corruption of his allies, made lateral transfer or retention of incumbents unlikely. We saw in our Lithuanian case how incumbents, including associates of the previous party boss, were selectively transferred from the party apparatus to state organs. The overall positive political legacy of Snechkus's regime encouraged the succeeding regime to cultivate experienced incumbents. They constituted a valuable resource often found lacking in any organizational setting. Occasionally these incumbents were moved into less powerful organizational slots, but they nevertheless retained their

Table 6.6 *Fate of incumbent ministers and raikom first secretaries, 1969–1974*

	Ministers		First secretaries		Akhundov associates	
Fate	N	(%)	N	(%)	N	(%)
Retained, promoted	15	(38)	24	(47)	1	(4)
Ousted, demoted, retired	20	(53)	26[a]	(51)	21	(96)
Died	1	(3)				
Unknown	3	(8)	1	(2)		
Total	39	(100)	51	(100)	22	(100)

[a]Several are unknown, but they were not reelected to the CC or the Auditing Commission.

When the incumbent ministers and first secretaries are combined and compared against the Akhundov associates, the following relational statistics result: Chi Square = 11.05; D.F. = 1; Significance Level = 0.00.

elite status. In Azerbaidzhan, such incumbents were not laterally transferred or demoted. They were purged.[25]

Did the leadership changes initiated by Aliev result in a team more capable of tackling the problems facing Azerbaidzhan? Biographical and career data and very minimal attitudinal information for selected leaders make a direct answer to this question difficult. Any evaluation of competence must be tentative. Nevertheless, the biographical data do reveal that members of the Aliev patronage network were, on average, better educated than the general Azerbaidzhani political elite of the 1970s. I have used education level as a surrogate measure for tapping expertise (and potential performance). Members of the Aliev network were well educated, with nearly all (97 percent) having completed a higher educational institution (compared to 83 percent of the overall population, and 91 percent of Akhundov network members). The differences in formal training among these groups are not statistically significant; but they suggest that the triumph of the Aliev network did not constitute the advance of a less qualified elite cohort.

Within five years of his succession, Aliev had formed an entirely new team of officials. Moscow's role had been critical, both in bringing an outsider into power and in providing support for his program of personnel and policy change. The feudal nature of political relations within the USSR explains why conditions were conducive to Aliev's reconstruction of the Azerbaidzhani party. A group of politicians from outside the AzCP leadership – from Nakhichevan and the republic's KGB joined with national authorities in attempting to revive the republic and its economy. As we shall see, with Moscow's support, this elite cohort was primed to do so.

Elite circulation and cadres discipline

The circumstances that brought about the Azerbaidzhani leadership change differed from those we observed in Lithuania. Different too was the Azerbaidzhani regime's personnel policy. The new Lithuanian regime consolidated its position in a slower and more regularized fashion and, once in place, exhibited a general stability of officials throughout its tenure. The new Azerbaidzhani leadership, on the other hand, faced a considerable amount of corruption at all levels. It required an ongoing policy of personnel rotation to limit the emergence of resistant groupings of officials in various institutional settings.

This strategy of regular movement and replacement of politicians characterized the entire Aliev period. These changes took place in the midst of an on-going republic-wide campaign that stressed cadres discipline. The need for broad-range leadership change was a major theme set out immediately after the July 1969 Plenum. Personnel turnover in regional party organizations, for instance, was linked publicly with a desire to raise the qualifications of cadres as well as with matters of party discipline. The Baku regional party First Secretary emphasized the problem of apparatchik motivation:

> Moreover, there come to mind examples of past years, when this or that member of the raikom, whom we knew from a most positive side, suddenly did not handle his assignments in a proper way, he lost, so to speak, initiative, a concern about work. And when they started to find this out, the explanation was simple: a man was given an assignment that he didn't feel like doing, or he simply did not have sufficient qualifications. (*Bakinsky Rabochy*, August 15, 1969)

The important economic problems confronting Azerbaidzhan were said to result from problems of motivation and leadership incompetence. Aliev commented at a Fall 1969 CC meeting that:

> The main reason for the serious defects in the development of the republic's economy is the low level of organizational work of some leading party, soviet, economic, trade union, komsomol and other organs, which do not provide the necessary action, initiative, and

> purposefulness in the struggle to mobilize the efforts of workers in
> fulfilling the social tasks before them. (*Bakinsky Rabochy*, September
> 18, 1969)

Tackling the economic dilemmas of the republic would begin with
the party and state apparats. The key to resolving the crisis in
republic and regional level leaderships was to strengthen the "discipline" of the responsible party workers. "Above all it is necessary to
raise the feeling of responsibility of every leader for that part of the
work which has been entrusted to him, raise the exactingness and
discipline in all the links of our economy" (*Bakinsky Rabochy* editorial, August 13, 1969). At the most basic level, this public discussion justified some alteration of the leadership's recruitment and
mobility practices. Just days after the July Plenum, a front-page
Bakinsky Rabochy editorial entitled "The Leninist Style" stressed the
importance of "the thoughtful selection, placement and upbringing
of cadres."[26] In reality this translated into the increased recruitment
of individuals who had spent much of their professional lives
outside the central party apparatus and who were tied more closely
with specific sectoral interests.

For those incumbent party leaders who proved effective in motivating economic growth and good party work, promotions were in
order. For instance, two First Secretaries, N. Kh. Abbasov and V.A.
Ismailov, whose rural regions were successful in increasing cotton
production, were lauded and given important promotions.[27] Abbasov, head of the Agdam raikom since 1965, was promoted in 1970 to
head the Sal'yan raikom. Ismailov, who had headed the Agdzhabe-
din raikom since 1968, was promoted into the AzCP CC in 1973.
These politicians had moved into the ranks of the political elite
during the Akhundov period, but their performance merited further
advance.

The policy of regular personnel turnover continued throughout the
1970s. There was an ongoing campaign to "maintain cadres' discipline", while attention was given to "strengthening the moral
character" of party leaders.[28] In reality, controlling regional officials
proved an ongoing challenge. Regional mafias had considerable
resources – economic and political – that were locally derived and
that enabled local bosses to secure the loyalty and assistance of local
subordinates and republic-level superiors. Regional party first secretaries continued to be replaced or transferred through the 1970s.[29]
Between 1975 and 1979, for example, first secretaries were replaced in
at least twenty-one Azerbaidzhani raiony.[30] A number of Aliev's

own associates were shifted in and out of several raikoms, with several of them then moving into positions of republic-level responsibility.[31] In general, the policy was to leave politicians in regional secretaryships for four or five years, and then transfer them. It was intended that they serve long enough to introduce organizational and policy changes, but not long enough to become comfortable or to develop their own locally ensconced entourage.

This strategy proved to be less than successful. In some cases first secretaries appointed after the July 1969 Plenum had to be removed due to "disciplinary problems." They had been in power eight or ten years, which proved long enough to develop their own local networks.[32] In other cases, however, questionable regional leaders simply were transferred or moved to Baku into CC or ministerial slots. The purpose of these cadres policies was clear: the extensive "family circle" developed by Aliev was not to be repeated by others.

This policy of cadres rotation also characterized the republic CC apparatus and the Council of Ministers. Between 1975 and 1979, seven of the fifteen CC departments underwent leadership changes, as did twenty-six of the fifty-one ministries and state committees. Officials were laterally moved from one organizational slot to another. Their tenure of service lasted only a few years before they were transferred to a new position within a different institution. Those who had assumed top policy-making positions within the Azerbaidzhani party apparatus by the latter 1970s often moved up in this fashion. Thus the influential AzCP secretaryship for propaganda and agitation was rotated among several officials. Aliev's first agit-prop Secretary, D.P. Guliyev, was promoted into this position after two years of heading the Ministry of Higher and Specialized Secondary Education. His successor, R.G.K. Mamed-zade, a close protégé of Aliev, served as head of the Administrative Organs Department (1970–71) and then as the head of the OPWD (1971–76) before assuming the same secretaryship. The third holder of this position under Aliev, K.M. Bagirov – who ultimately replaced Aliev as Azerbaidzhani First Secretary – previously served as the head of the Building and Urban Economy Department (1970–74) and then as First Secretary of the important Sumgait City party organization (1974–81).

Twelve of the thirty-five identified Aliev associates held at least two appointments in two different organizations during Aliev's tenure. In nearly all cases, these individuals held the first position – to which they generally were appointed sometime between 1970 and 1972 – for two to four years. They subsequently were transferred to another organization, one often involving similar sectoral concerns. Occasionally, an individual was recruited from a raikom first secretaryship to an important slot in Baku.[33] Meanwhile clients in junior CC apparatus positions were transferred to important slots in the periphery.[34]

Against the backdrop of a conscious policy of political elite circulation, there was a handful of politicians whose careers transcended the leadership upheavals of the late 1960s and 1970s. These politicians were highly educated and professionally experienced, and were strongly positioned within their institutional bases. Of the eight incumbent ministers and state committee chairmen who survived the political upheavals and for whom full biographical and career data are available, five held candidate or doctorate degrees.[35] Most served within their specialized sectors for much of their careers.[36] These officials were part of the governmental bureaucracy, although their institutions dealt with important policy matters. The available career data indicate that their careers were not made on the basis of close ties to top Azerbaidzhani leaders. Generally, they moved up their hierarchies slowly, reaching top positions only in their professional maturity. Their experience contrasts markedly with that of their CC apparatus counterparts, whose careers were tied to top politicians and whose mobility was rapid, both up and down the political hierarchy.

Political implications of the Aliev machine

How did Aliev and his network fare in their effort to rule Azerbaidzhan? We have seen that organizationally Aliev's network and governing coalition grew quickly and penetrated subordinate bodies. Remnants of the predecessor regime were quickly swept away. Within only a couple of years the new network had effectively reached into lower-level party organizations. Rival politicians and networks did not do well during the Aliev years. As incumbent party Secretary for Heavy Industry, Dzhafar G. Dzhafarov, Aliev's main rival, had considerable experience in the CC apparatus. But within two years of the 1969 succession, he was removed from power.

The Aliev network was able to extend its power when its members assumed high profiles in areas it did not otherwise penetrate. Aliev or his top protégés were almost always in attendance during lower-level regional party meetings – especially those meetings involving leadership changes. Throughout 1970, either Aliev or a protégé was present at the April 15 Nakhichevan ASSR, the May 8 Baku City, the July 4 Agdam Raikom, the October 14 Agdash Raikom, and the November 4 Kel'badzhar Raikom organizational meetings – all of which produced important leadership changes. By 1974, the fifth year of Aliev's power consolidation, a high number of important gorkoms and raikoms had held organizational meetings during which leadership changes occurred. The network's authority was revealed in the numerous regional and city party meetings held during just the first two months of that year: Aliev attended three such meetings, including those in Baku and Sumgait, while network members A.I. Ibragimov, I.A. Ibragimov, D.P. Guliyev, A.G. Kerimov, G.N. Seidov, and R.G. Mamed-zade – among others – attended at least one such meeting each. No other group of politicians attended even a fraction of this number of meetings. Even Second Secretary S.V. Kozlov only attended one such lower-level organizational meeting (Nasimin Region, February 1).

Meanwhile, alternative sources of power did not arise within Azerbaidzhan to more directly influence organizational questions or to contravene the initiatives of the republic party leader. There is no evidence that a rival network emerged during the 1969–82 period. Any political constraints on Aliev and his network originated in Moscow. The republic's second secretary often served as Moscow's on-the-spot representative. But these second secretaries were routinely transferred into and out of Azerbaidzhan upon completion of their duties. This regular turnover limited Moscow's influence.[37]

Aliev proved to be a self-confident party boss in tackling the spectrum of serious problems within the republic. From the beginning, he assumed a high public profile in detailing the many issues and in applying a hardline policy response. The proceedings of the July 1969 Plenum that elected Aliev were well publicized, as was his address. From this point on, the party leader dominated the Azerbaidzhani policy discussion as is evident both in the broad range of organizational, political, economic, and social issues with which he dealt, and in the variety and number of forums that he addressed. Aliev's role was similar to that of Grishkiavichus in Lithuania, though the exigencies of the Azerbaidzhani setting only augmented his power and authority.

As in the Lithuanian case, the party leader's public statements represented the republic's response to issues and concerns raised by Moscow. Central press organs had continued to criticize the republic's economic performance in early 1970, laying the blame on former officials.[38] Moscow's discussion of Azerbaidzhan's ills was explicit, as responsible institutions (e.g., the agriculture ministries and state committees) were being purged. While many Aliev associates criticized the former regime, it was Aliev himself who directly identified Akhundov, Alikhanov, Iskenderov, and many other top officials as responsible for Azerbaidzhan's problems.

A comprehensive examination of the policy discussion in open sources sheds little light upon the nature of power relations and policy making in the republic. But it does reveal that the First Secretary broadly outlined the new regime's policies, and that associates and coalition members spelled out the details that were relevant to their own domains of responsibility. Leading network members – especially party secretaries and influential *Buro* members – assumed relatively high public profiles. Those *Buro* members with governmental portfolios (the Supreme Soviet Chairman, the Chairman and the Deputy Chairmen of the Council of Ministers) enjoyed relatively high public profiles in terms of speeches and articles published, attendance at party organizational meetings, etc. Native republic party secretaries also enjoyed some public attention – certainly more than the republic second secretary.

Aliev focused on economic difficulties, especially the republic's low industrial and agricultural growth rates. He also called attention to a services sector that ranked as one of the weakest and least developed of any republic. Commensurate with the position taken by Moscow, Aliev identified existent but under-utilized material and labor resources; he did not call for additional inputs from Moscow. He broached "negative incentives" through a discipline campaign directed at both officials and workers.

The Azerbaidzhani policy discussion also reveals that organizational problems and lower-level corruption continued to command the leadership's attention throughout the duration of the Aliev regime. The case of the security apparatus is illustrative, as it became a focal point for public discussion of official incompetence and misrule. The Ministry of Internal Affairs was targeted for special public treatment, in part reflecting the Aliev group's efforts to wrest control of this KGB competitor from former rivals and associates of Akhundov. The republic Minister of Internal Affairs, M. Ali-zade, was removed shortly after Aliev's succession. Demoted to deputy director of the Azerbaidzhani Chief Supply Administration, he became the subject of further criticism in 1977 when he was removed from that position on the basis of corruption and patronage and subsequently expelled from the AzCP.[39] The purge of the Internal Affairs Ministry extended to other officials, including deputy ministers and the head of the Baku City Executive Committee's Internal Affairs Administration.[40] After the First Secretary publicly criticized their activities, fourteen directors of regional departments of the ministry were removed during the first years of the Aliev regime.[41]

Beyond the removal of corrupt officials, the economic problems that had placed Azerbaidzhan at or near the bottom of growth rates and productivity were identified and addressed by the Aliev coalition. The republic's industry and agriculture had previously grown slowly and performed poorly, but by the mid-1970s its relative position among the republics had improved significantly. The discipline campaign, combined with Moscow's support and the net inflow of resources, helped to offset the impact of the languishing petroleum industry. Azerbaidzhan's position among Soviet republics in economic productivity improved dramatically during the first five years of the regime. In industrial labor productivity, industrial productivity, and national income growth, the republic ranked fourth, sixth, and fourth respectively – standings that were considerably stronger than for the Akhundov period.[42] In fact the republic maintained its better-than-average standing among republics' growth rates throughout Aliev's tenure. Although Aliev complained of corruption and economic shortcomings until his departure for Moscow in December 1982, the republic's growth rates during his tenure surpassed those of both his immediate predecessors and successors.[43]

The Aliev leadership was ethnically homogenous and politically cohesive. Its style was domineering, but it did reap a decade of policy successes that were not lost upon the national leadership. Although Aliev did not exhibit the managerial or economic expertise expected to reform the republic, he did possess the political muscle and authority to impose his own solution. His discipline campaign and a policy of cadres circulation characterized the entirety of the Aliev period – and they did not occur without Moscow's approval. But the Aliev network and governing coalition were hardly creatures of Moscow. Far from it. The regime in Baku was a native Azerbaidzhani regime: one that enjoyed Moscow's support in return for political quiescence and a reinvigoration of the republic's economy. Nearly 80 percent of all leading Azerbaidzhani politicians were of the titular nationality, with less than 14 percent Slav.[44] All top government and party posts (except the Second Secretary) were held by ethnic

Azerbaidzhanis. Among the thirty-five identified associates of Aliev, thirty-three were Azerbaidzhani. Russian and Slavic cadres seldom filled positions that became vacant during the numerous leadership changes of the 1970s, and when they did, the positions were generally of marginal political importance.[45]

During the second half of the 1970s, Aliev assumed an increasingly national profile; his election as a Politburo candidate member in 1976 lifted him into the ranks of the top national leadership. His leadership qualities – especially his toughness in dealing with a complex set of problems – contributed to his political success. His regime's program of negative and positive incentives helped to spur the republic's economic and political turnaround. Moscow supported the regime throughout its tenure, though certain other non-Slavic republic regimes received similar support.[46] Above all, the regime owed its political success to Aliev's reliable and organizationally well-positioned patronage network. The institutional strength of that network, matched by its policy achievements, enabled Aliev's regime to govern for over a decade.

Aliev reconsidered and the period of reform

When Aliev was appointed USSR First Deputy Premier in December 1982, he immediately assumed a varied portfolio of responsibilities that included reform of the railway system and Soviet policy in the Middle East. After Aliev's departure from Baku, there was a half decade of stability in the republic's leadership and political life. His successor, Kiamran M. Bagirov, was a senior member of the Aliev machine. He had enjoyed rapid mobility under Aliev, heading a CC department, becoming First Secretary of the important Sumgait Gorkom, and serving as party Secretary for Propaganda and Agitation.

Bagirov continued Aliev's economic and cadres policies. During his tenure there was some regularized rotation of personnel, but the coalition fashioned by Aliev governed the republic. The Andropov discipline campaign with occasional national press accounts of Azerbaidzhani nepotism and corruption compelled some personnel changes.[47] Perhaps the most important changes came in December 1983, when three *Buro* members were removed, including a prominent Aliev protégé (V.A. Guseinov). However, in general, only officials heading scandal-ridden government agencies or regional party organizations were targeted for ouster.[48]

Under Bagirov, political newcomers generally were not recruited into vacated posts. When long-serving Supreme Soviet Chairman Khalilov retired in December 1985, he was replaced by another prominent regime member, S.B. Tatliyev. Although Tatliyev was not a close Aliev protégé like Khalilov, his selection signified cadres continuity, not change. Such continuity was evident throughout the top Azerbaidzhani leadership: among the fourteen *Buro* members confirmed at the XXXI AzCP Congress (February 1986), only two had not been in the republic's leadership ranks as of Aliev's last AzCP Congress in 1981; likewise, only one of six Secretariat members was not in the leadership ranks at that time. Except for the Second Secretary dispatched from Moscow, only one new face was to be found in the Bagirov team; all other senior party and government officials had advanced under Aliev's supervision in the 1970s and early 1980s.[49] After the 1986 Congress, thirteen of the identified Aliev associates were still CC/AC members. The Aliev machine still maintained its organizational grip on the republic.

After over a decade and a half of power consolidation, only Moscow could threaten the primacy of the ruling patronage network. Immediate post-Brezhnev period discipline campaigns had little impact. For Azerbaidzhan and other Muslim republics, only the considerable weight of the anti-corruption and reform drive of the Gorbachev regime would uproot unresponsive conservative republic leaderships. The process, however, proved slow and tortuous.

Central media accounts of corruption and policy inertia cited powerful officials in all of these republics, though the Azerbaidzhani leadership did not come under fire until 1987.[50] New pressures were applied on the Baku regime with the October 1987 ouster of Aliev. At the time he was one of the few remaining Brezhnev associates. While he attempted to promote himself as a policy reformer, his past record suggested otherwise.

Reemergent ethnic cleavages between Armenians and Azerbaidzhanis that centered on the Nagorno-Karabakh region complicated the Azerbaidzhani political scene, exacerbated the pressures brought on the Baku leadership with Aliev's fall, and led to Bagirov's ouster in May 1988.[51] Aliev and Bagirov, among others, were held responsible for the troubling conditions that were now causing massive public violence in the Nagorno-Karabakh.[52] Moscow quickly linked the dramatic outbreak of ethnic conflict in the region to Baku policies that were characterized as neglectful.[53] As in the past, when images of anti-Soviet nationalism were evoked to justify republic leadership changes (e.g., the 1959 ouster of Mustafayev), such themes were used after the Nagorno-Karabakh violence to pressure the republic's leadership. Even Bagirov's successor, A.R.Kh. Vezirov, manipulated these themes in his formal address to the XIX CPSU Conference (June 1988), placing "enormous blame" for the ethnic violence on the previous leadership.[54]

It was only in the wake of Aliev's ouster that a wave of more important personnel changes occurred in Baku. A few influential network members such as Z.M. Yusif-zade (AzSSR KGB head) were removed while other former associates such as I.N. Askerov (a head of the OPWD under Aliev) and I.A. Mamedov (once an AzCP Secretary) were publicly dishonored.[55] These changes were more than cosmetic, but additional pressure – especially from within the republic – was needed if the position of the network was to be seriously challenged. That pressure came with an August 14, 1988 *Bakinsky Rabochy* article that explicitly denounced the former leader. Detailing the failings of his economic and anti-corruption measures, the article criticized Aliev for his personality cult and his toadyism toward the now-discredited Brezhnev. Aliev became an important local symbol of the period of stagnation. Other media accounts – especially in the national press – amplified this theme.[56]

These attacks were a serious challenge to the governing network, but the Baku political scene was complex. With the February 1989 retirement of Azerbaidzhani Premier G.N. Seidov – an Aliev associate and the Secretary for Industry and Construction during Aliev's tenure – the network appeared to be in full retreat. But cadres decisions of the latter 1980s demonstrated its resilience, as other – albeit junior – members assumed responsible positions. Bagirov's successor as party leader, Abdul-Rakhman K. Vezirov, was himself a former associate of Aliev. Although he had been away from Baku for over a decade serving in several Soviet embassies (1976–88), his earlier rise in the AzCP apparatus had occurred under Aliev (1970–76).[57] Like his immediate past predecessors, Vezirov publicly attacked the corruption and economic problems that racked the republic. He criticized the previous regimes, but his characterizations were carefully worded and more balanced than those found in national media sources. For instance, in describing the republic's economic woes, he emphasized its lagging standard of living and poor consumer goods and services sector but he acknowledged its impressive past productivity growth rates. He articulated Moscow's contention that emergent ethnic problems were rooted in the past leadership's failed economic and anti-corruption measures. During his twenty-month stewardship, little of substance changed. In fact, Vezirov proved quite cautious in responding to *glasnost* and democratization, resisting many popular manifestations of reform in the republic.[58] The most important personnel decision Vezirov made during his tenure was to resurrect a prominent Aliev associate, V.A. Guseinov, to head the republic's KGB.[59]

Vezirov's inability to manage the worsening Azerbaidzhani–Armenian crisis led to still another succession in January 1990. The new party leader Ayaz N. Mutalibov had been the republic's Premier for nearly a year, and he had staked out a public position on the Nagorno-Karabakh problem that was fully commensurate with Moscow's stated line: i.e., that past policy mistakes made by Baku regimes necessitated the commitment of additional resources (by Moscow) to the autonomous province, but with the Nagorno-Karabakh remaining under long-term Azerbaidzhani political jurisdiction.[60] Like Vezirov, Mutalibov was a product of the Aliev regime, even if he was not a close associate of the former boss. He had risen to power in the 1970s, and although he was primarily a government (Gosplan) official during the 1980s, he was part of the republic's established political hierarchy. His 1990 elevation reflected the basic dilemma confronting national authorities who were attempting to deal with a resistant periphery: the dearth of rising new officials who genuinely adhered to *perestroika* and new policy norms. Mutalibov's past record and his initial steps as Azerbaidzhani leader suggested he had much in common with Bagirov and Vezirov: he was a new top leader, drawn from an established political cohort, who promoted essentially old-style policies.

The political and economic record of post-Aliev Azerbaidzhan was unsatisfactory from the national authorities' standpoint, necessitating a multifaceted strategy. Moscow waged a vigorous media campaign, oversaw several leadership changes, dispatched a leading troubleshooter (A.I. Vol'sky) and created a Special Administrative Committee to govern the troubled Nagorno-Karabakh, and regularly sent top leaders (including Ligachev and Razumovsky) to pressure senior republic officials. Nevertheless, the governing Azerbaidzhani network survived, albeit with some turnover of high-profile figures. And there was no evidence of more profound behavioral changes on the part of the republic's governing elite. Yet one important development of the 1980s – a result of the national reform effort – portended potential change in the long-term viability of patronage networks and the future conduct of Azerbaidzhani politics: the emergence of informal groups and the growing legitimacy for popular involvement in the republic's political life.

Motivated by the spirit of *perestroika* and reform, the Azerbaidzhani Popular Front and the more radical, pan-Turkic and pan-Islamic Dirchelish Party arose out of the Nagorno-Karabakh turmoil during the late 1980s. These groups had many concerns, including the protection of the environment, the status of Azerbaidzhani cultural and intellectual life, and ties with Iranian Azerbaidzhanis. Their emergence was striking given the absence of a participatory political culture and the fact that Azerbaidzhan had lacked a cultural or intellectual elite that would challenge the dominant political elite. Within weeks of their emergence these groups brought considerable pressure on Baku authorities. The Vezirov regime had very reluctantly acknowledged Popular Front interests, but only after mass demonstrations and the rapid spread of the front's membership into dozens of raions. The near complete collapse of public order – with the Popular Front demanding Vezirov's ouster – helped to bring him down in early 1990.[61]

As the new decade began, the Popular Front and other groups appeared to constitute new rivals to the old networks. The reform process and media campaigns had discredited past regimes: the poor condition of the economy and the fragile state of ethnic relations were clear to all. Meanwhile, the use of force by Soviet authorities had all but removed any lingering legitimacy of national – mostly Russian – authorities. The emerging non-Communist leadership from the Popular Front and the cultural-intellectual elite was ever more able to articulate broader Azerbaidzhani interests; but in 1990, with Mutalibov's succession, these forces faced yet another establishment member whose policy inclinations better approximated Aliev's political record than the Popular Front's draft program. Three years of national pressure, with mounting popular disaffection, still had not fully uprooted the political remnants of the *Alievshchina*.[62]

Patronage and center–periphery relations

From Moscow's point of view, the legacies of both the Azerbaidzhani and Lithuanian leaderships and patronage networks were complex and mixed. We have seen that ineffectual regimes – originally brought to power and sanctioned by the national leadership – were replaced by new regimes whose initial performance more fully corresponded to Moscow's expectations. But there were both payoffs and costs to network politics in the locales. Networks helped to unify the governing elite and provide some unity among members. That unity helped native party leaderships in both republics to pursue initiatives that altered subordinates' behavior; and, at least initially, these initiatives were compatible with Moscow's interests.

The networks and regimes supported by national authorities evolved through phases in which the balance of payoffs and costs shifted. During the phase of regime formation, as officials were rotated and power consolidated by the new leader, network expansion facilitated governance. Traditionally, new regimes ruled with Moscow's mandate, and they enjoyed an added discretion in promoting policy ends that were said to be Moscow's, but as regimes aged and networks attempted to maintain their position, policy inertia and corruption often set in. Politicians were motivated to maintain and expand their power bases and they encountered few if any constraints. In the cases we have examined, stagnation set in when networks became well-ensconced and regimes grew older. A once-effective Snechkus regime proved less capable in its final years, while the Akhundov leadership exhibited considerable complaisance and corruption. The Grishkiavichus and Aliev regimes were likewise subject to quite negative assessments after their patrons' departures. The presence of a Russian second secretary or other "supervisory personnel" made little difference. By and large, the policy formula developed in the early phase of the regime was applied with little modification throughout the regime's duration. The incrementalist tendency of the Soviet system was reinforced by this pattern of regime evolution. In the centralized and hierarchical Soviet system, the periodic movement of officials could only partially stem the negative consequences of network politics.

These studies also revealed that in the absence of fundamental system reform, the removal of patronage networks did not alter the conditions that led to their emergence. Short-term problems were sometimes addressed but long-term conditions remained the same. Where power was concentrated, networks operated seemingly unchecked, and Moscow's basic political and economic interests were protected. Removing an uncooperative, embedded network was difficult, even with strong national pressure. But strong national authorities did occasionally apply pressure and subnational leaderships were transformed.

The emergence of the strong patronage networks of Aliev and

Grishkiavichus was both an organizational triumph for these regional leaders and a reassertion of Moscow's will in the Soviet periphery. These regional patrons' policy programs were variants of the national program, and their power – at the time – enhanced Moscow's control, yet the experience of these and successor regimes reveals that the long-term relationship between center and periphery is dynamic and complex. The potential significance of regional networks changes if the center is less authoritative and less powerful. In the cases explored here, the national authorities possessed the power to coerce regional politicians and networks to make changes. The evidence indicates that such changes – whether in personnel or in policies – were forthcoming. This ability to coerce declined as the 1990s began, as regional leaderships proved less responsive to Moscow's interests. Brezhnev period network deference was giving way to Gorbachev era network resistance: the pressures of *perestroika* made the political dominance of regional networks within their own bailiwicks ever less certain. Lithuania was becoming increasingly *democratic* and Azerbaidzhan increasingly *chaotic*. If there were *rules* to the conduct of a new Soviet politics, they were neither uniform nor clear.

7   The logic of patronage in changing societies

There are few constants in political life, but one seemingly holds true regardless of time, place, or system type: politicians are primarily motivated by the pursuit of power and authority. Paraphrasing Anthony Downs, politicians formulate policies to advance their positions, rather than advance their positions so as to formulate policy.[1] Career building is central to decision makers and policy making. Politicians' interests join together because it suits their quest for power to do so.

Politicians use numerous formal vehicles to merge their careers as they advance their power interests. Among the most important are the bureaucracies, political parties, and interest associations that comprise the policy process itself. Beyond these, politicians' own skills and experience are critical to their ability to forge working relations with others; but informal institutional factors also condition the pursuit and application of power. Patronage networks are an extralegal means for politicians to pool their resources and direct them toward group ends. Network membership offers no guarantee of success, but obviously it can provide a politician considerable assistance in the quest for power and authority.

Gyula Jozsa's notion of a "roped party" offers an apt description of the basic nature of the patronage network as it operates in the traditional Soviet system.[2] The motivations and behavior of network members may be likened to those of a team of mountain climbers who are connected together with a protective rope, assisting one another as they make their way to the summit. The patronage network is essentially a coalition of individuals who share at least one goal and who agree to pool their resources in pursuit of that shared goal. The resources are position, expertise, and the ambition to promote one's own interests. The goal is career building, the maximization of political power, and the related ability to influence decision making. The network is a vehicle for upward mobility, with payoffs and costs incurred by members as the entire party advances. The strength of the group rests upon the ability and reliability of each member. One member can slip without the entire team falling; but the team requires a sure leader and a group of members who are working toward the common goal of reaching the political summit.

Career ambitions drive all climbers as they move toward the summit. Among groups of climbers, commonalities and differences will emerge. Often, these groups will champion different interests, hold different issue orientations. Groups may become allied or opposed; but the behavior and careers of all groups and members are subject to the norms dictated by the political opportunity structure. That opportunity structure channels all politicians' mobility efforts: it sets the behavioral parameters within which all politicians operate. Understanding the political opportunity structure – and how it may change – is the key to understanding the behavioral norms and motivations of political officials in the Soviet Union and elsewhere.

Ambition and career building in the Soviet system

The view from below

Our knowledge of the Soviet political opportunity structure and its paths to the summit is limited; but a few observations can be offered. First, the centralized and hierarchical nature of the traditional Soviet system has channeled aspirants' upward mobility through well-regulated and supervised career paths. This setting is very different from that of liberal democracies, where there are multiple political ambition outlets, where the system is open (at least in the formal sense), and where opportunity structures have not been unified. In liberal democracies, the politically ambitious have a varied set of mobility opportunities and are less dependent upon the narrow and self-interested judgments of a small, concentrated, and highly homogeneous political elite. The reality of institutional competition within the divergent elite and among societal interests only widens the range of options before aspiring politicians. Until recently, career advances in the Soviet system have not taken place across independent interests and institutions, but only within a unified set of hierarchies. The nomenklatura system was predicated upon central control over political mobility, with aspirants having little choice but to demonstrate deference to the top leadership. There was every incentive for the powerful to closely monitor careers, while there were few if any restraints upon them as they did so.

Given this political opportunity structure, it behooved those initiating careers to foster connections with the powerful. There were no explicit rules stopping them from doing so. On the contrary, political norms and expectations encouraged candidates to forge such ties. The reality that there were many aspirants and few slots in the decision-making process only heightened an aspirant's interest in establishing connections with those in the nomenklatura ranks. One young aspiring politician made these concerns clear to me as he tried to build his career in Moscow's party organization. For him, correctly understanding the political proclivities of various local and regional party first secretaries was critical as he linked up with a particular local party organization and began the arduous move up the hierarchy. He fully anticipated riding the coat-tails of a "far-sighted" politician with career potential (*perspektivnii politik*). Officials seeking advancement adopted certain common behavioral proclivities – being obeisant, cautious, and conservative in viewpoint. The result was a higher level of political elite attitudinal constraint. There were policy differences, but the system did not encourage them.

In any system, the ambitions of aspiring officials determine their career-building activities. Knowledge of the political opportunity structure helps us to infer those individuals' ambitions on the basis of positions they have held.[3] We may differentiate among ambitions by examining politicians' careers and tracing their patterns of mobility. This strategy is especially helpful in enabling us to identify those who have had the most influence over the political process. The political elite examined in the national and republic studies exhibited a range of ambition types. Comparison of careers reveals that up-and-coming politicians with *progressive ambition*, who most influenced the operations of the political system, were especially prone to use patronage connections to advance themselves. These politicians generally advanced within the party apparatus, linking themselves to upwardly mobile superiors. Their multifaceted career backgrounds reveal that they tended to be "generalists" who functioned in various political settings. During the Brezhnev and post-Brezhnev periods, these politicians were educated and experienced. Client "party hacks" were not a common phenomenon of these regimes.

Within the top political bodies there were also officials whose careers revealed *discrete* and *static* ambitions. Among CC/AC members were representative workers, milkmaids, and heroic figures. Their ambition was discrete in that they held only one political office and for a specified term. Seldom were these individuals tied to system-level patrons or parts of larger patronage networks. They were at best peripheral actors in the Soviet political drama. Politicians with static ambition were more politically significant if they made long-term careers in a single domain or held one position over an extended period. Many ethnic minority representatives made such careers. Some of these officials were constrained by Soviet political realities that minimized the mobility of non-Russians. We can, however, identify politicians who garnered a certain degree of authority and were able to maintain their elite status for a considerable time, but whose political ambition and career needs, relative to those of high-powered clients, appeared to be modest.[4] These politicians could be highly motivated, but their career tracks severely limited their ultimate mobility prospects.

In the Soviet Union as elsewhere, the political opportunity structure sets both the norms of career building and the expectations of thousands of individuals who seriously aspire to ascend the political summit. Examining that opportunity structure, we can determine which positions and institutions are the most effective conduits leading politicians to the upper echelon of the ruling elite. The earlier studies identified certain "springboard" positions and organizations, most being key slots and units within the party apparatus. Serving in key CC departments – such as the organizational–party work and general departments – enhanced opportunities for upward mobility. So did leading an important regional party organization. The experience of numerous incumbents in these organizational slots demonstrates that these positions provided the greatest opportunity for mobility to senior national positions.

Often these springboard positions were the organizational bailiwicks of already powerful system patrons. Those patrons were aware of their significance and carefully selected occupants. They cultivated associates whose prospects for further advancement were accordingly strengthened. In this rigid system – with many competing politicians with progressive ambition – the opportunity structure made patronage networks a most effective vehicle for mobility. Regardless of national regime, aspirants looking up the political hierarchy manipulated these connections to maximize their career prospects. Only a profound decentralization and democratization of the political system could alter these traditional norms.

The view from above

While there was a system logic compelling aspiring politicians to enhance their career prospects through patronage networks, there was a comparable rationale for established politicians to rely on these networks for their own power consolidation efforts. The political and institutional positions of more senior officials and their network members could be strengthened by recruitment and coalition-building activities. The ambitions of senior politicians entailed more than their own career advances, they entailed also the advances of other trusted and connected officials. A new leader – or any powerful politician – was compelled by the Soviet institutional structure and its informal rules to engage in personnel rotation and the careful cultivation of subordinates. While these activities began with a top leadership succession or a politician's advance, they continued throughout a politician's career. They involved the expansion of one's network – at least within one's own institutional domain – as well as the forging of alliances with other politicians and interests.

Expanded patronage networks helped to link the party and state hierarchies. They were important at all levels of authority. At the highest levels, a leader's ambitions embraced the consolidation of power within the party apparatus. The critical organs overseeing personnel and organizational matters were the important first targets for high-level personnel changes and the elevation of a powerful politician's associates. Those institutions responsible for the policy areas critical to the leader's programmatic interests (and authority) also merited attention. It was quite possible that the leader had earlier experience and some influence in such areas. Associates or politicians allied with the leader generally were responsible for filling the leadership voids in these areas. From this base of operation within the central party apparatus, the increasingly powerful patron could direct changes in lower-level party organizations as well as in the state bureaucracy. He or she was better able to form a government, a coalition of allied politicians that not only formulated policy, but could oversee its actual implementation.

These personnel placements were especially profitable to a system patron in the supervision and implementation of policy. Western pluralist notions of the policy process have focused on the input side, i.e., actual policy making. In these conceptualizations, attention is focused on the critical policy-making institutions (e.g., the Politburo) and the influence brought to bear on policy formulation by aggregated interests; but the output side of the ledger should not be ignored, especially in the traditional Soviet system. This system significantly limited the ability of politicians who were not at the highest decision-making levels to influence policy. If they had any influence, it was likely to be indirect and of an advisory nature. Any direct influence had to be applied at the implementation stage, when an official assumed a supervisory function. It was at this stage that what Downs calls "authority leakage" took place.[5] To minimize such leakage, a chief executive had to use personnel policy to gain more direct control over the institutions and positions that had assumed critical implementing and supervisory roles. In the Soviet-type system, bureaucracies carrying out policy were much more important to the top elite than nascent lobbies or interest groups, which could only influence policy formulation in an indirect way. Control over those bureaucracies – obtained by penetrating one's network into those bureaucracies – became a top political and career priority for a leader.

Once the network carved a niche for itself in the system, there was every reason to safeguard its political position. The integrity of the group became important and loyalty assumed a new importance. The loyalty of network members remained rational as long as the network helped members in their pursuit of power. Conditions could arise encouraging network members to forge political ties with other more powerful politicians. In fact, as the national study revealed, some successful politicians built careers through multiple linkages. In general, however, there had to be very real career-related incentives for politicians to jettison protective network associations; but there were some very powerful incentives for politicians not to violate this interdependent relationship. Any politician considering a shift from one network to another needed to weigh the gains of the new association against the costs of appearing even more careerist than the average official. In such a shift, a politician risked violating a basic norm of the Soviet polity and society: that of individual and group loyalty and reliability.[6] The Soviet-Russian political culture – essentially derived from a traditional peasant setting – placed a high value upon these qualities. Depending upon the circumstances, violation of such a norm could prove very costly to one engaged in long-term career building.[7]

The new politics

The decentralization of decision making and the democratization of the political process are fundamentally altering the traditional Soviet political opportunity structure and the behavior of Soviet politicians. As the political opportunity structure opens, its hierarchies become disentangled and more independent of one another. Whether the result is a more independent system of Soviets or the emergence of a multi-party system, organized and institutional interests become distinguishable; we can already differentiate ever more separate party, government, and parliamentary hierarchies. The central control that was the hallmark of the Soviet system is giving way to a more fractious politics. In the Soviet Union of the early 1990s we find a new system of *formal* institutional checks and balances that is enhancing the influence of once-powerless bodies. The informal checks and balances of patronage networks seem increasingly superfluous.

The new political arrangements of the Gorbachev period leave more institutional outlets available to aspiring politicians. Newly independent party, government, and parliamentary institutions become alternative career channels through which politicians may rise. The logic of these institutions' personnel recruitment and mobility – and the logic of their very operation – will vary. It is already evident that the qualities maximizing an aspirant's rise in one institution vary from those needed to excel in another. The reliability and deference so prized in the CPSU apparatus contrast sharply with the popular standing needed to advance to and in parliamentary bodies. Moreover, the traditional springboard positions within the CPSU apparatus that were once so attractive to the ambitious are naturally giving way to more influential elected parliamentary positions.

It is clear that the resources needed for career success differ given the norms of this changing political opportunity structure. Depending on the way power is organized, patronage connections may continue to be of importance. But circumstances vary considerably: the Lithuanian election results of early 1990 demonstrated the limited utility of patronage relations in a competitive electoral setting, yet strong pressures from Moscow have not been able to alter the importance of network connections in the formation of Azerbaidzhani regimes. The *new politics* of political accountability and reform require politicians to exhibit the "right" attitudes and at least the potential for the "right" performance, as Brazauskas found in Lithuania and Yeltsin has demonstrated in the RSFSR. Initial Soviet electoral results revealed no single set of preferred attitudes or behavior. Attitudes and behavior are judged, however, not in terms of organizational prowess but in ability to address the issue agenda. Indeed, the political strength of politicians such as Brazauskas and Yeltsin also rests on their ability to construct working coalitions of interests which, unlike past coalitions, are based more on issue positions and less on organizational or patronage considerations.

Events of the late 1980s and early 1990s revealed a continuing role for networks in Soviet political life. There are still opportunities for the powerful to sponsor at least like-minded allies, if not long-term protégés. Trusted subordinates continue to fill organizational slots, though they likely serve under the direct institutional purview of the senior official making the appointment. Gorbachev's own influence over the membership of the Presidential Council and Ryzhkov's influence over the Presidium revealed their institutional prerogatives. But in the Presidential Council, while a number of loyalists and senior allies were included, there were still pressures on Gorbachev to include some balance of representatives of diverse societal interests (e.g., the reformer A.E. Kauls and the conservative V.G. Rasputin). In the period of reform, the political world of Soviet executives is clearly more complex and uncertain.

The Soviet *second polity* in comparative perspective

A central contention of this study is that the pursuit of power in a constrained political opportunity structure encourages the flourishing of informal networks and extralegal arrangements. These conditions maximize the prospects of a *second polity*, structuring career-building and policy-making activities. A second important contention is that the traditional Soviet system has required these informal arrangements which provided the slack necessary for it to function. Other political systems, especially in so-called "developing" societies, also exhibit these phenomena. These societies have the objective conditions, sociopolitical traditions, and political culture that promote patronage networks. With so many of these societies also in the midst of rapid change, the Soviet experience assumes interest and relevance. The Soviet case is distinctive because power has been so concentrated and political mobility and decision-making channels have been so institutionalized, centralized, and formally defined. Top-level politicians enjoyed especially wideranging discretionary powers. Here, relations of domination and subordination naturally characterized elite political behavior, and these relations were reinforced by the bureaucratized decision-making process.

The Soviet-Russian political culture reinforced the tendency to rely on extralegal arrangements such as patronage networks. It was essentially a peasant political culture – though moderated by a modernization ethos – similar to many developing societies in which the elite and masses had common expectations of the political system. A "subject political culture" that encouraged deference to the elite and that favored values of collectivism and social responsibility within communities clearly accommodated patron–client networks.[8] The absence of other mechanisms permitting the expression and satisfaction of demands by a mass populace only reinforced the need for informal networks. In many developing societies inequality favoring the elite has been accepted and assumed. Politics has represented the means by which the guiding elite patrons legitimately, and in an unrestrained fashion, helped their subordinates and citizens realize desired political (and often economic) ends.[9]

Patronage relations were important when resources were scarce and access to them was concentrated in the hands of only a few. As the Soviet-Russian experience demonstrates, that scarcity may reflect not objective realities but subjective political conditions. There may be many existent resources in a society, but control over their distribution and use may be highly concentrated. The latifundia systems of the Mediterranean cultures are also illustrative, as they encouraged the development of more modern social networks and an ethos accommodating patronage networks.[10] Successful control of land and distribution of produce distinguished bosses and clients. The relative poverty of much of the population in the region enhanced the positions of those who distributed the resources. Very personalistic patron–client ties flourished on the basis of direct, but unequal, reciprocity in the exchange of goods and services. This pattern continued even as the latifundia systems evolved: formally political actors (e.g., party leaders, mayors, etc.) simply replaced landowners as the key gatekeepers to resources.

The actual manner of power concentration has varied considerably, in some cases favoring oligarchical arrangements such as are found in Latin America, and in others favoring a centralized national regime such as that of the Soviet-type system. The oligarchical political systems in many Latin American countries often permit the regional elite to assume dominant power positions, and not only on the local but also the national political scenes.[11] The boss or *cacique* utilizes the support of various elements of the local socioeconomic elite (e.g., landowners, allied clergy, and financiers) to assure himself a measure of autonomy *vis-à-vis* the national government while remaining the formidable political power source in his own community.[12] The *cacique* possesses the connections and access to various resources that make him an indispensable "representative" for the local community. Cliques of these bosses that represent regional interests actually serve as legislators in many Latin countries. They set government policy – not in the sense of sitting formally in a legal legislative body, but rather through hard bargaining with regional peers and national-level officials, who are all somewhat accommodating so as to maintain their privileged positions.[13]

The modernization and rapid development of many developing societies did not alter the relevance of informal connections to elite mobility and behavior. Often that development only contributed to the continuing importance of patronage networks in providing coherence and predictability in an unstable political environment. The Soviet-Russian case demonstrated this, for top Bolshevik leaders responded to the pressures of maintaining their newly found power by relying upon their "connections" and networks of loyal protégés in forming a ruling elite cohort. Regional bosses became the critical actors linking the national Bolshevik regime with the periphery. Bolshevik recruitment and governing norms rapidly came to approximate many norms of the previous tsarist regime and its bureaucracy.

In other modernizing societies the emergence of universal suffrage, the modern political party, and mass political elections has altered the political landscape. These mechanisms have linked many diverse elements, including the political center and the periphery, moderating the politics of patronage, faction, and personality. But many have not been immune to the factions and clientelistic connections that can assume a semi-integrative role. That role could be quite functional when regional and lower-level interests coincided with those of the national regime.

In many settings the advent of the modern political party has not altered the salience of patronage politics. While the monolithic one-party system helped to maximize the utility of informal networks, circumstances could also arise in multi-party systems where such informal clusters became politically significant. Comparable to the factions of powerful notables in Ancient Rome[14] and the groupings of politicians in early European and American political parties,[15] personalistic networks have represented alliances among individuals seeking common or interrelated goals. The coalition building and electoral success of contenders have been connected with patronage networks that provided ties to the localities. Parties' electoral success could be assured by their careful manipulation of voters through the allocation of development projects from the state.[16] Party patrons have attempted to maximize power and turn public institutions and resources to their own ends through favors exchanged for votes.[17] Such favors have ranged from the selection of personnel and the awarding of contracts to the propitious regulation of local economic and political life.[18] Through political parties, as new integrating mechanisms, traditionally favored elite elements could maintain their authoritative positions. The party leader – now in the position of local boss or chief – replaced the landowner and served in the capacity of regional or local patron.[19] Party politicians distributed goods or jobs for electoral success. Their power grew as the scope of the national government's activities expanded into the localities. The wide gulf that previously separated the center and periphery narrowed, as did the gaps between the localities comprising that periphery. Patrons linked their interests and localities to the center and to each other. Party-based patrons often supervised the application of national initiatives and programs in their own bailiwicks, such as occurred with the Congress Party and its regionally based elite in India.[20]

The Soviet-Russian experience was comparable, though the degree to which the regional patron's role mediated central and peripheral interests is questionable. We have seen that the Soviet system limited the prerogatives of regional politicians, though officials did possess some advocacy privileges on behalf of their local interests. Over time, however, lower-level officials and networks became more comfortable in pursuing their own interests. Whether sponsored by or simply tolerated by national authorities, lower-level networks learned the rules of the political game and how they were applied by those authorities.

Vestiges of patronage politics can also be found in more developed societies, including liberal democracies, where the political opportunity structure has been controlled by relatively narrow elements of the elite. Clusters of personal relations have emerged within institutions and organized groups such as party organizations. In these cases political power has become concentrated in the hands of a selectorate comprising the local or regional party leadership.[21] Under these conditions there has been a minimal check on the behavior of the party organizational leadership. Regional, local, and urban patronage machines, as exemplified by the Chicago politics of Mayor Richard Daley and the machines of powerful Louisiana governors, have functioned effectively because a certain democratic centralism – if the term may be applied – assured a patronage network unity in the face of external challenges.[22] Such political networks have been quite heterogeneous, bridging various ethnic groups and social classes. They possessed resources and were effective in helping network members secure access to the political and economic opportunity structures.[23] Often, the machine boss or patron could even control the preelection selection process of candidates.

What has existed in the patronage machines found in liberal democracies is what Samuel Eldersveld termed a "stratarchy" of power, where power is distributed within the organization through semi-autonomous layers.[24] These layers are hierarchically linked and reciprocally deferential. Similar to patronage networks in developing and Soviet-type systems, mutual need, mutual support, mutual respect, and much inter-echelon accommodation characterize a stratarchy. But we find in these machines, as in the patronage machines of the traditional Soviet system, what might be termed a "command model" of power distribution, with deference directed strictly upward. Even in the liberal democracies, conditions could encourage reliance on political networks to gain access to a society's opportunity structures. Networks could – on one level – help represent interests and integrate particular societal elements. When these societies address the issues of more complete representation and broader integration of interests, however, the dysfunctional qualities of networks tend to lessen their long-term viability.[25] In liberal democracies competitive elections and regime turnover provide the slack necessary for the democratic polity to function effectively.

Developments in Gorbachev's USSR echo this Western liberal–democratic experience. One need only contrast contemporary developments in Lithuania with those in Azerbaidzhan. In the former, mechanisms such as competitive elections and independent interest groups are widening the range of interests influencing the policy process. The utility of extralegal agencies such as patronage networks has become limited. In Azerbaidzhan, however, where political power remains concentrated and the political culture promotes informal means of interest representation, networks continue to flourish. The expansion of the Soviet party system does not signify the automatic demise of network politics.

But what of the modern state bureaucracy – a universal phenomenon of the twentieth century – and its relevance to politics and patronage? How does that bureaucracy affect the political opportunity structure and politicians' career ambitions? The traditional Soviet system assumed a developed and interconnected set of bureaucracies. The logic of those bureaucracies was not Weberian – indeed, there was always a good deal of what one scholar termed a "bureaucratic shapelessness" – but it did presume a certain regularization and routinization of behavior.[26] The Soviet experience exemplified that of many other developing societies, for as the national government and bureaucracy developed, many responsibilities of the regional elite were coopted. This tendency was only reinforced by the centralized structure of the policy-making process. Most modern bureaucracies have become more hierarchical and compartmentalized – though not to the same degree as the Soviet system. But their standard operating procedures have become more multifarious, and the need for a structuring or organizing mechanism to ensure their effective coordination has become ever more pronounced.

The Soviet experience demonstrates that patronage could assume a functional role in a complex bureaucratic setting if it enhanced elite attitudinal constraint and policy coherence. It was conducive to governance if (a) competing interests were brought together; (b) the prospects for shared policy positions were increased; and (c) the center's policies and interests were more likely to be pursued in the locales. But utility must be judged on the basis of desired ends. Patronage networks could promote system continuity and policy change, and both continuity and change could be seen in functional and dysfunctional terms. Likewise, patronage networks could aid system integration *qua* central control over potentially autonomous local actors, or they could create complacent, status quo oriented entities – driven by self interest – that only widen the gap between center and periphery.

The legacy of the Brezhnev regime reveals the complex impact of patronage relations. During the first half of the Brezhnev period (1964–75), patronage relations aided consensus coalition building, resulting in a policy program that simultaneously enhanced Soviet power and raised the population's standard of living. Yet in the succeeding years, patronage relations reinforced a conservative regime whose policies resulted in economic stagnation, social and political complacence, and the overextension of the Soviet global position. From the Gorbachev regime's perspective, the Brezhnev extended network proved quite dysfunctional. This judgment reflects not only the Gorbachev leadership's conception of Brezhnev's priorities and performance but also its own political interests and needs. Such judgments are variable and reflect different goals. And in the complex and bureaucratized modern political setting, mechanisms are still required to bridge interests and institutions. Thus, a Gorbachev regime that decried the nepotism of the Brezhnev era has also used connections and cultivated particular types of officials in its promotion of *perestroika*.

The logic of the bureaucratic-political setting in both the Brezhnev and initial Gorbachev regimes was similar: many officeholders were grouped together on the basis of past associations and common, interrelated, upward mobility. A politician's desire to function within a complex organization, to control it, and to influence its policies has required the cooperation of functionaries at lower levels. The hierarchical authority patterns of the developed bureaucracy have often reinforced the loyalty of officials at lower levels to those at higher ones. The informal relations that emerge out of these hierarchical interactions have even superseded the formal distinctions associated with putatively superior or subordinate positions.[27] The patron–client groups that emerge in such institutional settings have only benefited from the intra-organizational communications networks found in any bureaucracy. This is true in many national settings. Nathan demonstrated the success of Chinese officials in consolidating their positions through personalistic factions.[28] In China, patronage networks have facilitated the communication of policy priorities and the distribution of resources to subordinates operating at different organizational levels. They have also facilitated the transmission of lower-level demands to the top.[29] Here and elsewhere, regardless of political domain, officials in the role of patron could use the institutional resources at their command to strengthen their administrative positions. Officials who aspired to higher-level mobility often possessed the desire and means to manipulate appointments and forge alliances within their administrative domains. If the bases for connections and alliances were not only grounded in past associations and common experiences, but in common political and institutional interests, then the system would have profited from such informal endeavors. This has been especially true when group-level interests and system-level needs converged.[30]

Much of the literature on patron–client ties in developing societies has stressed the importance of the personal bond. Within the modern bureaucracy, the personal bond might or might not be a critical element tying careers together over the long haul. A personalized relationship based on past common experience has served as an adhesive. This, however, has been negated in those settings in which explicit rules of impartiality and impersonality counter the political implications of personal bonds. Clientelistic networks have been most likely to arise at the nexus between the public and private sectors in Western polities. This is due to the fact that there have been fewer – more informal – constraints operating on those officials and politicians found at these junctures. Powerful interest associates who link private and semi-private lobbies to the government bureaucracy exhibit forms of patronage behavior, but where civil service rules and norms have been less developed, the utility of such personal bonds could be enhanced by common views and goals between the parties. A commonality in views based on past experiences has made the bond stronger.

At the same time, the nature of the modern bureaucracy transforms the individual actor's role into one of cross-cutting responsibilities. A modern political functionary is, after all, not only a potential leader, but also an administrator, a policy advocate, an affiliate with sectoral, organizational, and geographic groupings, and a member of various demographically defined cohorts. As a result, the potential patron or client performs a range of tasks that likely differentiate that individual from other functionaries. As Michael Crozier argues, this set of roles corresponds to the hierarchical arrangements within the bureaucratic setting.[31] It presupposes interactions among individuals who assume superior and subordinate roles.

Regardless of national setting, it is fair to conclude that where explicit civil service codes and norms of behavior are absent, the modern bureaucracy is fertile ground for informal factions and clientelistic networks. This is especially true where essentially administrative bureaucracies are not separated from the actual political process – a reality of many developing countries, as well as of countries with the traditional Soviet-type political system.[32] In the USSR, where the bureaucracy and political system have become more meritocratic, patronage politics still thrive. Rational-technical theories are correct in contending that rules are more explicitly detailed and rigorously applied. Soviet political life has been normalized – and more routinized – during the past decades. In the absence of such system rules, there would be no sense of accountability and no generally accepted standards of behavior. Yet a rigid application of such rules would make all politicians and networks, including those at the top, highly vulnerable. Rules, however detailed, have been loose enough in their application to enable the governing elite to promote its interests.

The ubiquity of bureaucracy in socialist countries has caused a great dependence on formal organization and authority. Alfred Meyer once characterized the Soviet system as a "bureaucracy writ large."[33] This core feature has separated the traditional Soviet political setting from others. It helps to explain the salience of clientelistic networks in Soviet socialist countries. In the developing world even though the most traditional political systems have been transformed by the modern bureaucracy and political party, these institutions did not assume complete responsibility for resource distribution, sociopolitical integration, and other key tasks of the regime. Unlike the Soviet Union, there has been no interlocking set of institutions linking all actors and parts of the polity. The economic sector has remained, to varying degrees across these diverse polities, distinguishable from the political domain. While political parties and the national bureaucracy have interconnected various elements across policy-making levels in developing countries, they have not represented a monolithic structure assuming full responsibility across all issue domains. Regional power brokers, with autonomy from the center and interests distinguishable from the center, have often been able to continue as important political actors in their own right. Such local power brokers, operating as patrons in the regions, could assume important integrative and functional roles.[34] In the traditional Soviet system, however, the center and periphery were much more closely interconnected; the regional elite enjoyed less autonomy.

Thus we find that two conditions that cultivate informal political relations and clientelism have been manifested in rather different ways in Soviet and developing societies. First, while political power in the Soviet system has been concentrated in a stratified and hierarchical setting, it has been less concentrated in the more porous political-administrative structures found in most developing societies. Second, while there has been a single base of power and authority in the traditional Soviet system, there have been often alternative and competing bases of power in developing countries. Indeed, developing societies' relative lack of centralized power – and the absence of an all-powerful national government – has generally enhanced the bargaining positions of regional and lower-level network leaders who were competing to expand their powerbases. Ruling groups of the elite might monopolize political power in both systems, but their nature and composition have varied considerably.

Political development, a subject political culture, and the evolving modern bureaucracy ensure that clientelism will have continuing relevance to elite recruitment, mobility, and behavior. The manner of power distribution and the presence of checks on its manipulation by specific individuals and groups are the most important factors in predicting elite behavior and political clientelism. Highly concentrated power within an explicitly defined hierarchy insulates the elite's position and promotes networks. The absence of mediating mechanisms, such as competitive electoral processes that permit a rotation or replacement of politicians through extra-hierarchical means, further encourages such relations. When these two conditions – highly concentrated power and an absence of checks – are combined, the prospects for informal political associations are magnified.

The experience of the Soviet past reveals that for patronage networks to emerge and form the basis of governing coalitions, political power must be concentrated and centralized, though not excessively so. Both the dynamic 1920s and 1950s permitted Moscow to set broad policy lines while patronage networks emerged and thrived at all levels. The national leadership was strong enough to countenance change, but it needed local representatives in the central apparatus and locales to enforce its directives. These periods of power consolidation by the national regime were fully conducive to the proliferation of numerous networks. An era when forces are being mobilized (or remobilized) will especially afford the dynamism and fluidity permitting networks to thrive. From the standpoint of national leaders, such networks are functional to governance.

But as power becomes more concentrated at the top, the number and range of networks' activities will be constrained. This certainly proved true during the latter 1930s and after World War II, as members of networks – operating primarily beneath either Stalin or his top lieutenants – were more circumspect in advancing their

interests. Even Stalin's protégés proved vulnerable to the fluctu-
ations in his thinking and policy line.

The evolution of the USSR into a post-Stalin system maintenance
phase altered the politics of patronage networks. Not only coercion
but expectations of enhanced performance influenced the behavior
and career aspirations of officials. Subordinates were granted somewhat increased leeway in fulfilling their responsibilities. Throughout
the post-Stalin era, there has been increased room for political
maneuvering by lower-level officials and their networks, both in the
central apparatus and the locales. National leaders lacking the
hegemonic power of their Stalin era predecessors have cultivated
their ties to such officials and networks to strengthen their own
positions. The strategies adopted by national leaderships to channel
subordinates' behavior have varied. Khrushchev applied a personnel
rotation approach, while Brezhnev made use of personnel stability.
Both strategies helped new national leaderships to consolidate power
and apply new policy programs; both ultimately proved dysfunctional in the latter phases of those regimes, severely tainting the
legacies of the two leaders. The Gorbachev leadership's program of
political reforms has begun to fundamentally change the character
and utility of Soviet political patronage. In the first five years of the
regime the political opportunity structure was altered to permit a
wider range of interests to effect policy in more contentious ways.
Soviet politics have taken on a dynamism and spontaneity previously unknown. The experience of other societies suggests there
can be a future role for patronage politics in the new Soviet polity;
but a role that is more limited, circumscribed by more explicitly
developed institutional rules and elite norms.

An uncertain Soviet future

The democratization process, with its varying developments in
Moscow and the diverse locales, does not permit easy generalization
about the Soviet elite and policy process. My national, Lithuanian,
and Azerbaidzhani studies suggest different reform experiences and
alternative futures regarding the evolution of Soviet elite politics and
the role of patronage networks in regime formation and governance.
These studies anticipate a prolonged period during which institutional arrangements and political practices will differ considerably
among the diversity of regions comprising the USSR. There is every

likelihood that national politics will be influenced by norms that are not transferred to the republics.

How are we to assess the future of Soviet patronage politics? This is no easy task, as there is an ephemeral quality to patron–client networks. No institutionalized rituals or norms consecrate them or enhance their viability or visibility. Because networks encompass various settings and types of politicians, it is difficult to generalize about members' behavior and network norms. Beyond a politician's most intimate and long-term associations are more attenuated political relationships which form the bulk of an extended patronage network.

This volume has adopted a functionalist approach to patron–client relations, describing how they have been conducive to regime formation and governance in the Soviet system. The vagaries of Soviet bureaucracies – with their constant reorganizations and the imprecision with which responsibilities are delegated within and among them – have reinforced the utility of such relations. My analysis has revealed the payoffs of patronage both to network members and to the broader system and society. Yet this study has also revealed how patronage networks undercut governance, especially when networks obstruct and subvert regime policies and system goals. Every Soviet regime, whether at the national level or below, has come up against this reality.

The traditional Soviet system has required extra-legal networks to grease the bureaucratic engine. It has operated more effectively when informal networks were bridging individuals', groups', institutions', and sectors' interests. The system, however, has been changing; the imperatives for securing power and authority are being altered. Political reforms are permitting the emergence of other mechanisms that also bridge interests – mechanisms which in other national settings have proven more effective in allowing actors to openly join their interests and careers together. The triumph of interest groups and the emergence of political parties could signify the beginning of a new stage in Soviet political development. But the remarkable resilience of patronage networks in diverse societies suggests there may well be a place for patron–client relations in the Soviet *new politics*.

Appendix

Norms of leadership recruitment and coalition formation developed in this study are identified on the basis of a systematic analysis of elite biographies and career précis. The tradition of using collective biographies to analyze coalition behavior and elite politics goes back at least to Lewis Namier's work on British politics of the eighteenth and early nineteenth centuries.[1] His approach allowed him to identify coalitions of individuals and to examine the importance of patronage ties in matters of recruitment and policy. Other scholars followed his example, developing an analytical approach and literature identified as prosopography.[2] Useful for testing hypotheses about populations of elites, prosopography is especially appropriate for studying elite politics in closed societies. The paucity of elite biographical and attitudinal data only reinforces the appropriateness of a systematic investigation of norms and trends on the basis of available aggregated data. For the Soviet Union, minimal career and attitudinal data are available for national officials, while at lower levels elite data are practically nonexistent. Using collective biographies – to the extent that they are available – frees us from undue reliance upon individual cases and enhances the confidence we may have in the norms and trends identified.

In my studies, the political elite is understood to constitute politicians who wield decision-making authority at either the all-union or the republic level: (a) all members and candidate members of the all-union or the republic party central committee (CC), and (b) all members of the all-union or republic party central auditing commission (CAC). By including all CC/CAC members, I am automatically including the membership of the top policy-making bodies, the Politburo (or *buro* in the republics) and the Secretariat, as well as the top leadership within the Council of Ministers, the Supreme Soviet, and other major party and state institutions at the

242

national and/or republic levels. By definition, CC/CAC membership confers political elite status on individuals, even if their institutional affiliations are less prestigious. Indeed, token members of these bodies gain certain perquisites with inclusion, though they do not possess the influence enjoyed by those with strong institutional affiliations.

All CC/CAC members are treated as potential protégés or clients of the first secretary. I believe there are only marginal differences in the status of CC full and candidate members. While the full member officially has voting rights, available evidence suggests that the entire CC/CAC membership acts as a consultative body to the party Politburo and does not decide policy matters by vote – at least not during the period covered by this study. The same is true at the republic level, with the comparable memberships serving as consultative bodies made up of representatives of the republic's sectoral and territorial interests. The difference between the CC and the CAC as consultative bodies is likely minimal. The Central (or republic) Auditing Commission oversees the party discipline of members and candidates of the Communist Party. While the Auditing Commission's more focused institutional concerns make it of less direct importance to policy making, its membership's close ties to the central party apparatus, combined with the tendency for cross-organizational mobility between it and the CC, place the AC and CC on the same level. It is true that there is a rough hierarchy that differentiates these politicians into three ranks, with full CC members at the highest level, followed by candidate members, and then by members of the CAC. But combined, these three groups represent a locus of real decision-making power, at the all-union level and at the republic level.[3]

In order to establish that a patronage relationship between two individuals exists, two major conditions must be met. First, the two politicians must have been in geographic proximity for a given period of time during their careers. Second, a positive pattern in their promotions must be such that as patron X rises, his clients $x1$, $x2$, and $x3$ also rise with him, though they may be at various authority levels and rise at different rates. Certainly, the first condition is necessary if the relationship is to be a personal, reciprocal one, while the second is necessary if the relationship is to thrive in the political system and have any political significance.[4]

Measuring the mobility of politicians and assessing whether positional changes represent promotions, lateral moves, or demotions, can be tricky. This is especially true for the reform period of the late 1980s and 1990s. I weighted different positions in institutions according to (a) their degree of policy-relevant influence and responsibility, and (b) their degree of prestige. Evaluating positions within institutions was more straightforward. Titles suggest the relative positions of personnel within an institutional hierarchy (e.g., chairman, deputy minister, head of section, responsible worker in section x, etc.). Nevertheless, comparing positions across institutions is difficult, especially when considering whether a transfer to a qualitatively different job actually represents a promotion.

I utilize a scheme that differentiates the party and the state apparatuses. Using this scheme, I define promotion to represent two basic types of job transfer. First, mobility up any organizational hierarchy, from one level to any other level above that level, is treated as a promotion. Second, movement from a state or other apparatus position to a party position at that level or a higher level constitutes a promotion. This decision rule reflects my belief that as the primary policy-making and policy-supervisory hierarchy during the period under study, the party apparatus has been more powerful and more prestigious than any other apparatus.

I also identify two types of demotion. First, demotion constitutes any movement downward within or across the organizational hierarchies. A lateral move from the party hierarchy to another hierarchy also constitutes a demotion, though certain subtleties in mobility and norms of transfer are lost in the process. Assessing lateral movements of cadres is the most difficult aspect of evaluating elite recruitment and mobility. In many cases a lateral move could represent promotion, demotion, or simply transfer, such as in the case of a CC secretary for industry who is selected as chairman of a republic supreme soviet. Does movement from a critical post in the party apparatus (possibly position number three or four in that apparatus, after the first secretary, the second secretary, and perhaps ahead of the secretary for agriculture) to the most visible position within the governmental hierarchy represent a step up, across, or down? The decision rules suggest this is a promotion, as the individual moved from a second level position within the party apparatus to a top position within the state apparatus (albeit a less powerful position within the total configuration of institutions within the republic). But this is a tricky identification and, without first-hand information, judgment calls must be made.

These stipulations are sufficient for a first cut at elite mobility and clientelism, for individuals making careers meriting CC/CAC membership would have come into contact with one another as they were moving up from the regional and lower levels. Given the relatively small universe of a republic's political elite, it is difficult to imagine individuals moving up the political ladder without awareness of one another in a specific territorial or institutional setting. And given the limited number of political slots to be filled by top party leaders, reciprocal personal relationships will arise as former professional acquaintances from specific institutions and regions are recruited into positions of republic-level significance.

Although the biographical data for republic-level officials are scarce, two additional indicators of clientelistic ties – common educational experience and common experience in the Second World War – may further confirm the ties suggested by career indicators.[5] Common educational experience means having attended the same institution or university during the same time period. Common war experience means having served in the same region, in the same partisan group, or on the same front during World War II. Factoring these measures in not only underscores the ties identified through multiple measures, but also helps in distinguishing the duration of those ties.

Patronage ties based upon appointment and common past experience are captured by my measures. The strongest basis for such ties, common political beliefs grounded in common past experience, may only be measured through consideration of elite public statements. This is very difficult to accomplish at a subnational level given the paucity of attitudinal data. As a result, the two republic studies can only infer the policy implications of the republic party first secretaries' coalition-building efforts for the formative years of their new regimes. The Lithuanian and Azerbaidzhani studies rely upon the public statements of the republic first secretaries to indicate how their public posturing related to policy concerns. At the national level, however, limited attitudinal data for a larger population of officials are available. We can assess the relationships among patronage, coalition formation, and attitudes of Soviet officials.

One caveat should be noted in the identification of patronage networks. A powerful patron, upon reaching a higher level of authority, is in the position not only to recruit former protégés, but to sponsor relative newcomers to higher-level political circles. Such "newcomers" may not have served previously with that politician, but the rapid upward mobility of such personnel over a short time period suggests that, at the very least, those individuals enjoy the favor of the patron. I identify such individuals who enjoy rapid mobility under a patron within a short time period as "clients," distinguishing them from "protégés," or individuals who have worked with a politician-patron in the past and who continue to enjoy mobility under him in the present. This distinction between "protégé" and "client" is both necessary and useful. The "protégé" has a relatively more equal relationship with the patron that is based on shared common experience. The "client," however, moves up quickly in the hierarchy, has always been in a very subordinate position to the patron, and is consequently more dependent upon the patron. For the purposes of my studies, individuals who make two significant career advances under a patron during the *first* five-year period of the patron's tenure are identified as "clients." I have adopted George W. Breslauer's thinking that a new leader needs approximately five years to consolidate his power and form his own "team" in order to advance a policy program.[6] This is the critical period for a new leader and rapid promotions of subordinates are significant. Two distinct promotions for a politician during that all-important five-year period are strong evidence that the individual enjoys the confidence of his superior.

While adding an important dimension to the analysis, identification of clients is more difficult because it is not always clear who approves promotions. All available information is used in these studies to determine where individuals or political offices oversee others. Top-level KGB promotions during the Brezhnev period are a case in point. Although nearly all of the KGB deputy chairmen may have been formally elevated when Andropov headed that organization, Brezhnev and his group apparently enjoyed the institutional prerogatives to promote faction members into these positions. In addition, those officials had past associations with Brezhnev while lacking such associations with Andropov. Combined, these considerations led to the determination of Brezhnev network membership. Overall, application of my decision rules likely undercounts the total number of sponsored officials. But these decision rules yield very probable patron–client ties.

The MICRO Information Management System, developed by the Institute of Labor and Industrial Relations of the University of Michigan, was used in the systematic identification of patron–client ties. MICRO permits the coding of biographical and career data so that temporal, regional, institutional, and positional information can all be brought together in a single case. Each coded case represents one position held by an individual, with the following conditions: that a given politician A served between time T_1 and T_2 in region B, in institution C, with his/her position being D. A politician's career is made up of a number of such cases. All of these coded cases for all politicians can then be scanned and compared with the careers of others to identify patron–client ties.

To check the reliability of my coding rules and the results of the MICRO Program, selected samples of politicians were drawn from the Lithuanian and Azerbaidzhani elite populations. These samples – each with forty politicians – were not random; rather they were composed of the types of serious politicians found in the general populations (as opposed to milkmaids, workers, and others who would obviously not be coded as clients). The inter-coder reliability among three coders who examined these cases was 0.883 for the Lithuanian sample and 0.908 for the Azerbaidzhani sample. The degree of agreement between each two coders was as follows: for the Lithuanian sample, coders 1 and 2, 0.875; coders 2 and 3, 0.850; coders 1 and 3, 0.925; for the Azerbaidzhani sample, coders 1 and 2, 0.900; coders 2 and 3, 0.850; and coders 1 and 3, 0.975. The cases where the coders disagreed involved distinguishing between lateral and horizontal mobility of politicians who might, or might not, be clients of the new party first secretary.

The inter-coder reliability between the MICRO Program and the consensus coding of the three coders – 0.950 for both the Lithuanian and the Azerbaidzhani samples – was much higher than that between any one of the coders and MICRO. The fact that no one coder's coding agreed with that of MICRO as often as the consensus coding strengthens my confidence in the patron–client identifications made by the MICRO Program.

Biographical and career data

Elite biographical and career data were gathered from a number of sources, both Soviet and foreign. The basic sources for all politicians are the national and republic series, *Deputaty Verkhovnogo Soveta*, which provide career précis for all deputies of the relevant supreme soviet. I gained access in the Soviet Union to the 1965, 1968, 1971, and 1976 volumes for Azerbaidzhan, and the 1971, 1975, and 1980 volumes for Lithuania. All volumes of the national *Deputaty* were consulted. In addition, *Yezhegodniki* of the *Bol'shaya Sovetskaya*

Entsiklopediya were used, as were corresponding volumes for the two republics. Published obituaries in the central and regional press occasionally enabled me to update career files. The revived CPSU publication, *Izvestiya TsK KPSS,* was especially useful in locating précis for Gorbachev period officials.

Among English-language sources, I consulted the journal *Current Soviet Leaders,* 1974–79 (Mosaic Press), and Borys Lewytzkyj and Juliusz Stroynowski's volume, *Who's Who In The Socialist Countries* (New York: K.G. Saur Publishing Co., 1978). I also used various editions of Alexander G. Rahr's compilation, *A Biographic Directory of 100 Leading Soviet Officials* (Munich: Central Research, Radio Liberty, 1981, 1984, 1986, and 1988), to update files.

These sources yield biographical and career data for approximately 1,200 national politicians, covering the entire 1964–89 period. For Lithuania, the aggregated data for over 225 politicians span the period from 1971 to 1981. While most sources utilized were for the 1971–81 period, they provide information for many politicians of the earlier period, certainly from the mid-1960s on. Lithuanian media sources have been consulted to update this database to the extent possible for the period of the latter 1980s. For Azerbaidzhan, the aggregated data for over 400 officials span the period from 1965 to 1976. Again, many prominent figures of the earlier period are included in this population, with national and republic media sources consulted for post-Aliev developments.

The data collected for all politicians span both demographic and career considerations. They include an individual's year of birth, nationality, year of joining the Communist Party, level of education and institutional affiliation. They also include as complete an account of careers as possible, noting positions held, dates, and the places where the individual served.

Notes

1 The elite, patronage, and Soviet politics

1. Because the terms patronage and clientelism are understood to refer to the same phenomenon, they are used interchangeably throughout this volume.
2. Edwin A. Hollander and James W. Julian, "Contemporary trends in the analysis of leadership process," in W.E. Scott and L.I. Cummings, eds., *Readings in Organizational Behavior and Human Performance*, Homewood, Illinois: Irwin, 1973, pp. 432–41.
3. James MacGregor Burns, *Leadership*, New York: Harper and Row, 1978, p. 13.
4. As Robert Dahl has written, "homo politicus," by his nature, "deliberately allocates a very sizable share of his resources to the process of gaining and maintaining control over the policies of government." See Dahl, *Who Governs?*, New Haven: Yale University Press, 1961, p. 225.
5. See Jerome M. Gilison, "New factors of stability in Soviet collective leadership," *World Politics*, XIX, 4, July 1967, pp. 563–81, who argues that failure to achieve the desired ends of the group that a leader represents can cost that leader his legitimacy in their eyes. This certainly proved true in the political fate of Nikita Khrushchev.
6. This search for security is a critical factor underlying the behavior of politicians and is developed in Keith Legg, *Patrons, Clients, and Politicians: New Perspectives on Political Clientelism*, Berkeley: University of California, Institute of International Studies, Working Papers on Development, No. 3, 1976.
7. In certain national settings it is taken for granted that subordinates are tied personally to leaders. See for instance Minagawa's discussion of Japan (Shugo Minagawa, "Political clientelism in the USSR and Japan: a tentative comparison," *Nanzan hogaku*, 4, 1981, pp. 256–90).
8. For a comprehensive discussion of clientelism, see Steffen W. Schmidt, James C. Scott, Carl H. Lande, and Laura Guasti, eds., *Friends, Followers, and Factions: A Reader in Political Clientelism*, Berkeley: University of California Press, 1977. Also see René Lemarchand and Keith Legg, "Political clientelism and development," *Comparative Politics*, IV, 2, January 1972, pp. 149–78.

9. Eric R. Wolf, "Aspects of group relations in a complex society: Mexico," *American Anthropologist*, LVIII, 1956, pp. 1065–78.

10. Nobutaka Ike, *Japanese Politics: Patron Client Democracy*, New York: Knopf, 1972.

11. I am not interested in accounting for the specific actions of political actors, but rather the broad behavioral tendencies of groups of actors as they aspire to advance their careers and to influence the political process.

12. For a discussion of power distribution in the Russian *ancien regime*, see Richard Pipes, *Russia Under the Old Regime*, New York: Charles Scribner's Sons, 1974.

13. *Protektsiya* and *sviazi* have not only a political connotation, but can evoke a broader set of images which we would associate with a mafia. For a colorful and concrete description of these extralegal associations, see Konstantin Simis, *USSR: The Corrupt Society*, New York: Simon and Schuster, 1982. Also see Il'ya Zemtsov, *Partiya ili Mafiya*, Paris: Les Editeurs Reunis, 1976.

14. Gregory Grossman, "The 'Second Economy' of the USSR," *Problems of Communism*, XXVI, 5, September–October 1977, pp. 25–40.

15. T.H. Rigby, "Early provincial cliques and the rise of Stalin," *Soviet Studies*, XXXIII, 1, January 1981, pp. 3–28; p. 5.

16. Hahn's careful study of agriculture policy in the 1960s and the implications of top level debates on lower-level politics is suggestive. See Werner G. Hahn, *The Politics of Soviet Agriculture, 1960–1970*, Baltimore: The Johns Hopkins University Press, 1972.

17. The profound significance of contested seats in a powerful USSR Congress of People's Deputies and Supreme Soviet cannot be overemphasized as one ponders the consequences of the Gorbachev reform program.

18. Zygmunt Bauman contends that "for a peasant society, patronage is the way of life . . . It is a major functional prerequisite of peasant society . . ." See his "Comment on Eastern Europe," *Studies in Comparative Communism*, XII, 2 and 3, Summer/Autumn 1979, pp. 184–89.

19. For a detailed discussion of the material and political significance of dysfunctional network activities see Michael Voslensky, *Nomenklatura: The Soviet Ruling Class*, Garden City, New York: Doubleday & Co., 1984, especially pp. 178–97.

20. See Pipes, *Russia*, p. 284; a broader discussion of corruption is provided in chapter 11.

21. See Nicholas Lampert, *Whistleblowing in the Soviet Union*, New York: Schocken Books, 1985.

22. See Arnold J. Heidenheimer, ed., *Political Corruption*, New York: Holt, Rinehart and Winston, 1970, pp. 3–28.

23. Jerry F. Hough and Merle Fainsod, *How the Soviet Union is Governed*, Cambridge, Mass.: Harvard University Press, 1979, pp. 543–55.

24. Valerie Bunce and John M. Echols III, "Soviet politics in the Brezhnev Era: 'Pluralism' or Corporatism?" in Donald R. Kelley, ed., *Soviet Politics in the Brezhnev Era*, New York: Praeger, 1980, pp. 1–26.

25. Phillippe Schmitter, "Still the century of corporatism," *Review of Politics*, XXXVI, 1, 1974, pp. 85–131.

26. The notion of a political opportunity structure and its influence on elite behavior is developed by Joseph A. Schlesinger in *Ambition and Politics*, Chicago: Rand McNally and Co., 1966.

27. Comment made to the author during an interview conducted in Ann Arbor, Michigan, January 1984.

28. Richman identifies the important role of networks at the enterprise level, where the *krugovaya poruka* or mutual guarantee relationship requires party secretaries, managers, and other influentials to work together to prevent exposure of any extralegal behavior. See Barry M. Richman, *Soviet Management*, Englewood Cliffs: Prentice-Hall, 1965, p. 203.

29. For example, Frederic Fleron, "Representation of career types in the Soviet political leadership," in R. Barry Farrell, ed., *Political Leadership in Eastern Europe and the Soviet Union*, Chicago: Aldine Publishing Co., 1970, pp. 108–39.

30. Sharlet's analysis of the 1977 Soviet Constitution traces how these "rules" were multiplied and more explicitly developed during the Brezhnev era. Robert Sharlet, *The New Soviet Constitution of 1977: Analysis and Text*, Brunswick, Ohio: King's Court Communications, 1978.

31. Ellen Jones, "Committee decision making in the Soviet Union," *World Politics*, XXXVI, 2, January, 1984, pp. 165–88.

32. See George W. Breslauer, *Khrushchev and Brezhnev as Leaders*, London: George Allen and Unwin, 1982.

33. This argument also pertains to first secretaries at lower policy-making levels. Subject to the policy directives issued by national authorities, first secretaries set the issue agenda and assume responsibility for policy implementation within their prefects. Such a role follows from the logic of the party's leadership position, with political authority accorded to the party's top representative within a region or locality. Gorbachevian reforms may eventually alter this, but it is true for the period examined here.

34. See James H. Billington, *The Icon and the Axe*, New York: Vintage, 1970, pp. 44–77, for a discussion of Muscovite political traditions; and Marc Raeff, *Origins of the Russian Intelligentsia*, New York: Harcourt, Brace, Jovanovich, 1966, pp. 34–121, who examines the more centralized political system established by Peter the Great.

35. Walter M. Pintner and Don K. Rowney, eds., *Russian Officialdom: The Bureaucratization of Russian Society from the Seventeenth to the Twentieth Century*, Chapel Hill: The University of North Carolina Press, 1980.

36. Marc Raeff, "The Russian autocracy and its officials," *Harvard Slavic Studies* IV: *Russian Thought and Philosophy*, Cambridge, 1957, pp. 77–91.

37. Brenda Meehan-Waters, "Social and career characteristics of the administrative elite, 1689–1761," in Pintner and Rowney, *Russian Officialdom*, pp. 76–105.

38. Hugh Seton-Watson, "Russia and modernization," *Slavic Review*, XX, 4, 1961, pp. 583–88.

39. The *chinoproizvodstvo* system included both the *chiny*, or hierarchy of ranked titles assumed by individuals, and the *dolzhnosti*, or hierarchy of actual positions held by individuals. It not only established the levels of positions within the system, but also the criteria necessary for advancement to those levels. The system gave considerable power and authority to those atop the system, providing ample incentive for aspirants to form clientelistic relations with their superiors.

40. See Seymour Becker, *Nobility and Privilege in Late Imperial Russia*, DeKalb: Northern Illinois University Press, 1985.

41. Richard G. Robbins, Jr., *The Tsar's Viceroys: Russian Provincial Governors in the Last Years of the Empire*, Ithaca: Cornell University Press, 1987.

42. Walter M. Pintner, "The evolution of civil officialdom, 1755–1855," in Pintner and Rowney, *Russian Officialdom*, p. 198.

43. The emperor was always free to alter the Table and reclassify the ranking of positions and institutions so as to help favored individuals or groups.

44. Merle Fainsod, *How Russia is Ruled*, Cambridge: Harvard University Press, 1953, pp. 154–56.

45. See T.H. Rigby, *Lenin's Government: Sovnarkom 1917–1922*, Cambridge: Cambridge University Press, 1979, for a more detailed account of this early period of Soviet history and the reliance on clientelistic networks in recruitment.

46. The memoirs of prominent Soviet leaders have provided discussions of these regional struggles and patronage in the 1920s. See A. I. Mikoyan, *Dorogoi bor'by*, Moscow: Izdatel'stvo politicheskoi literatury, 1971, and N.S. Patolichev, *Ispytaniye na zrelost*, Moscow: Izdatel'stvo politicheskoi literatury, 1977.

47. Challenges associated with the "workers opposition" within the Communist Party combined with the growth of active resistance within the country as manifested in such events as the Kronstadt sailors' uprising of March 1921.

48. See Leonard Schapiro, *The Communist Party of the Soviet Union*, New York: Vintage Books, 1971, pp. 201–16.

49. Leonard Schapiro, *Communist Party*, 1971, pp. 250–51, and Fainsod, *How Russia is Ruled*, p. 166.

50. Isaac Deutscher, *Stalin: A Political Biography*, New York: Oxford University Press, 1967, pp. 217–27.

51. See Adam Ulam, *Stalin: The Man and His Era*, New York: The Viking Press, 1973, pp. 236–39.

52. See Deutscher, *Stalin*, pp. 98–101, Evan Mawdsley, *The Russian Civil War*, Boston: Allen and Unwin, 1987, pp. 89–91, and Ulam, *Stalin*, pp. 16–17, 172.

53. Schapiro, *Communist Party*, p. 242.

54. By the XI Party Congress (April 1922), the rules were in place giving central organs control over the selection and placement of lower-level party cadres. CC instructors and Moscow-appointed local secretaries together confronted local party organizations to force acceptance of national policy and cadres decisions.

55. See Robert V. Daniels, "Stalin's rise to dictatorship, 1922–29," in Alexander Dallin and Alan F. Westin, eds., *Politics in the Soviet Union: 7 Cases*, New York: Harcourt, Brace, and World, 1966, pp. 1–38, and Sheila Fitzpatrick, "Stalin and the making of a new elite, 1928–1939," *Slavic Review*, XXXVIII, 3, September 1979, pp. 377–402.

56. Kaganovich sponsored, among others, Bulganin, Khrushchev, and Malenkov.

57. See Merle Fainsod, *Smolensk Under Soviet Rule*, Cambridge: Harvard University Press, 1953, pp. 191–93, and J. Arch Getty, *Origins of the Great Purges: The Soviet Communist Party Reconsidered, 1933–1938*, Cambridge: Cambridge University Press, 1985, pp. 163–71.

58. For a discussion of one such network, that of Lavrenty Beria, see Charles H. Fairbanks, Jr., "Clientelism and higher politics in Georgia, 1949–1953," in Ronald Suny, ed., *Transcaucasia: Nationalism and Social Change*, Ann Arbor: The University of Michigan Press, 1983, pp. 339–68, and Boris Nicolaevsky, *Power and the Soviet Elite*, Ann Arbor: The University of Michigan Press, 1975, pp. 120–29.

59. Chubar, Kossior, Postyshev, and Rudzutak were all eventually executed, while Kuibyshev and Ordzhonikidze died under suspicious circumstances.

60. An important organizational base of support about which we know little was Stalin's personal secretariat. It apparently reviewed all policy matters, drafted all policy proposals, monitored the flow of documentation through the various party bodies, and oversaw cadres recruitment. See Abdurakhman Avtorkhanov, *The Communist Party Apparatus*, Cleveland: Meridian Books, 1968, pp. 102–7.

61. One strategy that enhanced the Stalin network's influence in state bureaucracies was appointing protégés to political commissariat positions just beneath top officials of non-party organizations. Thus in 1928, Ordzhonikidze was appointed as a vice chairman of the Sovnarkhom under Rykov, Kaganovich was appointed vice chairman of the Trade Unions Council under Tomsky, and Savelev was appointed to a deputy position immediately beneath the editor-in-chief of *Pravda*, Bukharin. These appointees were responsible to Stalin as well as to the Second Secretary and Stalin associate Molotov.

62. Note Stalin's speech delivered at the February/March 1937 CC Plenum. See Joseph Stalin, *Sochineniya*, I, 1934–40, edited by Robert H. McNeal, Stanford: Hoover Institution, 1967, pp. 230–31.

63. See Robert Conquest, *Power and Policy in the USSR*, New York: Harper and Row, 1967, and Myron Rush, *Political Succession in the USSR*, 2nd edn, New York: Columbia University Press, 1968.

64. See Conquest, *Power and Policy*, for a discussion of Khrushchev's "Ukraine machine."

65. For example, Dmitry Polyansky, from Krasnodar; Aleksei Kirichenko, from Rostov; and Yekaterina Furtseva, from the Moscow gorkom.

66. E.g., Andropov (Kuusinen), Polyakov (Khrushchev), Ponomarev (Suslov), Rudakov (Khrushchev), and Titov (Podgorny).

67. Former Ukrainian associates of Khrushchev, Y.N. Zarobian and Z.T. Serdiuk, were selected in the early 1960s to head the Armenian and Moldavian party organizations. A.P. Kirilenko and I.Kh. Yunak were among the Khrushchev associates recruited to head provincial party organizations (Sverdlovsk and Tambov, respectively).

68. See Roman Kolkowicz, *The Soviet Military and the Communist Party*, Princeton: Princeton University Press, 1967, on Khrushchev's significant connections in the military and how they were manipulated in the 1950s.

69. See Brezhnev's account of protégés fighting the influence of Khrushchev rival Kozlov's clients in Kazakhstan in the 1950s and 1960s, *Tselina*, Moscow: Politizdat, 1979.

70. See Barbara Ann Chotiner, *Khrushchev's Party Reform*, Westport: Greenwood Press, 1984.

71. See Myron Rush, *Succession*, pp. 101, 118–120, and 126.

72. Lithuania does not contain oblasts or autonomous regions which are politically tied to the central administration in Moscow. This is important in choosing Lithuania because it means administrative complexities of political accountability do not arise as they do in larger republics with semi-independent administrative units (e.g., Ukraine and Kazakhstan).

73. Azerbaidzhan contains an autonomous oblast, but its political and economic importance make it more comparable to an RSFSR krai (territory). The republic party first secretary, similar to the leader of a RSFSR obkom, is directly accountable to Moscow for the republic and its subordinate political units.

74. See the appendix, pp. 243–47, for a discussion of the approach by which elite populations were drawn and patronage norms analyzed.

2   Networks and coalition building in the Brezhnev period

1. Valerie Bunce, *Do New Leaders Make A Difference?* Princeton: Princeton University Press, 1981.

2. The rapid generational shift in the Soviet leadership and an especially pressing policy agenda coming out of the Brezhnev period clearly accelerated this timetable for Gorbachev and his associates. But as chapter 4 will indicate, more radical reform initiatives emerged only after the Gorbachev regime consolidated its position.

3. For the most comprehensive study of the policy programs of the two leaders, see George W. Breslauer, *Khrushchev and Brezhnev as Leaders*, London: George Allen and Unwin, 1982. Also see Alexander Yanov, *Detente After Brezhnev: The Domestic Roots of Soviet Foreign Policy*, Berkeley: Institute of International Studies, University of California, 1977, and Jerry F. Hough and Merle Fainsod, *How the Soviet Union is Governed*, Cambridge: Harvard University Press, 1979.

4. This total CC/CAC membership figure excludes the Politburo and Secretariat patrons, though these politicians are elected members of the CC. For a discussion of the decision rules used in identifying protégés and clients, see the appendix, p. 242.

5. To identify such connections would require assumptions which would transform this study into one of mere conjecture. For instance, how can one systematically study the accountability of certain regions and institutions to particular politicians? Often, such accountability is arbitrary and reflects the unique career past of a particular politician (e.g., Suslov's oversight of Stavropol and the inferred connections with Gorbachev). For a discussion of dilemmas in identifying patronage ties, see John H. Miller, "Putting clients in place: the role of patronage in cooption into the Soviet leadership," in Archie Brown, ed., *Political Leadership in the Soviet Union*, Bloomington: Indiana University Press, 1989, pp. 54–95.

6. Michael P. Gehlen and Michael McBride, "The Soviet Central Committee: an elite analysis," *American Political Science Review (APSR)*, LXII, 4, December 1968, pp. 1232–41; quotation from p. 1232.

7. E.g., the Altai Krai and the Arkhangel'sk, Crimean, Kemerovo, Kuibyshev, Novgorod, Novosibirsk, Odessa, Riazan, Rostov, Ul'yanovsk, and Yaroslavl Oblasts.

8. E.g., such ministries and state committees as the Automobile Industry, Electronics Industry, Machine Tool and Tool Building Industry, Aviation Industry, Shipbuilding Industry, Shipping, Transport Construction, Coal Industry, Gas Industry, Foreign Trade, Education, Communication, Finance, and Trade.

9. The high election and reelection average for the heroes group is not surprising considering their important legitimating role. However, the figures for the military and the national functionaries are more noteworthy because these groups can also assume an important representative and public role. The career prospects for regional party leaders were quite good, assuming that their subordinate party organizations and regions remained stable. Analysis of the career backgrounds of non-Slavic ethnic minority leaders indicates they often remained as party bosses for long time periods. Most came to power during the first half of the Brezhnev era, holding on through the remainder of the 1970s and into the 1980s. A significant number were replaced only after Brezhnev's death.

10. Excluded from the table are Politburo and Secretariat members who were retired or dead by the XXIII Congress in 1966: Leonid Il'ichev, Anastas Mikoyan, Aleksandr Rudakov, Nikolai Shvernik, Vitaly Titov (who is only included in the population of Podgorny CC clients), and Leonid Yefremov.

11. Brezhnev moved into the CC in 1952, while nearly all of his protégés joined afterwards. He was a Politburo candidate member in 1952, while his protégés only joined that body or the Secretariat in the later 1950s (Kirilenko in 1957). Besides Kirilenko, no Brezhnev protégé advanced into these top bodies until Ustinov's election in 1965.

12. A useful account of the Dnepropetrovsk group as a regional elite cohort is laid out in Joel Moses, "Regional cohorts and political mobility in the USSR: the case of Dnepropetrovsk," *Soviet Union*, III, 1, 1976, pp. 63–89.

13. Ustinov was selected a candidate member at the March 1965 CC Plenum, while Shcherbitsky was returned to the Politburo as a candidate member at the December 1965 Plenum. The Kazakh party leader, Kunaev, joined the Politburo as a candidate member at the Party Congress in 1966.

14. Kunaev and Shcherbitsky.

15. Grechko was elected a full member at the April 1973 Plenum; Ustinov was elected a full member and Aliev a candidate member at the Party Congress in 1976; Chernenko was promoted to full member in November 1978; and Tikhonov was promoted to full member in November 1979.

16. The promotion of Chernenko was especially important, not only because of his extremely close working relationship with the General Secretary, but because his secretarial portfolio included responsibility for questions of security and order within the central party apparatus, as well as oversight of information gathering, routing, and documentation.

17. The importance of Kapitonov's position and his relationship with Brezhnev are underscored by the fact that he was so quickly retired from his central party apparat duties in early 1983, within months of Brezhnev's death. Control over the Organizational-Party Work Department has been fundamental to a leader's control over the party apparatus. Kapitonov assumed a crucial role in the Brezhnev regime for the very reason that, through him, Brezhnev was able to promote many protégés and clients.

18. Franklyn Griffiths, "A tendency analysis of Soviet policy-making," in H. Gordon Skilling and Franklyn Griffiths, eds., *Interest Groups in Soviet Politics*, Princeton: Princeton University Press, 1971, pp. 335–77.

19. The year 1969 is an appropriate time point for considering the relative standing of patronage networks, both because the regime had consolidated power and because none of the major post-Khrushchev leaders had departed from the scene. It should be noted that the relative representation of different institutions and levels of authority within these various networks varied little between 1969 and the 1970s.

20. E.g., V.V. Matskevich, the Agriculture Minister, who was resurrected by Brezhnev after Khrushchev had demoted him; F.D. Voronov, a Dnepropetrovsk protégé, who served as Minister of Ferrous Metallurgy; N.V. Goldin, who served as Minister of Construction of Heavy Industry Enterprises; and Y.P. Slavsky, who was resurrected in 1965 as Minister of Medium Machine Building.

21. Bodiul was rewarded for his efforts by being transferred to Moscow in December 1980 as a deputy chairman of the Council of Ministers. This advance occurred within days of Kosygin's death – and would be reversed within a short period after Brezhnev's death.

22. Among other Brezhnev associates elevated to CC membership were his personal aides, G.E. Tsukanov (1966), A.M. Aleksandrov-Agentov (1971), A.I. Blatov (1976), and V.A. Golikov (1981), who collectively represent a significant proportion of all Brezhnev clients identified here.

23. George W. Simmonds, ed., *Soviet Leaders*, New York: Thomas Y. Crowell Company, 1967, Michel Tatu, *Power In The Kremlin*, New York: The

Viking Press, 1970, and Werner G. Hahn, *The Politics of Soviet Agriculture, 1960–1970*, Baltimore: The Johns Hopkins University Press, 1972.

24. E.g., the careers of two network members, N.T. Kozlov and V.K. Mesiats, were closely interconnected. Both attended the Timiriazev Institute in the early 1930s, advancing through the Moscow gorkom in the 1950s and 1960s. During the 1970s and 1980s both served in the agricultural sector as USSR ministers.

25. Both V.A. Demchenko and A.M. Kalashnikov served as RSFSR Council of Ministers Deputy Chairmen.

26. V.K. Mesiats served as USSR Minister of Agriculture and K.I. Brekhov became USSR Minister of Chemical and Oil Machine Building.

27. Little has been published in Soviet sources about the functions of this and other organs dealing with cadres affairs. An exception is an article by a first deputy head of the CC General Department: K. Bogoliubov, "Vazhnaia, neot'emlemaia chast obshchepartiinogo dela," *Partiinaya zhizn*, no. 20, October 1981, pp. 19–27.

28. Kapitonov had served earlier in the CC department responsible for RSFSR cadres appointments.

29. These included V.G. Afanas'yev, V.I. Stepanov, and K.I. Zarodov (who was also chief editor of *Problemy Mira i Sotsializma* from 1968 to 1982).

30. It was Suslov, for instance, who journeyed to Vilnius in late Fall 1973 to deliver an important criticism of the Lithuanian leadership that came just months before an important Lithuanian leadership succession. Throughout his entire eighteen-year tenure as party boss, Brezhnev never made an official visit to the Baltic republics.

31. V.P. Lein, for example, experienced rapid mobility after 1959, when Pel'she became Latvian party First Secretary. Four years after Pel'she's move to Moscow, Lein was appointed RSFSR Minister of Food Industry. A year later, in 1971, he was elected to the CC.

32. Y.I. Kuskov and V.V. Zagladin.

33. Michael Voslensky contends that Shelepin originally was the intended replacement for Khrushchev when the October 1964 coup occurred. Only the fear of Shelepin's expanding base of political support altered this arrangement. See Michael Voslensky, *Nomenklatura*, New York: Doubleday, 1984, pp. 255–61.

34. N.G. Yegorichev, head of the Moscow gorkom until 1967, was posted to Denmark in 1970; N.N. Mesiatsev, Secretary of the USSR Union of Journalists, was posted to Australia that same year; I.I. Udal'stov, a deputy head of the CC Ideology Department, was moved to diplomatic slots in Czechoslovakia and Greece; and V.S. Tikunov, who had served with Shelepin and Semichastny in the Komsomol and the KGB, was "retired" to ambassadorial work in Romania, Upper Volta, and the Cameroons in the late 1960s and 1970s.

35. V.Y. Semichastny, who was Shelepin's "right-hand man," departed from the KGB in 1967, becoming a deputy chairman of the Ukrainian Council of Ministers (for sport). V.N. Yagodkin, who was a Moscow city party secretary (for ideological questions), was "promoted" in 1976 to a deputy

ministerial position in the Ministry of Education. B.F. Korotkov, the party First Secretary in Perm, was simply retired "for health reasons" in 1972, at the age of 45.

36. The Donetsk organization is an important one in Ukraine, and its support for Podgorny was critical to his position in the republic. Such subnational patronage networks were not dealt with here. But this does not mean that they were not politically relevant. Postwar Ukrainian politics, for instance, had been influenced by the political struggles among the Kiev, Khar'kov, Dnepropetrovsk, and Donetsk networks.

37. *Partiinaya zhizn*, no. 15, 1965, pp. 23–25.

38. Titov served as party Second Secretary in Kazakhstan under Brezhnev's protégé and the new Kazakh party First Secretary, Dinmukhamed Kunaev.

39. Shelest's first major party job was as the Khar'kov city Secretary for defense industry (1940).

40. Shelest was very much a representative of Ukrainian interests in Moscow. As Borys Lewytzkyj has noted, during Shelest's leadership in the republic, "he tried to preserve and expand (the) Ukraine's achievements. When he was ousted in 1972, it was explained that Shelest had engaged in localism (*mestnichestvo*) and had pursued narrow national interest." See Borys Lewytzkyj, *Politics and Society in Soviet Ukraine, 1953–80*, Edmonton: Canadian Institute of Ukrainian Studies, University of Alberta, 1984, p. 140.

41. L.M. Shevchenko and V.V. Kortunov both became CAC members while serving as aides to Podgorny in the Supreme Soviet Presidium.

42. A few, however, such as A.P. Botvin and G.I. Vashchenko, while closely linked to Podgorny, Titov, and Shelest, were able to accommodate themselves to their successors and survived. Indeed, Vashchenko not only served as the first deputy chairman of the Ukrainian Council of Ministers, but became USSR Minister of Trade in January 1983.

43. The political mentor of this group, Kirill Mazurov, discusses many of this network's members in his memoirs, *Nezabyvaemoye*, Minsk: "Belarus'," 1984.

44. See Amy W. Knight, "Pyotr Masherov and the Soviet leadership," *Survey*, XXVI, 1, Winter 1982, pp. 151–68. For a comprehensive analysis of Belorussian elite politics during the Brezhnev period, see Michael Urban, *An Algebra of Soviet Power*, Cambridge: Cambridge University Press, 1989.

45. This point is developed in chapter 3 on the policy consequences of patronage networks and coalition building.

46. For example, Kirillin and Lesechko supported the efforts at securing greater technology through foreign imports. Both stressed greater investment of resources into research and development of technologies. Kirillin's background was in the area of science and technology, and he dealt with energy questions. He was a member of the USSR Academy of Sciences and linked to its department of technological sciences. Lesech-

ko's career included experience in the foreign trade area, and also in machine building.

47. Both of Kosygin's client Vice Chairmen, Kirillin and Lesechko, were retired in 1980 when Kosygin himself stepped down from power.

48. These include the Belorussian politician Tikhon Kisilev, the Georgian party bosses Vasily Mzhavanadze and Eduard Shevardnadze, the long-time Uzbek party leader Sharaf Rashidov, and the Leningrad party leader Grigory Romanov.

49. Foreign Minister Andrei Gromyko's influence was narrowly focused, while both Dmitry Polyansky and Gennady Voronov – their standing tied to the agricultural sector – had their authority limited during the early Brezhnev period.

50. E.g., Viktor Chebrikov.

51. E.g., Y. M. Tiazhel'nikov and N.V. Bannikov.

52. Given the lack of systematic regional-level economic data, this is the lone measure that reflects the importance of regions.

53. See Peter Frank, "Constructing a classified ranking of CPSU provincial committees," *British Journal of Political Science*, IV, 2, April 1974, pp. 217–30.

54. Correlating the ranked positions of the top regional party organizations over the period from 1966 to 1982 reveals that the relative positions of the various regional party organizations were consistent over time. The same fifteen regional party organizations had the highest membership figures throughout this period; correlating their ranked positions resulted in an R of 0.980.

55. See party Secretary Ivan Kapitonov's report to the Party Congress, *XXV S'ezd KPSS: Stenograficheskii otchet*, vol. I, Moscow, 1976, p. 295.

56. Of the twenty-five most important regional units, leadership changes took place in the following fifteen: Moscow City, Moscow Oblast, Azerbaidzhan, Rostov, Krasnodar, Gorky, Dnepropetrovsk, Kuibyshev, Volgograd, Kiev City, Bashkir ASSR, Cheliabinsk, Voronezh, Minsk, and Latvia.

57. An analysis of variance test for the 140 regions results in an F statistic of 2.9079 and a significance statistic of 0.058.

58. Many of the officials heading intermediate-sized regional party organizations survived the period of power consolidation and subsequently benefited from the regime's stability of cadres policy. They generally retired honorably or died in office, not suffering the political disgrace experienced by many of their predecessors during the Khrushchev period.

59. These seventeen regional party organizations were: Moscow City, Moscow Oblast, Azerbaidzhan, Donetsk, Krasnodar, Gorky, Sverdlovsk, Dnepropetrovsk, Khar'kov, Saratov, Kiev City, Volgograd, Voronezh, Cheliabinsk, Voroshilovgrad, Minsk, and Latvia.

60. An analysis of variance for two populations of regional party organizations (led by nonclients/clients, 1976), by political importance of those

party organizations, yielded an F-statistic of 17.284 and a significance level of 0.0001.

61. Grechko, Kosygin, Kulakov, Masherov, Pel'she, and Suslov.
62. Mazurov, Mzhavanadze, Podgorny, Polyansky, Shelepin, Shelest, and Voronov.
63. Retention of elite status was based upon whether a member of the CC/CAC was (re)elected to CC/CAC membership at the Party Congress following the death or retirement of the patron. For purposes of this calculation, it did not matter whether the person's membership was full or candidate, but rather whether s/he was returned to one of these top party organs. A number of the clients who were ousted in fact retained positions of some significance. However, if they were removed from the CC/CAC they were considered to have been demoted.
64. For purposes of differentiating between "apparatchiki" and "administrators," the entire careers of politicians were examined, with those who spent 50 percent or more of their careers in purely organizational party positions identified as the former, and all others identified as the latter.
65. The one apparatchik who survived was the Belorussian politician, Aleksandr Aksionov. Aksionov had political connections to two Politburo members, Shelepin and Masherov, and survived both politicians' departures from the political scene.
66. Mikhail Gorbachev's career is often cited in this regard, as he ascended the political hierarchy by way of connections to a number of top politicians: Kulakov, Suslov, and finally, Andropov.
67. Illustrative is the career of the Krasnodar party boss, S.F. Medunov. Medunov moved up under Polyansky, having served with him in the Crimean obkom in the 1950s. He became the Krasnodar First Secretary in 1973, at the height of Polyansky's national prominence. With Polyansky's fall in 1975, Medunov came under political attack, ostensibly on matters of his oblast's poor productivity and corruption. Nevertheless, he forged connections with Brezhnev and these helped him to survive. It was only in summer 1982, when the Brezhnev group was on the defensive with the General Secretary's illness, that he was demoted, and to the position of USSR Deputy Minister for Fruit and Vegetables. His ouster came swiftly after Brezhnev's death, when he was expelled from the CC (June 1983).
68. See Seweryn Bialer, Stalin's Successors, Cambridge: Cambridge University Press, 1980, especially chapter 6, and Jerry F. Hough, Soviet Leadership in Transition, Washington D.C.: The Brookings Institution, 1980, especially chapter 3.

3   Patronage and the Brezhnev policy program

1. On this point, See Lewis J. Edinger and Donald D. Searing, "Social background in elite analysis: a methodological inquiry," APSR, LXI, 2, June 1967, pp. 428–45.

2. For example, see Dina Spechler, "Internal influences on Soviet foreign policy: elite opinion and the Middle East," Hebrew University Research Paper, no. 18, 1976, and Thane Gustafson, *Reform in Soviet Politics: Lessons of Recent Policies on Land and Water*, Cambridge: Cambridge University Press, 1981.

3. Peter Hauslohner, "Prefects as senators: Soviet regional politicians look to foreign policy," *World Politics*, XXXIII, 1, October 1980, pp. 107–233, and George W. Breslauer, "Is there a generation gap in the Soviet political establishment? Demand articulation by RSFSR provincial party first secretaries," *Soviet Studies*, XXXVI, 1, January 1984, pp. 1–25.

4. In particular, see George W. Breslauer, *Khrushchev and Brezhnev as Leaders: Building Authority in Soviet Politics*, London: George Allen & Unwin, 1982.

5. Seweryn Bialer raises an important question about the power of a general secretary when he asks, "power for what?" The general secretary has extensive resources, but their ultimate utility will depend upon his goals. If he is working within the system, promoting more incremental change, his level of power will likely be great. If he is attempting, however, to transform that system, as through a radical program of domestic reform, his power will be less certain. Brezhnev's political preferences – encouraging stability, gradualism, and accommodation – only enhanced his position within the elite. See Bialer, *Stalin's Successors*, Cambridge: Cambridge University Press, 1980, p. 71.

6. Karel Kaplan has written about the dominant role of the party first secretary, arguing he "is not just primus inter pares, but more powerful than that." See Kaplan, "The anatomy of a governing Communist Party, Part I: the Secretary General," *Berichte*, no. 19, 1983. In a related monograph, Kaplan assesses the input of Politburo members to political deliberations as entailing "observations" rather than overt policy advocacy. See Kaplan, "The anatomy of a governing Communist Party, Part II: the Politburo," *Berichte*, no. 26, 1983.

7. For contrasting perspectives on when the conditions are most opportune for policy reform in the Soviet-type system, see Valerie Bunce, 1981; Philip G. Roeder, "Do new Soviet leaders really make a difference? Rethinking the 'Succession Connection'," *APSR*, LXXIX, 4, December 1985, pp. 958–76; and the exchange between Bunce and Roeder, "The effects of leadership succession in the Soviet Union," *APSR*, LXXX, 1, March 1986, pp. 215–24.

8. An especially critical period when Brezhnev was on the defensive came in the mid-1970s, just before the XXV CPSU Congress. Domestic and foreign policy setbacks, including a troubled agricultural sector which contributed to the poor fulfillment of the ninth five-year plan (1971–75), led the party leader to recast a number of his initiatives. See Breslauer, *Khrushchev and Brezhnev*, pp. 202–44.

9. See Werner G. Hahn, *The Politics of Soviet Agriculture, 1960–1970*, Baltimore: The Johns Hopkins University Press, 1972, pp. 182–99, for a detailed discussion of Brezhnev's agricultural policy.

10. For a discussion of the ideological logic underlying this theoretical notion, see James P. Scanlan, *Marxism in the USSR: A Critical Survey of Current Soviet Thought*, Ithaca: Cornell University Press, 1985, pp. 232–40. The historical development of "developed socialism" is discussed in Alfred B. Evans, Jr., "Developed socialism in Soviet ideology," *Soviet Studies*, XXIX, 1977, pp. 409–28.

11. The term was first used by Mikhail Suslov but came to be linked with the Brezhnev policy program.

12. An important project, the Baikal–Amur railroad, represented a useful symbol which was manipulated to support a number of Brezhnev concerns: in particular, the development of the eastern zones, the development of production complexes, and the more efficient distribution of materials. But while Brezhnev was prominently associated with this extensive project, it entailed region-specific concerns not addressed by most national officials. Thus, reference will be made to the BAM project, but it is not treated here as a central plank in the Brezhnev program.

13. Note the CC plenums in December 1977, July and November 1978, November 1979, and October 1980.

14. Constraints operating on Supreme Soviet election candidates in their public statements influence all of the candidates. Any resultant bias affects the entire population of speakers. By employing these speeches in determining candidates' issue positions, we avoid the problems of differences in intended audience and function of speech. These problems arise when comparing different types of speeches delivered by different types of politicians.

15. At the XXIII Party Congress Brezhnev already assumed a leading role. Unlike past congresses when many Politburo members delivered addresses, only two – Kosygin and Podgorny – did so, and they spoke in their official guises as head of government and head of state. A convenient time point to identify Brezhnev's heightened dominance is 1970, with the publication of the first two volumes of his collected speeches and articles. *Leninskim kursom: rechi i stat'i*, Politizdat, Moscow, 1970.

16. For instance, the proportion of full CC members who were retained at a party congress rose from 49.6 percent at Khrushchev's last congress in 1961 to 83.4 percent at the height of Brezhnev's power at the XXV Party Congress in 1976.

17. See Hahn, *Soviet Agriculture*, pp. 165–6.

18. Rush, citing the Khrushchev–Bulganin division of sectoral responsibilities, argued that Brezhnev gained primary responsibility for agriculture, while Kosygin did so for industry. Whether or not this was the case, policy changes heightened expectations of a revived economy. See Myron Rush, *Political Succession in the USSR*, 2nd edn, New York: Columbia University Press, 1968, pp. 224–26.

19. This permitted strengthening of the state planning organ, Gosplan, and also the industrial ministries. These changes came at the expense of

Khrushchev's regional councils, sovnarkhozy, which were soon to be abolished.

20. This required several tasks, ranging from acquiring new machines and equipment, and chemicals and fertilizers, to efforts to raise land fertility and expand the program of land reclamation.

21. Interest in developing a post-Stalin Soviet constitution emerged long before Brezhnev became party leader. The drafting of a comprehensive document began under Khrushchev, and by the early 1970s the Brezhnev regime was giving it serious attention. See Jerome Gilison, "Khrushchev, Brezhnev, and constitutional reform," *Problems of Communism*, XXI, 5, September–October 1972, pp. 69–78, and Robert Sharlet, *The New Soviet Constitution of 1977*, Brunswick, Ohio: King's Court, 1978.

22. These ranged from greater ideological orthodoxy at home, to the need for the most advanced military technology as a deterrent.

23. Podgorny spoke about increasing the wages for rural and also urban workers, including collective farmers. He expressed an interest in increasing the funding for housing, and also for health care and education.

24. These and other discussions reflected regional and local conditions and concerns. Kunaev discussed Kazakhstan's water shortage problem and the necessity of a land reclamation program to facilitate a more efficient use of water. In Ukraine, Shcherbitsky argued that further investment was called for if grain yields were to be increased.

25. Indeed, Mazurov, along with Kosygin, was a leading member of the national administrative elite, with the two men expressing similar policy preferences throughout the later 1960s and 1970s.

26. Such new management principles included expanding the productive independence and initiative of republics, oblasts, enterprises, kolkhozy and sovkhozy.

27. Although Masherov supported doubling capital investment, his discussion of agriculture stressed conservation of already existent resources and capacities.

28. For a discussion of Voronov's views on mechanized links as appropriate units, see Hahn, *Soviet Agriculture*, pp. 207–24.

29. Andrei Kirilenko and Konstantin Katushev, for instance, moved up in highly industrialized regions, assuming responsibility for this broad sector at the national level. Dmitry Ustinov made a career in the defense armaments area.

30. Kunaev discussed these issues as they related to the Kazakh economy, while Shcherbitsky did likewise for Ukraine.

31. Shelepin lost his seat in the party Secretariat in 1967, being transferred to the top trade unions position for an eight-year stint before his ouster in 1975.

32. Their position may have been basically unchanged, but simply muted. Masherov did express concern over the importance of raising the standard of living.

33. The nonproliferation treaty was cited by Podgorny as evidence of the benefits of careful negotiation with Western countries.
34. Andropov became KGB head in 1967 and a member of the Politburo in 1973. His personal connections – both when he served in the KGB and later – often included individuals who also were members of the Brezhnev group (e.g., Viktor Chebrikov, the future head of the KGB). Solomentsev enjoyed mobility under Brezhnev, becoming a CC department head, a party secretary, and a candidate member of the Politburo within the first seven years of Brezhnev's rule. Several politicians who worked closely with Brezhnev and who were members of his network also had career ties to Solomentsev (e.g., Y.M. Tiazhel'nikov and N.V. Bannikov).
35. For example the accelerated chemicalization, land reclamation, and integrated mechanization programs.
36. This included raising rural wages, increasing payments to collective farmers for produce, and more broadly providing goods and services in the countryside.
37. Voronov was on the defensive by the end of the 1960s, with the ousters in early 1971 of two of his top protégés, RSFSR First Deputy Premier K.G. Pysin and RSFSR Deputy Premier A.Y. Biriukov, predating his own removal as RSFSR Premier by just a few months. While he remained a Politburo member until April 1973, Voronov's influence was quickly dissipating.
38. See Breslauer, *Khrushchev and Brezhnev*, pp. 200–19.
39. The lack of a reference did not necessarily signify opposition to a Brezhnev policy plank. In some cases, for instance, regional leaders did not touch upon certain national policy concerns. But a politician opposing an initiative associated with the General Secretary did not openly oppose it. Rather, it was ignored, therefore no support was provided. In this regard, I viewed a reference as signifying support.
40. Shelepin was ousted in May 1975, while Shelest and Voronov had been removed a few years earlier. Polyansky was retired from the leadership in 1976, with Podgorny removed as Soviet President in 1977 and Kirill Mazurov retired in 1978.
41. See William H. Riker, *The Theory of Political Coalitions*, New Haven: Yale University Press, 1962. The rapid decay of Brezhnev's network was revealed by Kirilenko's quick and unexpected retirement just days before Brezhnev's death.
42. See Zhores A. Medvedev, *Andropov*, New York: W.W. Norton and Company, 1983, and Elizabeth Teague, "Kirilenko at 75 and Chernenko at 70: what chance does either have of succeeding Brezhnev?," *Radio Liberty Report*, no. 356, September 9, 1981.
43. Romanov supported the energy initiatives and the creation of more territorial industrial complexes, but little else. As in 1975, Gromyko supported the foreign policy line without even vaguely supporting Brezhnev's domestic program.

44. Among the three group patrons, Kapitonov lost his CPSU Secretariat portfolio for cadres matters very soon after Brezhnev's death, with Grishin removed as Moscow party boss three years later, and Demichev kicked upstairs as a Vice-Chairman of the USSR Council of Ministers.

4 Patronage, Gorbachev, and the period of reform

1. Aleksandr Yakovlev was the first authoritative politician to use the term *civil society*. See *Novoye vremia*, no. 24, 1989, p. 6.
2. Others have traced the logic of Gorbachevian reforms and the political struggles that have surrounded them. See Archie Brown, ed., *Political Leadership in the Soviet Union*, Bloomington: Indiana University Press, 1989, and John Gooding, "Gorbachev and democracy," *Soviet Studies*, XLII, 2, April 1990, pp. 195–231.
3. E.g., the confirmation of a new government, the approval of cost-accounting for the Baltic republics, entertaining serious legal and economic reforms, and tackling such pressing problems as pensions and the taxing of cooperatives.
4. The Supreme Soviet formally or informally rejected twelve nominees, including the incumbent Culture Minister (V.G. Zakharov), who was tied to Ligachev and who had held his position for three years, and several designated chairmen of the State Committee for Environmental Protection.
5. *Pravda*, July 21, 1989.
6. The executive presidency and Presidential Council (created March 1990) provide reformers with yet another institutional means by which to bypass resistant forces in the party–state apparatus as they promote increasingly radical policies.
7. *Pravda*, August 5, 1989.
8. By Fall 1989, even republic party first secretaries were subject to secret ballot, multi-candidate elections, as demonstrated in the selection of Ukrainian First Secretary Vladimir Shcherbitsky's successor, Vladimir Ivashko.
9. Defeated in a single-candidate Congress of People's Deputies election in March 1989, Solov'yov was removed from the Leningrad party leadership post in July and from the Politburo in September. A public outcry following an exposé of his activities on the popular television program "600 Seconds" led to his expulsion from the CPSU in February 1990.
10. See *Materialy XIX Vsesoyuznoi Konferentsii*, Moscow: Politizdat, 1988, p. 126, and *Pravda*, July 5, 1988.
11. See, for instance, the articles by O. Borodin in *Izvestiya*, January 12, 1989, and L. Onikov in *Pravda*, July 10, 1989.
12. See the discussion by V. Skvirsky, A. Butakov, and A. Gorenkov, *Kommunist*, 18, December 1989, pp. 21–27, and by V. Krivoruchenko, *Partiinaya zhizn*, no. 6, March 1990, pp. 21–24.

13. In the Council of Ministers, all but four of the seventy-four members had been appointed since March 1985, and these incumbents had long-standing associations with their domains of responsibility: V.G. Chirskov (Minister of Construction of Petroleum and Gas Industry Enterprises since 1984), Y.A. Izrael (Chairman, State Committee for Hydrometeorology since 1978), N.S. Konarev (Minister of Railways since 1982), and E.K. Pervyshin (Minister of Communications since 1974).

14. See the articles by the cadres Secretary, Georgy Razumovsky, in *Kommunist*, no. 9, June 1987, pp. 3–13, and in *Pravda*, December 24, 1987.

15. E.g., Deputy Premier L.I. Abalkin, an economist, Minister of Justice V.F. Yakovlev, a legal scholar, and the non-Communist Chairman of the State Committee for Environmental Protection, N.N. Vorontsov, all selected in 1989.

16. Thus, as of March 1990, four republic party first secretaries had followed Gorbachev's lead and were also chairing their republics' supreme soviets (Georgia, Kazakhstan, Lithuania, and Turkmenistan).

17. The 1990 public protests that brought down several regional party leaderships (e.g., Chernigov, Donetsk, and Volgograd) revealed an increasingly dynamic situation where incumbent officials had to be responsive to local constituents if they were to maintain their elite standing. These pressures transcended Moscow's ability to orchestrate the ousters of local officials.

18. The December 1989 trial and ultimate twelve-year sentence meted out to the former Uzbek First Secretary I.B. Usmankhodzhayev was an especially powerful statement that even high party officials are accountable.

19. Valerie Bunce and Philip G. Roeder, "The effects of leadership succession in the Soviet Union," *APSR*, LXXX, 1, March 1986, pp. 215–24.

20. See Archie Brown, "Andropov: discipline and reform," *Problems of Communism*, XXXII, 1, January–February 1983, pp. 18–31, and Jerry F. Hough, "Andropov's first year," *Problems of Communism*, XXXII, 6, November–December 1983, pp. 49–64. *Pravda*, December 19, 1985, contained the first personal attack on Brezhnev.

21. See Archie Brown, "Gorbachev: new man in the Kremlin," *Problems of Communism*, XXXIV, 3, May–June 1985, pp. 1–23.

22. The most notable was the Minister of Interior, N.A. Shchelokov, who was ousted in December 1982.

23. Explicit criticism of Rashidov came under Gorbachev, when Uzbek First Secretary Usmankhodzhayev blamed him for the republic's rampant corruption (*Pravda*, January 28, 1986).

24. Ligachev's rise under Andropov to a party secretaryship and to head the CC Organizational–Party Work Department was an especially critical step in the rooting out of Brezhnev associates and other incumbents. By 1984 his political clout was such that he continued to oversee cadres matters under Chernenko.

25. S.A. Afanas'yev (Minister of Heavy and Transport Machine Construction), V.V. Bakhirev (Minister of Machine Building), and I.F. Dmitriyev (Head, CC Department of Defense Industry).

26. E.g., G.V. Kolbin, Yakov Riabov, and Nikolai Ryzhkov.
27. E.g., B.T. Goncharenko, I.G. Grintsov, E.V. Kachalovsky, and B.V. Kachura.
28. Shcherbitsky's successor as First Secretary, Vladimir Ivashko, however, could not be considered a member of his entourage.
29. Y.N. Balandin, V.M. Borisenkov (who retired in November 1989, less than six months after Demichev's departure from the CC), and M.I. Khaldeyev.
30. Zimyanin and Andropov had worked together earlier in their careers, so Zimyanin and his associates fared well in the turbulent 1980s. Indeed, a Zimyanin client, B.I. Stukalin, was appointed as CC Propaganda Department Head immediately after Andropov's succession, in December 1982.
31. These retirements also included ten Brezhnev period Politburo and Secretariat members: Aliev, Demichev, Dolgikh, Gromyko, Kapitonov, Kuznetsov, Ponomarev, Solomentsev, Tikhonov, and Zimyanin. For a listing, see *Pravda*, April 26, 1989.
32. Chi-square results and significance levels for the varied networks of officials are as follows: for Brezhnev network apparatchiki, chi-square = 0.21 (0.65 level of significance); all Brezhnev network administrators were removed, precluding an application of these associational measures; for extended Brezhnev network apparatchiki, chi-square = 0.05 (0.83); for extended Brezhnev network administrators, chi-square = 0.02 (0.89); and chi-square = 0.00 (1.00) for both the client-apparatchiki and the client-administrators to all other networks.
33. E.g., V.V. Zagladin, the long-time advisor to Soviet party leaders, and B.T. Batsanov, the long-serving head of the USSR Premier's Secretariat.
34. E.g., V.A. Karlov (Head, CC Department of Agriculture and Food Industry), T.B. Guzhenko (Minister of the Ocean Fleet), and such oblast First Secretaries as A.F. Gudkov (Kursk), I.E. Klimenko (Smolensk), and M.Z. Shakirov (Bashkir ASSR).
35. Leonid Il'ichev, who had been closely tied to Khrushchev and who first joined the CC in 1952, was still a CC candidate member some thirty-nine years later in 1990.
36. For instance, USSR Deputy Premiers V.K. Gusev and I.S. Silayev, RSFSR Deputy Premiers A.A. Babenko and L.A. Gorshkov, and long-time First Deputy Head of the CC Organizational-Party Work Department Y.Z. Razumov.
37. We should recall Gorbachev's considerable powers as unofficial Second Secretary during Chernenko's thirteen months in power, as well as his political prerogatives during Andropov's tenure.
38. The time period between party congress elections to the CC/CAC is five years.
39. For comparative purposes, 91 percent of the "nonclient" apparatchiki and 94 percent of the "nonclient" administrators had higher education, with 21 percent and 35 percent respectively having advanced degrees. Among these "nonclients," 68 percent of apparatchiki and 63 percent of administrators joined the CPSU after 1952. "Nonclient" apparatchiki also

tended to serve in many institutional settings (7.6 average), whereas "nonclient" administrators tended to serve in fewer such settings (5.8 average).

40. He became a Deputy Head of the CC Agricultural Department in 1980, subsequently rising to First Deputy Head of the CC Agricultural and Food Industry Department, and in April 1987 he became USSR Minister of Khleboprodukty.

41. See Maniakin's comments on this in *Pravda*, September 24, 1987.

42. See his address to the XIX Party Conference, *Pravda*, June 30, 1988. Compare these comments with those to the April 1989 CC Plenum, *Pravda*, April 27, 1989.

43. George G. Weickhardt, "Gorbachev's record on economic reform," *Soviet Union/Union Sovietique*, XII, 3, 1985, pp. 251–76.

44. Two other up-and-coming agriculture officials who were Gorbachev clients but not CC/CAC members are Y.P. Belov, the Tadzhik Second Secretary since January 1984, and D.D. Berkov, a Stavropol official who was appointed Uzbek party Secretary for Agriculture in August 1988. Both once served under Gorbachev in the CC Agriculture and Food Industry Department.

45. In March 1990, with Gorbachev's election as the USSR's first executive President, Luk'yanov advanced to become Chairman of the Supreme Soviet and Congress of People's Deputies.

46. Other influential figures who became members of Gorbachev's "kitchen cabinet" of personal advisors include former party Secretary Anatoly Dobrynin, the Americanist G.A. Arbatov, retired Marshal S.F. Akhromeyev, MPA Head A.D. Lizichev, and the Head of the Institute of Marxism–Leninism, G.L. Smirnov. Such academics as A.G. Aganbegian and T.I. Zaslavskaya have also been important members.

47. Fiodor Burlatsky's selection as chief editor of *Literaturnaya Gazeta* in March 1990 was yet another example of an ally assuming a post critical to Gorbachev's long-term policy interests.

48. One cannot discount the importance of the CC Institute of Social Sciences, once under Burlatsky, and the journal, *Voprosy filosofii*, once edited by Frolov, as sources of personnel and ideas that underlay the *new thinking*.

49. E.g., see his article in *Izvestiya*, June 30, 1988.

50. He was chief of the Agro-Industrial Complex Department of the Council of Ministers Administration of Affairs (1981–83) when Gorbachev was the party Secretary overseeing this sector.

51. See his articles in *Partiinaya zhizn*, no. 22, 1988, pp. 30–37, and *Kommunist*, no. 2, 1989, pp. 12–21.

52. The Gorbachev regime troubleshooter G.V. Kolbin, while not a client, did serve under Shevardnadze as Georgian Second Secretary (1975–83) before his rise to national prominence.

53. George W. Breslauer, "All Gorbachev's men," *The National Interest*, no. 12, Summer 1988, pp. 91–100.

54. Among his reforms were the "Abasha" agricultural initiative intended to merge agricultural associations while using material incentives to spur on peasants' productivity. He was also an early advocate of opinion polling.

55. One such politician not included in my population of CC/CAC members is Y.P. Voronov, who first developed ties with Yakovlev in the later 1950s and 1960s. Resurrected to head the CC Culture Department (1986) and to "restructure" this sector, he subsequently became chief editor of *Literaturnaya gazeta* (1988).

56. He retired from this post in April 1989, in the wake of the reorganization of the CC apparatus.

57. See Medvedev's lead article in *Kommunist*, no. 2, 1988, pp. 3–18. Also his co-authored article (with the reformist economist and USSR Deputy Premier Leonid Abalkin) in *Voprosy ekonomiki*, no. 3, 1988, pp. 3–21.

58. See his comments to the April 1989 CC Plenum, *Pravda*, April 27, 1989.

59. Nearly a decade after leaving Tomsk, another Ligachev client, V.I. Zorkal'tsev, still held down Ligachev's old bailiwick as party boss.

60. Among these G.S. Kabasin, V.N. Konovalov, N.A. Mit'kin, Y.N. Pogorelov, V.I. Smirnov, and V.P. Sobol'yev.

61. E.g., Deputy Premier B.Y. Shcherbina, who also worked in Western Siberia in the 1960s, and who articulated policy views similar to those of Ligachev.

62. Andropov had drawn upon the support of Kirilenko and his associates in his struggle with Chernenko to assume Brezhnev's mantle. Kirilenko's retirement in 1982 was honorable. See *Pravda*, November 23, 1982.

63. Noteworthy were his role in the December 1988 Armenian earthquake disaster and the Summer 1989 miners' strikes. Poll results revealed Ryzhkov's solid standing with the Soviet populace (*Argumenty i fakty*, no. 26, 1989).

64. *Pravda*, July 21, 1989.

65. For a thorough discussion of Belorussian network politics, see Michael E. Urban, *An Algebra of Soviet Power*, Cambridge: Cambridge University Press, 1989.

66. Mazurov was retired in 1978 and Masherov died in 1980. Zimyanin, a CPSU Secretary for nearly a dozen years until his 1987 retirement, was less directly tied to the Belorussian politics of the 1970s and 1980s.

67. Other Sliun'kov associates who moved up include M.A. Kniaziuk, A.A. Reut, and N.A. Stashenkov.

68. E.g., V.V. Grigor'yev, A.S. Kamai, and A.A. Malofeyev.

69. His successor, Y.Y. Sokolov, who was selected over several Sliun'kov associates, shared Gorbachev's political and economic thinking. Urban, *Soviet Power*, argues that Sliun'kov likely supported him as a replacement (see pp. 133–34).

70. An important client of Zaikov is I.S. Belousov, a Deputy Premier and Chairman of the Governmental Military–Industrial Commission, whose

career has flourished since Zaikov became Leningrad First Secretary and a senior national figure.

71. A number of CC/CAC members were associates of Viktor Chebrikov, the one-time KGB chief, senior Secretary, and Politburo member, and the fallen Leningrad party leader Yury Solov'yov.

72. He had worked with Politburo member and senior Secretary Zaikov in the Leningrad military–industrial sector in the early-to-mid 1960s.

73. See his comments in *Krasnaya zvezda*, March 7, 1989, and *Izvestiya*, September 16, 1989. For a useful discussion, see Dale R. Herspring, *The Soviet High Command, 1967–1989*, Princeton: Princeton University Press, 1990.

74. E.g., the Chief of the General Staff and First Deputy Defense Minister, M.A. Moiseyev , and Deputy Defense Ministers V.M. Arkhipov and I.M. Tret'yak.

75. Among Gorbachev network members we find Afonin (Socio-Economic), Bakatin (Legal Affairs), Boldin (Party Organization and Cadres Policy), Cherniayev (International Affairs), Frolov (Ideology), Kruchina (POCP), Primakov (International Affairs), Skiba (Agrarian), Vlasov (Socio-Economic), and Volodin (Agrarian) as important commission members.

76. The memberships of other special CC commissions (e.g., on the repressions of the Stalin period, the publication of party documents, and the preparation of party historical materials) have also been dominated by members of the extended Gorbachev network. E.g., see *Izvestiya TsK KPSS*, no. 1, January 1989, p. 6, and no. 2, February 1989, pp. 7 and 121.

77. See their comments to the April and July 1989 CC plenums.

78. E.g., contrast the public positions of Deputy Premier Abalkin, favoring more radical economic reform, with those of party Secretary Medvedev.

79. Luk'yanov was subjected to very tough questioning – and a two-day delay – before being confirmed in a split vote on May 27, 1989. Kalashnikov, whom the Supreme Soviet refused to approve as a first deputy premier and head of the government's food program in June 1989, encountered subsequent challenges in his Volgograd bailiwick and was publicly forced out of office in January 1990.

80. See the *Moscow News*, no. 4, 1989, exposure of former Moldavian Second Secretary V.I. Smirnov, a reputed reformer (though with connections to Ligachev) whose rapid advance had resulted from his anti-corruption activities in Uzbekistan. Praised by some as a *perestroika* generation reformer, he fell from power and became the subject of a well-publicized investigation.

5   Patronage and regime formation in Lithuania

1. *Voprosy partiinoi raboty*, Moscow: Politizdat, 1959, p. 371.

2. For a personal account of Snechkus's formative years within the LCP, see M. Bordonaite, *Tovarishch Matas*, Vilnius: Mintis, 1986.

3. Between November 1944 and March 1946, Mikhail Suslov chaired the Lithuanian Bureau of the AUCP CC, with Viktor Shcherbakov succeeding him as bureau head until it was disbanded in March 1947.

4. See Jonas Zinkus, *Lithuania*, Vilnius: Encyclopedia Publishers, 1986, especially pp. 147–69 and 186–229.

5. V. Stanley Vardys, ed., *Lithuania Under the Soviets: Portrait of a Nation, 1940–65*, New York: Praeger, 1965, p. 115; and R.J. Misiunas and R. Taagepera, *The Baltic States: Years of Dependence, 1948–1980*, Berkeley: University of California Press, 1980, pp. 141–44.

6. Abdurakhman Avtorkhanov, *The Communist Party Apparatus*, New York: Meridian Books, 1968, pp. 174–75.

7. The intense struggle between Grishkiavichus and Ferensas was related to the author by several LCP officials who have been close observers of the republic's politics.

8. Grishkiavichus was a native Lithuanian, born in 1924. He became involved in Komsomol activities in his teens, fleeing in 1941 when the Germans invaded. He served in the Red Army and became involved in the Lithuanian partisan movement during the last stages of the war. He joined the LCP in 1945, and after the war worked as a journalist. He attended the higher party school in Vilnius and served in the LCP CC apparatus (1948–51). It was in 1956 that he achieved his first responsible political position as a secretary of the Vilnius gorkom. By 1960 he had become Second Secretary of the Vilnius gorkom, and in 1964 was chosen to head the LCP OPWD. Overseeing cadres selection for seven years, he made connections with many of those who assumed leading positions in his own regime. In 1971 he was tapped as the First Secretary of the Vilnius gorkom, a position he held until his February selection as the LCP boss.

9. In an important speech delivered in November 1973, the republic second secretary identified deficiencies in transportation as well as problems in the organization and monitoring of industrial production as responsible for the Lithuanian economic slowdown of the early 1970s.

10. *Sovetskaya Litva*, June 1, 1977.

11. Some have contended that by 1980, Lithuania had more samizdat per capita than any other Soviet republic. See Misiunas and Taagepera, *The Baltic States*, p. 243.

12. See *The New York Times*, May 22, 26, 28 , and June 8, 1972.

13. The politicians who replaced incumbent LCP secretaries averaged 49 years of age. Incumbent CC department heads averaged 49 years of age, while their replacements averaged only 47 years of age.

14. Mikalauskas had been in the CC since 1956, while Petkiavichius had been a party *Buro* member from 1954 to 1960.

15. Petkiavichius was elevated to full *Buro* membership at the XIX Congress of the LCP (*Sovetskaya Litva*, January 26, 1986).

16. When these changes are combined with those that took place in other organizations connected with Ferensas, we see that a serious effort was

made to remove elements supportive of Grishkiavichus's rival. Leadership changes occurred in the republic komsomol and CC departments and ministries responsible for heavy and light industry, transportation, and construction: all institutions with which Ferensas had previous ties.

17. Relative agricultural importance was measured on the basis of the total amount of grains and vegetables produced in each region. The relative industrial importance was measured on the basis of the total number of industrial workers in each region. These two figures were used to calculate the percentage of total agricultural and industrial productivity for each region, and the resultant figures were summed to arrive at a figure for each region's overall economic productivity. All figures used are from 1974, the year of the Lithuanian succession. See *Ekonomika i kul'tura Litovskoi SSR v 1974 godu*, Vilnius: Mintis, 1975, pp. 209–26.

18. These figures are from *Kommunisticheskaya Partiya Litvy v tsifrakh*, Vilnius: Mintis, 1976, pp. 162–65.

19. Donna Bahry, *Outside Moscow: Power, Politics, and Budgetary Policy in the Soviet Republics*, New York: Columbia University Press, 1987.

20. This was made clear in the Lithuanian Second Secretary's speech to the XVII Plenum of the Lithuanian CC, *Sovetskaya Litva*, March 15, 1975.

21. Valerie Bunce, *Do New Leaders Make a Difference?*, Princeton: Princeton University Press, 1981.

22. See Augustine Idzelis, "Branch-territorial dichotomy and manifestations of republic interests in Lithuania," *Lituanus*, XXIX, 2, 1983, pp. 5–25.

23. See *Radio Liberty Research Report*, March 25, 1974.

24. See Brezhnev's speeches in Kiev (*Pravda*, July 27 and 28, 1973), and his speech to the Kazakh party *aktiv* in Alma-Ata (*Pravda*, August 16, 1973).

25. E.g., see Gail Lapidus, "Ethnonationalism and political stability: the Soviet case," *World Politics*, XXXVI, 4, July 1984, p. 568.

26. See Avtorkhanov, *Communist Party Apparatus*, p. 176.

27. The average tenure of republic party second secretaries who served during the period 1955–80 was 3.8 years. The more important republics (e.g., Kazakhstan and Ukraine) experienced more frequent turnover than the less important republics (e.g., Estonia and Turkmenistan). But in all cases there was a regularized rotation of second secretaries.

28. Of all republic second secretaries who served between 1955 and 1980, only 20 percent had served previously in the republic to which they were dispatched. Only 19 percent were transferred to new positions in that same republic. Most were transferred from Moscow (approximately 52 percent) and returned to Moscow (43 percent).

29. Brezhnev's speech came in Kazakhstan on the twentieth anniversary of the celebrated *tselina*, virgin lands, campaign. See *Pravda*, March 16, 1974.

30. In particular, see his Supreme Soviet campaign election speech, *Sovetskaya Litva*, June 9, 1974.

31. *Sovetskaya Litva*, October 2, 1974.

32. *Sovetskaya Litva*, January 11, February 8, and June 4, 1975.

33. In stark contrast, of the five major organizational plena held by leading gorkoms and raikoms between the end of February 1974 and mid–1975, the LCP Second Secretary only attended one. See *Sovetskaya Litva*, February 26, 1974, when Kharazov attended a Vilnius gorkom meeting.

34. Ibid., April 13, 1975.

35. Ibid., June 11, 1975.

36. Ibid., May 22, August 4, September 24, and October 27, 1974.

37. In a speech delivered when Ferensas was demoted, Grishkiavichus heavily criticized sectors of the economy for which Ferensas had been responsible, especially trade, construction, light industry, and consumer goods. See *Sovetskaya Litva*, June 2, 1977.

38. See Ibid., August 31, September 21, and November 1, 1974.

39. Ibid., March 15, 1975.

40. This is especially evident when comparing Kharazov's profile with that of his successor, Dybenko. In 1979, for instance, at a point when Grishkiavichus had fully consolidated his position, Dybenko offered no major speeches (as published in *Sovetskaya Litva*).

41. E.g., training agricultural specialists, increasing LCP membership, and improving the work of PPOs. See *Sovetskaya Litva*, September 12, 1974, and March 15 and June 18, 1975.

42. See *Narodnoye khoziaistvo SSSR v 1985g*, Moscow: Finansy i Statistika, 1986, pp. 102–5, and *Narodnoye khoziaistvo SSSR za 70 let*, Moscow: Finansy i Statistika, 1987, pp. 133–5.

43. See Misiunas and Taagepera, *The Baltic States*, pp. 239–59.

44. *Sovetskaya Litva*, December 2, 1987.

45. Ibid., December 8, 1988.

46. For a detailed discussion, see V. Stanley Vardys, "Lithuanian national politics," *Problems of Communism*, XXXVIII, 4, July–August 1989, pp. 53–76.

47. See *Sovetskaya Litva*, August 14, 16, and 18, 1988.

48. Ibid., January 27, 1988.

49. *Pravda*, July 2, 1988.

50. Songaila's successor, Al'girdas Brazauskas commented at the first Sajudis Congress on October 23 that these changes had in fact been initiated by Sajudis and only subsequently supported by the LCP.

51. See *Sovetskaya Litva*, October 27, 1988, for detailed coverage of the October LCP CC Plenum and the leadership change.

52. *Sovetskaya Litva*, October 22, 1988.

53. See Alfred E. Senn, "Toward Lithuanian independence: Al'girdas Brazauskas and the CPL," *Problems of Communism*, XXXIX, 2, March–April 1990, pp. 21–28.

54. *Sovetskaya Litva*, October 23, 1988.

55. By the end of 1989, editions of the officially sanctioned Sajudis newspaper, *Atgiminas*, had risen to over 100,000.

56. The more radical Lithuanian Freedom League, the non-Lithuanian Yedinstvo, and the *green* movement also influenced that agenda and Sajudis.

57. See *Pravda*, October 26, 1988 and February 22, 1989.
58. See Shepetis's comments to the LCP CC Plenum, *Sovetskaya Litva*, June 28, 1989.
59. See *Sovetskaya Litva*, January 10, 1990, for the LCP's new program.
60. See Brazauskas's comments in *Sovetskaya Litva*, December 2, 1989.
61. *Pravda*, February 9, 1990.
62. The August 23 formation of a human chain linking over 1 million Balts to commemorate the 50th Anniversary of the Molotov–Ribbentrop Pact was an especially dramatic symbol of this emergent Baltic solidarity.
63. See *Atgiminas*, July 17, 1989, *Komjaunimo Tiesa*, October 17, 1989, and *Sovetskaya Litva*, January 10 and March 8, 1990.
64. See Brazauskas's comments during a November 17, 1989 radio interview that the LCP no longer consulted with the CPSU on cadres decisions.

6 Azerbaidzhan and the Aliev network

1. For general discussions, see Alexandre Bennigsen, "Several nations or one people?" *Survey*, XXIV, 3, Summer 1979, pp. 51–64, and Nancy Lubin, *Labour and Nationalism in Soviet Central Asia*, London: Macmillan, 1984.
2. Michael Rywkin, *Moscow's Muslim Challenge*, Armonk, New York: M.E. Sharpe Inc., 1982, especially chapters 8 and 9.
3. See James Critchlow, "'Corruption,' nationalism, and the national elite in Soviet Central Asia," *Journal of Communist Studies*, IV, 2, June 1988, pp. 142–61.
4. See Frank Huddle. "Azerbaidzhan and the Azerbaidzhani," in Zev Katz, Rosemarie Rogers, and Frederic Harned, eds., *Handbook of Major Soviet Nationalities*, New York: Free Press, 1975.
5. *Narodnoye khoziaistvo SSSR*, Moscow: Izdatel'stvo "Statistika," 1960 and 1970.
6. *Istoriya Azerbaidzhana*, Azerbaidzhani Academy of Science, Baku: Izdatel'stvo ELM, 1979, p. 200.
7. For a discussion of this period and Akhundov's weak response, see Steven E. Hegaard, "Nationalism in Azerbaidzhan in the era of Brezhnev," in George W. Simmonds, ed., *Nationalism in the USSR and Eastern Europe*, Detroit: University of Detroit Press, 1977, pp. 188–99.
8. His predecessor, Imam D. Mustafayev, party First Secretary from 1954 to 1959, also became a full member of the Azerbaidzhani Academy of Sciences as well as Director of the Azerbaidzhani Institute of Genetics and Selection upon his ouster.
9. A similar strategy was applied in nearby Soviet Georgia, where the Minister of Internal Affairs, Eduard Shevardnadze, was selected to head and clean up another corrupt party organization. See Amy W. Knight, *The KGB: Police and Politics in the Soviet Union*, Boston: Unwin Hyman, 1988, pp.88–89.

10. First Secretary from 1933 to 1953, Bagirov was removed and expelled from the AzCP at the July 1953 CC Plenum. He was ultimately sentenced to death and executed in 1956 for "high treason, acts of terrorism and participation in a counterrevolutionary organization" (*Bakinsky Rabochy*, May 27, 1956).

11. Akhundov expected to be promoted into the USSR Academy of Sciences, but ended up settling for the Azerbaidzhani Academy of Sciences. See Il'ya Zemstov, *Partiya ili mafiya?*, Paris: Les Editeurs Reunis, 1976, pp. 68–69.

12. *Pravda*, December 16, 1969. He did not formally become a full member until the XXIV Party Congress in 1971.

13. Kozlov, who had served in the Vladimir Oblast party organization from 1956 through 1962, worked in the CPSU CC apparatus during the five years before his assignment to Baku. He returned to Moscow in March 1977 when he was appointed a secretary of the All-Union Central Council of Trade Unions. His solid standing in the party was reflected in his election to CC candidate membership in 1971.

14. All but one of these remaining incumbent CC department heads would be retired during the remainder of Aliev's tenure.

15. The absence of comparable data for raikom first secretaries precludes an examination of their turnover rates for the pre- and post-succession periods.

16. G.Kh. Ibragimov, selected as Agriculture Secretary in early 1970, had served in the Nakhichevan ASSR during the previous decade. G.N. Seidov, the new Industry Secretary, and D.P. Guliyev, the new Propaganda Secretary, were recruited in 1971; both were also elected to *Buro* membership.

17. K.A. Khalilov, selected to chair the Supreme Soviet in December 1969, had been the Azerbaidzhani Finance Minister for over a decade. A.I. Ibragimov, the new Council of Ministers Chairman, had served in various capacities in the Council of Ministers for twenty years before his promotion. Both had previous KGB experience and both had working relations with Aliev.

18. These data are from an Azerbaidzhani Communist Party statistical volume, *KP Azerbaidzhana v Tsifrakh*, Baku, 1976.

19. I.e., Baku, Nagorno-Karabakh Oblast, Kirovabad, Nakhichevan ASSR, Sumgait, Kazakh, Sal'yansk, Shekinsky, Lenkoransk, and Shamkhorsk.

20. Soviet sources limit us to a single measure for regional economic importance: the average number of workers (both blue and white collar) by cities and administrative regions of the republic. These figures provide a single indicator for a number of concomitants of relative economic importance: size of population and levels of industrialization and urbanization. Unfortunately, industrial and agricultural productivity figures are not available at the regional and city levels for Azerbaidzhan in the late 1960s and 1970s. Data are from *Narodnoye khoziaistvo Azerbaidzhanskoi SSR v 1970 godu*, Baku, 1971, pp. 246–47.

21. James H. Oliver, "Turnover and 'Family Circles' in Soviet administration," *Slavic Review*, XXXII, 3, September 1973, pp. 527–45.
22. B. Michael Frolic, "Soviet urban political leaders," *Comparative Political Studies*, II, 4, 1970, pp. 443–64.
23. Supreme Soviet Chairman M. Iskenderov was quickly retired in late 1969 (*Bakinsky Rabochy*, December 25, 1969), while the 53-year-old Chairman of the Council of Ministers, E.N. Alikhanov, "resigned for health reasons" in early 1970 (TASS, April 18, 1970).
24. In his address to the 1971 AzCP Congress, Aliev explicitly criticized numerous Akhundov associates as well as the former First Secretary himself. Indeed, ten of the total twenty-two Akhundov associates identified in this study were singled out for criticism in the speech.
25. As was found in Lithuania, these ousters were not related to incumbents' ages. For the 1969–74 period, the average ages of retired government ministers (56.3 years) and regional first secretaries (47.6 years) were only marginally higher than those for new appointees (49.3 and 43.4 years respectively). Indeed, those incumbents from the previous regime who retained their positions were, on average, nearly the same ages as their ousted peers (53.5 years for retained government ministers, and 43.7 years for retired regional first secretaries).
26. *Bakinsky Rabochy*, July 19, 1969.
27. *Bakinsky Rabochy*, November 22, 1969.
28. See Aliev's article in *Literaturnaya Gazeta*, November 18, 1981, where he pointed with pride to the transformation of the "moral-political atmosphere" of Azerbaidzhan under his leadership.
29. See Elizabeth Fuller, "Corruption and retribution in Azerbaidzhan," *Radio Liberty Report*, 413/82, for a discussion of leadership changes in the period after Aliev's consolidation of power.
30. My data are less complete for the late 1970s so this figure likely undercounts the actual number of regions affected by change. The actual figure probably includes more than half of all regions.
31. B.S. Kevorkov was transferred from the OPWD to serve as the Kirov raikom First Secretary (1970–3) and then as the First Secretary of the Nagorno-Karabakh Obkom (after 1973). A.R.Kh. Vezirov, the future AzCP First Secretary, served as the Kirovabad city party leader, and was subsequently selected to head the CC Industrial-Transport Department.
32. Kazakh region First Secretary I.L. Abbasov, appointed in 1972, was ousted in January 1979 on charges of "cadres policy abuse" (*Bakinsky Rabochy*, January 5, 1979). S.A. Sailov, who had been First Secretary in the Kasum-Ismail (1969–74) and Shemakharich (1974–77) regions, was ousted on the grounds of nepotism and abuse of his official position, (*Bakinsky Rabochy*, August 16, 1977). His case was of such severity that he was expelled from the party and investigated by the republic procuracy (*Bakinsky Rabochy*, December 23, 1977).
33. Thus, the Sumgait city party First Secretary S.K. Abbasaliyev was brought to Baku after three years to head the republic's Central Statistical Committee. Five years later he was selected to chair Gosplan.

34. An OPWD inspector, G.G. Gubatov, was dispatched to head the Dashke-san regional party organization and then subsequently to head the Ali-Bairamli gorkom.

35. Most officials had some higher education. Instances of degrees being purchased or earned through relatively vacuous correspondence courses have been cited, but the suggestion of graduate work and degrees probably did reflect advanced training. The fact that in these five instances the area of specialty of the advanced study corresponded with the sector of professional experience only underscored the relevance of that higher education to political durability.

36. For instance, Agriculture Minister M.R. Khalilov had served in that position since 1965, having spent the bulk of his career in the agricultural sector. While he had some experience in the CC apparatus, most of his past service was in the Ministry of Agriculture. He continued in this position until 1977, when he retired at the age of 60.

37. All three Azerbaidzhani Second Secretaries, S.V. Kozlov, Y.N. Pugachev, and V.N. Konovalov, had previously worked in the CPSU CC apparatus and all three were Russian by nationality. None had experience in Azerbaidzhan before being transferred there as Second Secretary – a pattern typical of party second secretaries in all republics.

38. See *Pravda* articles published January 3, January 28, and February 27, as well as the CPSU CC and USSR Council of Ministers resolution of July 25.

39. See Aliev's speech of April 21, 1977, *Bakinsky Rabochy*, pp. 1–4.

40. Purged March 1970. *Pravda* published an article by its Baku observer, L. Tairov, January 28, 1970, criticizing the Ministry.

41. See Aliev's speech of July 31, 1975 in *Bakinsky Rabochy*, pp. 2–6.

42. *Narodnoye khoziaistvo SSSR*, Moscow: Izdatel'stvo "Statistika," 1974, pp. 181, 194, and 574.

43. See Aliev's address to the last AzCP CC Plenum of his tenure, *Bakinsky Rabochy*, October 24, 1982.

44. Though constituting 9.4 percent of the republic's population (1970), Armenians only accounted for 4.9 percent of my CC/AC population – a discrepancy suggestive of the ethnic problems that would surface in the late 1980s.

45. Russian and Slavic elements were over-represented in top military posts: many Russian and Slavic officers who were nominally members of the Azerbaidzhani CC/AC served in the Baku military district, the Caspian naval forces, or the Transcaucasian frontier forces. Of the twenty-one CC/AC members with military affiliations, nineteen or 90 percent were Russian or Ukrainian, most of these officers remained in these positions for four or five years before being transferred out of the republic. The nature of their mission and the brevity of their stay made them marginally relevant to the local political scene.

46. Brezhnev's support for the Aliev regime was vividly expressed during three highly publicized visits in October 1970, September 1978, and September 1982. But Kunaev (Kazakhstan) and Rashidov (Uzbekistan) also benefited from the long-term patronage of the General Secretary.

47. See *Pravda*, January 31, March 28, and April 8, 1983. *Bakinsky Rabochy* also addressed the nepotism problem, April 12, 1983.

48. E.g., F.I. Kengerli, Minister of Railroads, F.R. Salmanov, Minister of the Cotton-Processing Industry, and I.S. Shamiyev, Minister of Procurements; R.G. Alekperov, Udzhary First Secretary, and K.N. Ragimov, Nakhichevan First Secretary.

49. Among the more prominent was R.E. Mekhtiyev, who had been a head of the CC Organizational–Party Work Department under Aliev, and who was elevated into the *Buro* and Secretariat by Bagirov.

50. See *Izvestiya*, August 5, 1987, and *Pravda*, September 25 and October 31, 1987.

51. The strife in the Nagorno-Karabakh also brought down the region's long-ruling leader (since 1973), B.S. Kevorkov. A Russified Armenian, Kevorkov had gained the confidence of Aliev and his regime. His record of leadership revealed him as Baku's representative in the overwhelmingly Armenian region rather than as that region's spokesperson to the Azerbaidzhani leadership.

52. The long-ruling Armenian party boss K.S. Demirchian was also criticized severely, with his regime publicly associated with nepotism and corruption. See *Pravda*, January 18, 1988 and *Izvestiya*, July 28, 1988.

53. *Pravda*, March 21, 1988. Note Gorbachev's comments to a special session of the Supreme Soviet dealing with the Nagorno-Karabakh, *Pravda*, July 20, 1988.

54. *Pravda*, June 30, 1988.

55. *Bakinsky Rabochy*, December 13, 1988.

56. For especially detailed accounts see *Literaturnaya Gazeta*, September 21, *Pravda*, October 10, and *Sotsialisticheskaya Industriya* October 23, 1988. *Glasnost* permitted even the "retired" Aliev to publicly defend his tenure as republic leader and to dissociate himself from the ethnic problems that subsequently arose in Azerbaidzhan in a speech to the April 1989 CC Plenum (*Pravda*, April 27, 1989).

57. That Vezirov was an ethnic Azerbaidzhani from the Nagorno-Karabakh may have played a role in his elevation, though he proved ineffectual in dealing with the conflict there.

58. See his comments in *Pravda*, April 27, 1989. Threats he made against the Popular Front and its leadership were reported in *Kommunist* (Yerevan), October 10, 1989.

59. I.I. Gorelovsky, a former CPSU CC official, had been dispatched to head the KGB between August 1988 and August 1989. He had replaced one long-time Aliev confidant, but his successor was yet another member of the old Aliev network.

60. See *Izvestiya*, February 19, 1989.

61. Vezirov's public humiliation was especially evident in the immediacy of the steps taken to expel him from the AzCP. See *Pravda*, January 26, 1990.

62. For a detailed discussion of the Aliev legacy, see *Pravda*, February 4, 1990.

7   The logic of patronage in changing societies

1. Anthony Downs, *Inside Bureaucracy*, Boston: Little, Brown and Company, 1967, p. 28.
2. See Gyula Jozsa, "Politische Seilschaften in der Sowjetunion," *Berichte*, no. 31, 1981.
3. See Joseph Schlesinger, *Ambition and Politics*, Chicago: Rand McNally and Co., 1966. I have drawn upon Schlesinger's work in differentiating types of ambition among Soviet politicians.
4. E.g., Foreign Trade Minister Patolichev held his position since 1956. His memoirs, *Ispitaniye na zrelost'* (Moscow: Politizdat, 1977), indicate that he was quite motivated in his early career, but having carved out a niche within the top elite, he did not advance further. The careers of politicians such as Chernenko and Solomentsev reveal that age and seniority did not necessarily cause a politician's ambition to dissipate. Politicians' careers often took off at age 60 or older.
5. Anthony Downs, *Inside Bureaucracy*, pp. 134–5.
6. For a careful consideration of the development and influence of such behavioral norms, see Robert Axelrod, "An evolutionary approach to norms," *APSR*, LXXX, 4, December 1986, pp. 1095–111.
7. The case of Dmitry Shepilov is illustrative. Cultivated by Khrushchev, he rapidly advanced into the Presidium and Secretariat. But he joined with Khrushchev rivals in an effort to remove the Soviet leader. Their defeat ended Shepilov's brief tenure at the political summit; he was summarily demoted to a university lectureship. Khrushchev's sneering references to Shepilov reminded all of the costs resulting from a subordinate's betrayal of a patron. See Robert Conquest, *Power and Policy in the USSR*, New York: Harper and Row, 1967, p. 13.
8. Gabriel A. Almond and Sidney Verba, *The Civic Culture*, Princeton: Princeton University Press, 1963.
9. See Goran Hyden and Colin Leys, "Election politics in single-party systems" (unpublished paper, c. 1977), who note in the case of East and Central Africa that such a political culture "accepts inequality as natural and sees politics as a means of solving individual and local problems through the provision of support for the right patron."
10. See Jeremy Boissevain, "Patronage in Sicily," *Man*, I, 1, March 1966, pp. 18–33; J.G . Peristiany, ed., *Contributions to Mediterranean Sociology*, The Hague: Mouton and Col, 1968; and Luigi Graziano, "A conceptual framework for the study of clientelistic behavior," *European Journal of Political Research*, IV, 1976, pp. 149–74.
11. See Arnold Stricker and Sidney M. Greenfield, eds., *Structure and Process in Latin America: Patronage, Clientage and Power Systems*, Albuquerque: University of New Mexico Press, 1972, and Thomas V. DiBacco, ed., *Presidential Power in Latin American Politics*, New York: Praeger, 1977.
12. Robert Kern, *The Caciques: Oligarchical Politics and the System of Caciquismo in the Luso-Hispanic World*, Albuquerque: University of New Mexico Press, 1973.

13. See Robert E. Scott, "Political parties and policy-making in Latin America," in Joseph LaPalombara and Myron Weiner, *Political Parties and Political Development*, Princeton: Princeton University Press, 1966, pp. 331–67.

14. See Lily Ross Taylor, *Party Politics in the Age of Caesar*, Berkeley: University of California Press, 1949, and Christian Meier, *Caesar*, Berlin: Severin and Siedler, 1987. Taylor argues that such networks were critical in a leader's efforts to come to power and to maintain it. Patronage was also critical in linking the center and periphery in the vast empire.

15. As LaPalombara and Weiner noted, "To speak of political parties in Europe . . . before the middle of the nineteenth century is to speak very loosely indeed," LaPalombara and Weiner, *Political Parties*, p. 8.

16. See S.G. Tarrow, *Peasant Communism in Southern Italy*, New Haven: Yale University Press, 1967, especially, pp. 330–31.

17. Alex Weingold, "Patrons, patronage and political parties," *Comparative Studies in Society and History*, X, 4, July 1968, pp. 377–400.

18. Raymond E. Wolfinger, "Why political machines have not withered away and other revisionist thoughts," *Journal of Politics*, XXXIV, 2, May 1972, pp. 365–98.

19. Guenther Roth, "Personal rulership, patrimonialism, and empire building," *World Politics*, XX, 2, 1968, pp. 194–206.

20. Myron Weiner, *Party-Building in a New Nation*, Chicago: University of Chicago Press, 1967, and Frederick G. Bailey, *Politics and Social Change in Orissa in 1959*, Berkeley: University of California Press, 1963.

21. See Nobutaka Ike, *Japanese Politics: Patron-Client Democracy*, 2nd edn., New York: Alfred A. Knopf, 1972.

22. I am using the term "machine" here in the sense of Banfield's definition that a machine "is a party of a particular kind: one which relies characteristically upon the attraction of material rewards rather than enthusiasm for political principle." Edward C. Banfield, *Political Influence*, New York: The Free Press of Glencoe, 1961, p. 237. On the Daley machine, see Milton L. Rakove, *Don't Make No Waves, Don't Back No Losers: An Insider's Analysis of the Daley Machine*, Bloomington: Indiana University Press, 1975; on the patronage system of Louisiana Governor Edwin W. Edwards, see Clyde C. Vidrine, *Just Takin' Orders: A Southern Governor's Watergate*, LA: Vidrine, 1977.

23. The number of patronage slots controlled by a politician and his machine is one important consideration in determining access to those opportunity structures. The number could vary tremendously, with no correlation between a patron's level of authority and number of slots. For instance with over 35,000 patronage slots available, Mayor Richard Daley's Chicago machine enjoyed disbursement of great resources. See Melvin A. Kahn and Frances J. Majors, *The Winning Ticket: Daley, the Chicago Machine, and Illinois Politics*, New York: Praeger, 1984, p. 55.

24. Samuel J. Eldersveld, *Political Parties in American Society*, New York: Basic Books, 1982, especially pp. 99, 133–34.

25. One machine member's distinction between "honest" and "dishonest" graft revealed an appreciation of the mixed functional and dysfunctional consequences of political machines. William L. Riordan, *Plunkett of Tammany Hall: A Series of Very Plain Talks on Very Practical Matters*, New York: Dutton, 1962, pp. 3–6.

26. Seweryn Bialer, *Stalin's Successors: Leadership, Stability, and Change in the Soviet Union*, Cambridge: Cambridge University Press, 1980, pp. 16–17.

27. Shugo Minagawa, "Political clientelism in the USSR and Japan: a tentative comparison," *Nanzan hogaku*, IV, 4, 1981, pp. 256–90.

28. Andrew J. Nathan, "A factionalism model for CCP politics," *The China Quarterly*, no. 53, March 1973, pp. 34–66.

29. Tang Tsou, "Prolegomenon to the study of informal groups in CCP politics," *The China Quarterly*, no. 65, January 1976, pp. 98–114, and Lowell Dittmer, "Bases of power in Chinese politics: a theory and analysis of the fall of the Gang of Four," *World Politics*, XXXI, 1, October 1978, pp. 26–60.

30. Lindblom's discussion of incrementalism as a natural consequence of the complex bureaucratic setting suggests there are objective limits to which bureaucratic functioning can be made coherent. The nature of the modern bureaucracy will set the parameters within which a leader and his team strive for greater policy effectiveness and coherence. Charles E. Lindblom, "The science of muddling through," *Public Administration Review*, XIX, 2, Spring 1959, pp. 79–88.

31. Michael Crozier, *The Bureaucratic Phenomenon*, Chicago: The University of Chicago Press, 1964.

32. See Steffen W. Schmidt, "Bureaucrats as modernizing brokers? Clientelism in Colombia," *Comparative Politics*, VI, 3, April 1974, pp. 425–50.

33. Alfred G. Meyer, *The Soviet Political System: An Interpretation*, New York: Random House, 1965, p. 458.

34. John Duncan Powell, "Peasant society and clientelistic politics," *American Political Science Review*, LXIV, 2, June 1970, pp. 411–25.

Appendix

1. Lewis B. Namier, *The Structure of Politics at the Ascension of George III*, London: Macmillan, 1929.

2. See Lawrence Stone, "Prosopography," *Daedalus*, C, 1, 1971, pp. 46–79; N.C. Phillips, "Namier and his method," *Political Science*, XIV, 1, March 1962; Richard Pares, *George III and The Politicians*, London: Royal Historical Society, 1951; and Herbert Butterfield, *George III and The Historians*, London: Collins, 1957.

3. See Mary McAuley, "The hunting of the hierarchy: RSFSR obkom first secretaries and the Central Committee," *Soviet Studies*, XXVI, 2, October 1974, p. 477; and Jane Shapiro, "Candidate membership in the CPSU Central Committee: stepping-stone to glory or obscurity," *Comparative Politics*, VI, 4, July 1974, pp. 601–16.

4. See Philip Stewart, Robert L. Arnett, William T. Ebert, Raymond E. McPhail, Terrence L. Rich, and Craig E. Schopmeyer, "Political mobility and the Soviet political process," *APSR*, LXVI, 4, December 1972, pp. 1269–90.

5. For suggestive evidence of the relevance of the war experience to networks see Kirill Mazurov, *Nezabyvayemoye*, Minsk: "Belarus," 1984, and G.N. Kupriyanov's account of the events and personalities (including Yury Andropov) in Karelia in *Za liniei Karel'skogo fronta*, Petrozavodsk, 1975.

6. George W. Breslauer, "Political succession and the Soviet policy agenda," *Problems of Communism*, XXIX, 3, May–June 1980, pp. 34–52.

Select bibliography

Armstrong, John A., *The Soviet Bureaucratic Elite: A Case Study of the Ukrainian Apparatus*, New York: Praeger, 1959.

Avtorkhanov, Abdurakhman, *The Communist Party Apparatus*, Cleveland: Meridian Books, 1968.

Axelrod, Robert and William Zimmerman, "The Soviet press on Soviet foreign policy: a usually reliable source," *British Journal of Political Science*, XI, 2, April 1981, pp. 183–200.

Bahry, Donna, *Outside Moscow: Power, Politics, and Budgetary Policy in the Soviet Republics*, New York: Columbia University Press, 1987.

Bialer, Seweryn, *Stalin's Successors: Leadership, Stability, and Change in the Soviet Union*, Cambridge: Cambridge University Press, 1980.

Blackwell, Robert E., "Cadres policy in the Brezhnev era," *Problems of Communism*, XXVIII, 2, March–April 1979, pp. 29–42.

Blackwell, Robert E. and William Hulbary, "Political mobility among Soviet obkom elites: the effects of regime, social backgrounds, and career development," *American Journal of Political Science*, LVII, 4, November 1973, pp. 721–43.

Breslauer, George W., *Khrushchev and Brezhnev as Leaders: Building Authority in Soviet Politics*, London: George Allen and Unwin, 1982.

"Political succession and the Soviet policy agenda," *Problems of Communism*, XXIX, 3, May–June 1980, pp.34–52.

"Is there a generation gap in the Soviet political establishment? Demand articulation by RSFSR provincial party first secretaries," *Soviet Studies*, XXXVI, 1, January 1984, pp. 1–25.

"Provincial party leaders' demand articulation and the nature of center–periphery relations in the USSR," *Slavic Review*, XLV, 4, Winter 1986, pp. 650–72.

Brown, Archie, ed., *Political Leadership in the Soviet Union*, Bloomington: Indiana University Press, 1989.

Bunce, Valerie, *Do New Leaders Make a Difference?* Princeton: Princeton University Press, 1981.

Bunce, Valerie and Philip G. Roeder, "The effects of leadership succession in the Soviet Union," *American Political Science Review*, LXXX, 1, March 1986, pp. 215–24.

Ciboski, Kenneth N., "Ambition theory and candidate members of the Soviet Politburo," *Journal of Politics*, XXXVI, 1, February 1974, pp. 174–83.

Clark, William A., *Soviet Regional Elite Mobility after Khrushchev*, New York: Praeger, 1989.

Colton, Timothy J., *The Dilemma of Reform in the Soviet Union*, New York: Council on Foreign Relations, 1984.

Conquest, Robert, *Power and Policy in the USSR*, New York: Harper and Row, 1967.

D'Agostino, Anthony, *Soviet Succession Struggles: Kremlinology and the Russian Question from Lenin to Gorbachev*, London: Allen & Unwin, 1987.

Daniels, Robert V., "Stalin's rise to dictatorship, 1922–29," in Alexander Dallin and Alan F. Westin, eds., *Politics in the Soviet Union: 7 Cases*, New York: Harcourt, Brace, and World, 1966, pp. 1–38.

Edinger, Lewis J. and Donald D. Searing, "Social background in elite analysis: a methodological inquiry," *American Political Science Review*, LXI, 2, June 1967, pp. 428–45.

Fainsod, Merle, *How Russia is Ruled*, Cambridge: Harvard University Press, 1953.

Fairbanks, Charles H., Jr., "Clientelism and higher politics in Georgia, 1949–1953," in Ronald Suny, ed., *Transcaucasia: Nationalism and Social Change*, Ann Arbor: The University of Michigan Press, 1983, 339–68.

"Bureaucratic politics in the Soviet Union and in the Ottoman Empire," *Comparative Strategy* VI, 3, 1987, pp. 333–62.

Farrell, R. Barry, ed., *Political Leadership in Eastern Europe and the Soviet Union*, Chicago: Aldine Publishing Co., 1970.

Fitzpatrick, Sheila, "Stalin and the making of a new elite 1928–1939," *Slavic Review*, XXXVIII, 3, September 1979, pp. 377–402.

Frank, Peter, "The CPSU obkom first secretary: a profile," *British Journal of Political Science*, I, 1, 1971, pp. 173–90.

"Constructing a classified ranking of CPSU provincial committees," *British Journal of Political Science*, IV, 2, April 1974, pp. 217–30.

Gehlen, Michael P. and Michael McBride, "The Soviet Central Committee: an elite analysis," *American Political Science Review*, LXII, 4, December 1968, pp. 1232–41.

Gelman, Harry, *The Brezhnev Politburo and the Decline of Detente*, Ithaca: Cornell University Press, 1984.

Getty, J. Arch, *Origins of the Great Purges: The Soviet Communist Party Reconsidered, 1933–1938*, Cambridge: Cambridge University Press, 1985.

Gilison, Jerome M., "New factors of stability in Soviet collective leadership," *World Politics*, XIX, 4, July 1967, pp. 563–81.

Goble, Paul, "Soviet ethnic politics," *Problems of Communism*, XXXVIII, 4, July–August 1989, pp. 1–14.

Gooding, John, "Gorbachev and democracy," *Soviet Studies*, XLII, 2, April 1990, pp. 195–231.

Graziano, Luigi, "A conceptual framework for the study of clientelistic behavior," *European Journal of Political Research*, IV, 1976, pp. 149–74.

Gustafson, Thane, *Reform in Soviet Politics: Lessons of Recent Policies on Land and Water*, Cambridge: Cambridge University Press, 1981.

Gustafson, Thane and Dawn Mann, "Gorbachev's first year: building power and authority," *Problems of Communism*, XXXV, 3, May–June 1986, pp. 1–19.

"Gorbachev's new gamble," *Problems of Communism*, XXXVI, 4, July–August 1987, pp. 1–20.

Hahn, Werner G., *The Politics of Soviet Agriculture, 1960–1970*, Baltimore: The Johns Hopkins University Press, 1972.

Hajda, Lubomyr and Mark Beissinger, eds., *The Nationalities Factor in Soviet Politics and Society*, Boulder: Westview Press, 1990.

Harasymiw, Bohdan, *Political Elite Recruitment in the USSR*, New York: St. Martin's Press, 1984.

"Nomenklatura: the Soviet Communist Party's leadership recruitment system," *Canadian Journal of Political Science*, II, 4, December 1969, pp. 493–512.

Hauslohner, Peter, "Prefects as senators: Soviet regional politicians look to foreign policy," *World Politics*, XXXIII, 1, October 1980, pp. 197–233.

Heidenheimer, Arnold J., ed., *Political Corruption*, New York: Holt, Rinehart and Winston, 1970.

Hill, Ronald J., *Soviet Political Elites: The Case of Tiraspol*, New York: St. Martin's Press, 1977.

Hodnett, Grey, *Leadership in the Soviet National Republics*, Oakville, Ontario: Mosaic Press, 1978.

"The obkom first secretaries," *Slavic Review*, XXIV, 4, December 1965, pp. 636–52.

"Succession contingencies in the Soviet Union," *Problems of Communism*, XXIV, 2, March–April 1975, pp. 1–21.

Hough, Jerry F., *The Soviet Prefects*. Cambridge: Harvard University Press, 1969.

Soviet Leadership in Transition, Washington D.C.: The Brookings Institution, 1980.

"The Brezhnev era: the man and the system," *Problems of Communism*, XXV, 2, March–April 1976, pp. 1–17.

Hough, Jerry F. and Merle Fainsod, *How the Soviet Union is Governed*, Cambridge: Harvard University Press, 1979.

"Gorbachev consolidating power," *Problems of Communism*, XXXVI, 4, July–August 1987, pp. 21–43.

Istoriya Azerbaidzhana, Azerbaidzhani Academy of Sciences, Baku: Izdatel'stvo, ELM, 1979.

Jones, Ellen, "Committee decision making in the Soviet Union," *World Politics*, XXXVI, 2, January 1984, pp. 165–88.

Jowitt, Ken, "Soviet neotraditionalism: the political corruption of a Leninist regime," *Soviet Studies*, XXXV, 3, July 1983, pp. 275–97.

Jozsa, Gyula, "Politische Seilschaften in der Sowjetunion" (Political 'Roped Parties' in the Soviet Union), *Berichte*, no. 31, 1981.

Kaplan, Karel, "The anatomy of a governing Communist Party, Part I: the Secretary General," *Berichte*, no. 19, 1983.
  "The anatomy of a governing Communist Party, Part II: the Politburo," *Berichte*, no. 26, 1983.
Kelly, Donald R., ed., *Soviet Politics in the Brezhnev Era*, New York: Praeger, 1980.
Knight, Amy W., "Pyotr Masherov and the Soviet leadership: a study in kremlinology," *Survey*, XXVI, 1, Winter 1982, pp. 151–68.
Kolkowicz, Roman, *The Soviet Military and the Communist Party*, Princeton: Princeton University Press, 1967.
Lampert, Nicholas, *Whistleblowing in the Soviet Union*, New York: Schocken Books, 1985.
Lane, David, ed., *Elites and Political Power in the USSR*, Aldershot: Edward Elgar, 1988.
LaPalombara, Joseph, ed., *Bureaucracy and Political Development*, Princeton: Princeton University Press, 1967.
LaPalombara, Joseph and Myron Weiner, eds., *Political Parties and Political Development*, Princeton: Princeton University Press, 1966.
Legg, Keith, *Patrons, Clients, and Politicians: New Perspectives on Political Clientelism*, Berkeley: University of California, Institute of International Studies, Working Papers on Development, no. 3, 1976.
Lemarchand, Rene and Keith Legg, "Political clientism and development," *Comparative Politics*, IV, 2, January 1972, pp. 149–78.
Lewytzkyj, Borys, *Politics and Society in Soviet Ukraine, 1953–80*, Edmonton: Canadian Institution of Ukrainian Studies, University of Alberta, 1984.
Linden, Ronald, *Khrushchev and the Soviet Leadership: 1957–1964*, Baltimore: The Johns Hopkins University Press, 1966.
Lowenhardt, John, *Decision Making in Soviet Politics*, London: The Macmillan Press, 1981.
  The Soviet Politburo, New York: St. Martin's Press, 1982.
McAuley, Mary, "The hunting of the hierarchy: RSFSR obkom first secretaries and the Central Committee," *Soviet Studies*, XXVI, 2, October 1974, pp. 473–501.
Miller, John H., "Cadres policy in nationality areas: recruitment of CPSU first and second secretaries in non-Russian republics of the USSR," *Soviet Studies*, XXIX, 1, January 1977, pp. 3–36.
Miller, Robert F., "The politics of policy implementation in the USSR: Soviet policies on agricultural integration," *Soviet Studies*, XXXII, 2, April 1980, pp. 171–94.
Minagawa, Shugo, "Political clientelism in the USSR and Japan: a tentative comparison," *Nanzan hogaku*, IV, 4, 1981, pp. 256–90.
Misiunas, Romuald J. and Rein Taagepera, *The Baltic States: Years of Dependence, 1948–1980*, Berkeley: University of California Press, 1980.
Moses, Joel C., *Regional Party Leadership and Policy-Making in the USSR*, New York: Praeger, 1974.

"Regional cohorts and political mobility in the USSR: the case of Dne-propetrovsk," *Soviet Union*, III, 1, 1976, pp. 63–89.

"Regionalism in Soviet politics: continuity as a source of change, 1953–1982," *Soviet Studies*, XXXVII, 2, April 1985, pp. 184–211.

Nicolaevsky, Boris, *Power and the Soviet Elite*, Ann Arbor: The University of Michigan Press, 1975.

Oliver, James H., "Turnover and 'Family Circles' in Soviet administration," *Slavic Review*, XXXII, 3, September 1973, pp. 527–45.

Pintner, Walter M. and Dan K. Rowney, eds., *Russian Officialdom: The Bureaucratization of Russian Society from the Seventeenth to the Twentieth Century*, Chapel Hill: The University of North Carolina Press, 1980.

Powell, John Duncan, "Peasant society and clientelistic politics," *American Political Science Review*, LXIV, 2, June 1970, pp. 411–25.

Pronin, I.I., editor, *Rukovodiashchiye kadry: podbor, rasstanovka i vospitaniye*, 2nd edn, Moscow: Mysl', 1981.

Richman, Barry M., *Soviet Management*, Englewood Cliffs: Prentice-Hall, 1965.

Rigby, T.H., *Communist Party Membership in the U.S.S.R., 1971–1967*, Princeton: Princeton University Press, 1968.

Lenin's Government: Sovnarkom 1917–1922, Cambridge: Cambridge University Press, 1979.

"The Soviet leadership: towards a self-stabilizing oligarchy," *Soviet Studies*, XXII, 2, October 1970, pp. 167–91.

"The Soviet regional leadership: the Brezhnev generation," *Slavic Review*, XXXVII, 1, March 1978, pp. 1–24.

"Early provincial cliques and the rise of Stalin," *Soviet Studies*, XXXIII, 1, January 1981, pp. 3–28.

Rigby, T.H., Archie Brown, and Peter Reddaway, eds., *Authority, Power and Policy in the USSR*, London: The Macmillan Press, 1980.

Rigby, T.H., and Bohdan Harasymiw, eds., *Leadership Selection and Patron-Client Relations in the USSR and Yugoslavia*, London: George Allen & Unwin, 1983.

Robbins, Richard G., Jr., *The Tsar's Viceroys: Russian Provincial Governors in the Last Years of the Empire*, Ithaca: Cornell University Press, 1987.

Roeder, Philip G., "Do new Soviet leaders really make a difference? Re-thinking the 'Succession Connection,'" *American Political Science Review*, LXXIX, 4, December 1985, pp. 958–76.

Ross, Dennis, "Coalition maintenance in the Soviet Union," *World Politics*, XXXII, 2, January 1980, pp. 258–80.

Rush, Myron, *Political Succession in the USSR*, 2nd edn., New York: Columbia University Press, 1968.

Rywkin, Michael, *Moscow's Muslim Challenge*, Armonk, New York: M. E. Sharpe Inc., 1982.

Schapiro, Leonard, *The Communist Party of the Soviet Union*, New York: Vintage Books, 1971.

Schlesinger, Joseph A., *Ambition and Politics*, Chicago: Rand McNally and Co., 1966.

Schmidt, Steffen W., Laura Guasti, Carol H. Lande, and James C. Scott, eds., *Friends, Followers, and Factions: A Reader in Political Clientelism*, Berkeley: University of California Press, 1977.

Schmitter, Phillippe, "Still the century of corporatism," *Review of Politics*, XXXVI, 1, 1974, pp. 85–131.

Schwartz, Joel J. and William R. Keech, "Group influence and the policy process in the Soviet Union," *American Political Science Review*, LXII, 3, September 1968, pp. 840–51.

Shapiro, Jane, "Candidate membership in the CPSU Central Committee: stepping-stone to glory or obscurity," *Comparative Politics*, VI, 4, July 1974, pp. 601–16.

Skilling, H. Gordon and Franklyn Griffiths, eds., *Interest Groups in Soviet Politics*, Princeton: Princeton University Press, 1971.

Spielman, Karl F., "Defense industrialists in the USSR," *Problems of Communism*, XXV, 5, September–October 1976, pp. 52–69.

Stewart, Philip D., Robert L. Arnett, William T. Ebert, Raymond E. McPhail, Terrence L. Rich, and Craig E. Schopmeyer, "Political mobility and the Soviet political process," *American Political Science Review*, LXVI, 4, December 1972, pp. 1269–90.

Tatu, Michel, *Power In The Kremlin*, New York: The Viking Press, 1970.

Ulam, Adam, *Stalin: The Man and His Era*, New York: The Viking Press, 1973.

Urban, Michael E., *An Algebra of Soviet Power: Elite Circulation in the Belorussian Republic 1966–1986*, Cambridge: Cambridge University Press, 1989.

Vardys, V. Stanley, "Lithuanian national politics," *Problems of Communism*, XXXVIII, 4, July–August 1989, pp. 53–76.

   ed., *Lithuania Under The Soviets: Portrait of A Nation, 1940–65*, New York: Praeger, 1965.

Weingold, Alex, "Patrons, patronage and political parties," *Comparative Studies in Society and History*, X, 4, July 1968, pp. 337–400.

Welsh, William, "Elites and leadership in communist systems: some new perspectives," *Studies in Comparative Communism*, IX, 1 and 2, Spring/Summer 1976, pp. 162–86.

White, Stephen, "Communist systems and the 'Iron Law of Pluralism,'" *British Journal of Political Science*, VIII, 1, January 1978, pp. 101–17.

   "'Democratisation' in the USSR," *Soviet Studies*, XLII, 1, January 1990, pp. 3–24.

Index

302

303

The following series titles are now out of print: